Studies in
Political Economy of Development

Studies in
Political Economy of Development

by
IGNACY SACHS

PERGAMON PRESS
OXFORD · NEW YORK · TORONTO · SYDNEY · PARIS · FRANKFURT

U.K.	Pergamon Press Ltd., Headington Hill Hall, Oxford OX3 0BW, England
U.S.A.	Pergamon Press Inc., Maxwell House, Fairview Park, Elmsford, New York 10523, U.S.A.
CANADA	Pergamon of Canada, Suite 104, 150 Consumers Road, Willowdale, Ontario M2J 1P9, Canada
AUSTRALIA	Pergamon Press (Aust.) Pty. Ltd., P.O. Box 544, Potts Point, N.S.W. 2011, Australia
FRANCE	Pergamon Press SARL, 24 rue des Ecoles, 75240 Paris, Cedex 05, France
FEDERAL REPUBLIC OF GERMANY	Pergamon Press GmbH, 6242 Kronberg-Taunus, Pferdstrasse 1, Federal Republic of Germany

First edition 1980

British Library Cataloguing in Publication Data
Sachs, Ignacy
Studies in political economy of development.
1. Latin America—Economic policy
2. Underdeveloped areas—Economic policy—
Case studies
I. Title
338.98   HC125   79–40488

ISBN 0–08–022495–4

First published in France by Flammarion, 1977, under the title *Pour Une Economie Politique Du Developpement.*

Printed and bound in Great Britain by William Clowes (Beccles) Limited, Beccles and London

IN MEMORIAM MICHAL KALECKI

Contents

Introduction

The crisis of development is also a crisis of development theory. Economic growth alone, however rapid, cannot solve social problems and
banish misery and unemployment. To start a long-term development
process requires more than a partial modernization of the production
apparatus and the mirage of unbridled urbanization which often result
in the lowering of the quality of life of most town dwellers.

The imitative model which favoured the course followed earlier by
industrialized countries is worn out. Cultural dependence and intellectual self-colonization which constitute the extreme form of this model
do not prevent imitative growth from proceeding at a more rapid rate
than that registered in the past in capitalist countries. But importing
into poor countries a model of accumulation and of society founded
on inequality only emphasizes the inegalitarian nature of growth. As
long as the élites of these countries can afford to consume as much
or more than their counterparts in rich countries the vast majority
of the fringe population will be forced to live on a derisory income.

Growth through inequality results in the waste of scarce resources
allocated for superfluous production, and also in underutilization of
land belonging to owners of large estates and overexploitation of land
belonging to small farmers. It is therefore doubly destructive from the
ecological point of view.

Instead of the present imitative growth which is inegalitarian and
destructive we advocate *endogenous development* geared to the satisfaction
of the essential needs of the entire population and the protection of
natural resources and of the environment. But we should rather speak
of *developments* as the diversity of ecological, historical, cultural, and
sociopolitical contexts must be reflected in plurality of strategies.

The *economics* of growth are on trial. The time has come once more for the *political economy* of development, for abandoning the elegance of mechanistic models and the simplifications of *homo economicus* for the sake of understanding the decision processes and evaluating the relative strength of economic and social factors, their behaviour, and strategies. The task is relatively easy as long as we are dealing with hypothetical models of a competitive free market or with collectivist economy of the socialist type. It becomes much more difficult in the case of mixed economies in developing countries in which both models are present, economies marked moreover by the coexistence and interpenetration of asynchronisms, or, to put it more simply for purposes of analysis, by the coexistence of traditional and modern sectors.

The time has also come for committed planning which does not hide behind the screen of technicality and political neutrality. While helping the decision-makers to think in alternatives, it does prepare the ground for their options which commit the future of society, without however claiming that it can achieve optimum conditions. Development is multidimensional; the various aims and criteria of evaluation chosen by a society have no common denominator; planning is not a province of economy but it does have an economic dimension. That is why political economy can be of service to the planner, provided it throws off the yoke of *economics* and embraces in its field of vision *all* the levers (and not investment alone) as well as the whole social and ecological dimension of growth; thus, while placing the adjective "economic" before the noun it leads to *economic policy* and over and above that, to *structural reform*.

The texts collected in this volume were written over a period of a dozen years in Warsaw and later in Paris. They were mostly commissioned by the United Nations, their specialized agencies, and other international organizations. Originally written in English (but difficult to obtain), they were for the first time published as a single volume in a French translation in 1977. They are meant as a contribution to the recently opened field of the political economy of development and of the theory of planning in a mixed economy. We have preferred to keep to the original versions so as to maintain the autonomy of each text. In some cases this makes for repetition and some of the figures are out of date, but in any event they are only intended to indicate relative values. It seems useful to us to show how the same concepts—e.g. that of "perverse growth"—work in various contexts and circumstances. Moreover, we wished to preserve the form imposed by the very nature of these studies primarily designed to provide a basis for friendly dialogue with planners and policy-makers of developing countries.

This volume is dedicated to the memory of the late Michal Kalecki to whom I owe a great intellectual debt. My thanks go to the international organizations for their permission to reproduce these texts and for their assistance in preparing them.

Ignacy Sachs

CHAPTER 1

Some Considerations of Long-term Planning in Mixed Economies (1968)

This chapter draws inspiration from ideas and methods elaborated by Professor Michal Kalecki and discussed by him in the following four essays, published in successive volumes of *Essays on Planning and Economic Development* of the Warsaw Centre of Research on Underdeveloped Economies:

"An outline of a method of constructing a perspective plan"[1]

"Problems of financing economic development in a mixed economy"[2]

"Main differences between developed and underdeveloped capitalist economies"[3]

"Determination of the rate of growth of the socialist economy under conditions of unlimited surplus of labour"[4]

By *mixed underdeveloped economies* is meant economies having a significant, though not necessarily large, but in any case dynamic, public sector and a large private sector where elements of traditional and modern economies coexist both in rural and urban areas. Hence there is a possible subdivision of the private sector into the modern and the traditional (often treated as a household subsector). Wherever necessary a further subdivision may be introduced between domestic and foreign-owned subsectors of the private sector, but we should always

---

[1] *Essays on Planning and Economic Development*, vol. I, Warsaw, 1963, pp. 19–22.
[2] *Essays on Planning and Economic Development*, vol. II, Warsaw, 1965, pp. 37–50.
[3] *Essays on Planning and Economic Development*, vol. III, Warsaw, 1968.
[4] *Ibid.*

These papers were reprinted in *Essays on Developing Economies*, The Harvester Press, England, and Humanities Press, Inc., U.S.A., 1976; the second paper is also in *Selected Essays on the Economic Growth in the Socialist and the Mixed Economy*, Cambridge University Press, 1972.

bear in mind that an economic system cannot be treated as an arithmetic sum of its parts (thus, for instance, the coexistence of traditional and modern sectors modifies the working of the latter).

Such mixed underdeveloped economies show at the same time various similarities and marked differences both with respect to socialist and developed capitalist economies. In particular:

(a) They are, like the socialist economies, supply-determined in the main, i.e. their rate of growth is limited by lack of productive capacities, with the difference that owing to institutional reasons they usually show less capacity to overcome the bottlenecks, due to a greater inelasticity of supply of food and a lesser efficiency of controls on investment and foreign trade.

(b) Though supply-determined, in the main they share with the developed capitalist economies the problem of insufficient effective demand for some categories of goods. Thus, side by side with difficulties arising from the fact that the supply of "essentials" grown by agriculture (i.e. staple food) lags behind the demand, so that the economy is beset by inflation and capital goods are in short supply (mostly when limited capacity to import them is misallocated to projects with high prospective rates of individual return and low social priority), "essentials" and "semi-essentials" of industrial origin may be operating much below their actual capacity due to a lack of demand. The same may apply to some export-oriented production (mostly to products from perennial cultures, where the ability to adjust supply to demand practically does not exist) due to inadequate foreign markets. As for industrially produced "luxuries" (mostly durables, such as motorcars, household appliances, etc.), the market composed of a small but moneyed élite is shallow but willing to pay high prices so as to attract excessive investment in such branches to the detriment of the rest of the economy. Such an expansion may generate a dangerous euphoria with respect to the state of the economy and the impact of industrialization. In the long run, however, the excessive growth of the L sector will adversely affect the growth potential of the economy, so that we are really in the presence of a perverse growth.[5]

[5] Because of import restrictions in many developing countries there is considerable deferred demand for L goods at the moment of starting home production of the same. This makes investment in L industries still more attractive, but after some years saturation of the market may occur.

As a result of the above-mentioned features the financing of non-inflationary, fairly rapid growth in a mixed economy poses three problems:

(a) Adequate supply of food;
(b) Proper handling of scarce foreign exchange resources;
(c) Equitable social distribution of the burden of investment.

The first two problems arise in all the economies, irrespective of their socioeconomic pattern, but they are likely to be felt much more intensely in an underdeveloped mixed economy. This is due to the combination of high-income elasticities of demand for food and a high propensity for imports, on account of the lack of domestic production of capital goods with institutional rigidities in agriculture and structural imbalances in the international division of labour.[6]

Problem (c) can in theory be handled in a socialist economy, where wages and prices are centrally controlled,[7] but a free-market capitalist economy is characterized by a clearly regressive distribution of income, so that a corrective intervention of the State is called for in order to protect the poor strata of population from excessive exploitation. In a mixed underdeveloped economy capitalists will try, as a rule, to get the best of two worlds, namely a conspicuously high standard of personal consumption and a fair amount of private investment, financed out of public savings accumulated at the expense of the working people and/or an unnecessary high inflow of external resources. Inflation helps to achieve this aim by reducing the real income of wage earners and increasing the profit margin of traders and industrialists. Thus, a socially acceptable incomes policy will require as a minimum, on the one hand, curbs to be put on the rate of growth of personal consumption (including investment in luxury housing) of the moneyed élite and, on the other, public investment to be stepped up. Of course, inflation is ruled out.

A reasonable solution of the above-mentioned problems requires

---

[6] A small group of oil exporters, while successful as far as international division of labour is concerned, quite frequently mishandled their foreign exchange income by placing it in Western banks and securities instead of promoting development in their own territories.

[7] In reality the crucial political decision is that of allocation of income into consumption and investment; once it has been taken the rest is a mere technicality.

effective planning and this, in turn, rests on the following three conditions:

(a) _Control of investment through licensing_ with respect to major and medium-sized projects, in order to prevent investment considered undesirable either because it does not fit into the plan or because of wrong location. Lack of such controls and reliance on a market allocation of investment will, as a rule, bring about a heavy concentration of investment in the L industries turning out goods (mostly durables) and services (e.g. sumptuary housing) belonging to the category of "luxuries" and in regions which are already more developed than the rest of the country.

The reasons for such distortion of the investment pattern are easy to identify: on the one hand, L industries, enjoying a most effective protection from foreign competition due to balance-of-payments difficulties and the consequent import restrictions, and working for a market of well-to-do people ready to pay excessively high prices for prestige goods, are likely to show rates of return to capital which are higher and quicker than any other investment opportunity (short of usurious money-lending). On the other hand, new investment is more likely to be located in areas already developed, which thus provide some external economies.

Both these trends, if left uncorrected, will add to the lopsidedness of the economy. To the extent to which excessive investment in L industries draws on scarce resources of the country (foreign exchange, scarce materials, and skills, as well as food, which constitutes the main counterpart of wages), it prevents the simultaneous expansion of some other industries turning out capital goods, raw materials, and intermediate goods, as well as consumer goods belonging to the category of "essentials". Though in the short run the expansion of L industries may bring about an increase in the national income and add to employment,[8] such a pattern of growth will prove deceptive in the long run, as it will slow down the rate of development of the industries which, contrary to the L industries, contribute to the "growth potential" of the country.

---

[8] Entirely new industries always add to employment while factories which displace existing artisan-type production may, on the whole, reduce the total employment in industries and crafts.

That is why we propose to call "perverse growth" that spontaneous pattern of growth which is based on market allocation of investment. As for the regional imbalances, again, if left uncorrected, they will become ever more acute because the process of uneven development is a self-cumulative one. Richer regions (or urban areas) will grow richer, setting out migratory movements and an asymmetrical pattern of economic interregional relations, which in the limiting case may turn out to be of a colonial-like nature.

Now, "negative" measures (controls) should go hand in hand with "positive" measures consisting of a reasonable policy of fiscal, credit, and other incentives to the private sector, which engages in projects enjoying high social priority, and of the readiness of the government to carry out through public investment all the projects included in the plan which are left unattended by private capitalists, as well as those which from the very outset were meant to stay in the public sector. Public investment in public sector enterprises (as opposed to private sector financing from public sources) has some definite advantages, as the public sector may be geared to the implementation of plans while private entrepreneurs can at best only be induced to do it, and only to the extent to which the macroeconomic interest coincides with their individual profit-seeking goal.[9] That is why the policy of incentives to the private sector should be very carefully weighed, bearing in mind that, if it becomes too expensive for the State, it might be better to expand the public sector instead.

(b) *Control of foreign trade and foreign exchange operations, including capital movements*. Foreign currency is, so to speak, the joker in the planning game, as practically all the bottlenecks (with the exception perhaps of the medium-level skills) can be overcome by imports so long as there is the capacity to finance them. In a great many cases difficulties

---

[9] A good instance of the evasiveness of the private sector to macroeconomic considerations is that of the choice of technologies. Social cost-benefit and entrepreneurial cost-benefit criteria seldom coincide. A private capitalist may find it advantageous or expedient (because such a ready-made technique is offered to him from abroad) to introduce a highly capital-intensive technique in a country beset by employment problems. This will happen either because, enjoying a monopolistic position on the market, he is free to fix his prices in such a way as to get a fair margin of benefit whatever the costs of production and/or because the opportunity cost of capital to him is low, contrary to what it should be, because of a wrong government policy of incentives to private-domestic and foreign capital.

due to foreign trade set, in the last instance, a ceiling to the overall rate of growth of the economy. Under no circumstances should the sensitive area of contacts between the national and world economies be left to the free interplay of market forces. The attitude of those who commit themselves to planning in the internal sphere but yield to the pressures of the advocates of free trade in the realm of foreign economic relations is doubly inconsistent. To accept free trade really means opening the back door to the doctrine of a free-market economy which is incompatible with planning and discoursing on the organization of world markets, while giving up the organization of one's own country's foreign trade means putting the cart before the horse. The doctrine of free trade has always been a weapon in the hands of the stronger against the weaker partners, not to speak of the fact that advanced industrial countries who would like to compel the developing countries to abide by this doctrine are the first to abandon it for a beggar-my-neighbour policy as soon as they feel embarrassed by balance-of-payments difficulties.

A comprehensive foreign trade policy can be worked out only against the background of the plan and, at the same time, should be an integral part of such a plan. Reliance on such criteria alone, e.g. import substitution or preference of capital over maintenance imports, may lead to dangerous complications as neither import substitution of L goods nor new investment in the L industries is desirable, while maintenance imports for the existing industries turning out goods necessary to the smooth functioning of the economy should be given high priority.

To be effective such a policy must:

   (i) Operate some kind of controls on imports, preferably licensing.[10]

  (ii) Subject to close scrutiny and regulations the operations of foreign-owned enterprises, in order to avoid excessive outflow of profits both legal and illegal (through overpricing of imports and foreign technical services and underpricing of exports), so as to reduce the gap between real foreign currency income and apparent foreign currency income, as registered by trade statistics alone.[11]

[10] Of course, different technical solutions are possible, a multiple exchange rate system being a substitute for or a complement to selective licensing of imports.

[11] To the extent to which the situation can be made to improve in this respect, the capacity to import of the country considered will increase, other conditions (i.e. volume of trade and terms of trade in their current meaning) remaining the same.

(iii) Operate a selective system of export duties and/or (whatever the actual case) of export subsidies.

We see no harm in subsidizing some exports so long as an uncompetitive price is the only obstacle to enter the foreign market (which usually it is not). The policy-makers will only be faced with the decision of how far they are ready to go along with their subsidies or, in other words, how much net marginal domestic cost per unit of foreign currency earned they are ready to pay. This means weighing the advantage arising from the additional capacity to import with the need to spend a greater relative share of the national income as the export counterpart to finance imports. Of course, the alternative solution, namely saving foreign currency by means of additional import substitution, should also be brought into the picture. No prejudice should be attached to either of them, except that import substitution is a safer risk, other conditions being equal (i.e. the net domestic cost per unit of foreign currency earned through exports or saved through import substitution are approximately equal). Let us observe that the above argument can be easily transposed to the realm of selection of foreign-trade-oriented investment; all we need then is to compare the effectiveness of investment into projects which earn through exports or save through import substitution the same net amount of foreign currency.[12] Such comparison between industries turning out all kinds of different goods is possible, as foreign currency provides the common denominator, and from the point of view of optimization of foreign trade it is irrelevant what specific good is being sold abroad or ceases to be purchased from outside (provided it fits into the plan).

The uncertainty inherent in foreign trade operations cannot be altogether eliminated with the means mentioned above, but the national economy becomes more fit to make the best use of the opportunities offered by trade and to adapt itself to the changing conditions of the world markets. We should perhaps add here that some degree of stability can be instilled, even in foreign trade, by means of concluding bunches

---

[12] Of course, we must reduce investment outlays and current production costs to a simple index. This can be done by means of dividing the investment outlays by the "recoupment period" or the inverse of the national cost of capital, fixed in such a way as to ensure the full utilization of such labour for which there is an adequate food supply to guarantee the planned real wage.

of long-term export and import contracts,[13] stipulating the volume of future transactions and the prices or the modalities of price fixation which are conceived in such a way as to reduce the amplitude of their fluctuations. Governments of the parties concerned should guarantee, either directly or indirectly, the implementation of such a contract if they are to become effective instruments of action.

(c) *Indirect control of the price line* (except for fluctuations motivated by shifts in terms of trade which are *vis major*) by means of appropriate agricultural policies, meant to ensure equilibrium between supply and demand on the market for staple foods, the main counterpart to wages. For the developed countries, Professor M. Kalecki proposed an administrative control of prices and freeing of wages, so that any increase in nominal wages[14] obtained by the trade-unions would be tantamount to a genuine redistribution of income in favour of workers. But in underdeveloped countries the situation is different: so long as essentials are in short supply all attempts to keep prices stable by administrative measures will prove to be in vain and will only bring about speculation and the black market. Theoretically, one could think of rationing. Such a form of distribution requires, however, a very smooth and integer organization, and even then a reasonable supply of essentials per head of population. Thus, for practical purposes it must be ruled out in mixed economies, as there would not be much chance of enforcing a distribution system encroaching drastically upon the consumption of the upper classes (who also eat essentials) while improving the lot of poor people, not only in relative terms but also in absolute terms. The only way left is, therefore, the one suggested at the beginning of the paragraph, namely respecting the income elasticities of demand for essentials and supplying staple foods in sufficient quantities to keep the prices stable. A comprehensive agricultural policy must therefore be built into the plan, combining institutional measures dealing with land tenures and commercialization (freeing the peasant from the domination of landlords, traders, and money-lenders), technical assistance, and investment. The utmost attention should be given to the

[13] We insist on bunches of contracts, because package deals give scope for exchanging concessions and arriving at a reasonable distribution of gains between partners.

[14] He made this point at an Italian–Polish Roundtable on Planning, held in Ancona in May 1965.

problems of peasant agriculture, to the extent to which it is possible to activate it, and to draw on its underutilized potential, consisting mainly of reserves of family labour, with little external investment. This is a less expensive way of achieving simultaneously the treble aim of increasing the supply of essentials, reducing the pace of rural migration to towns, and widening the domestic market for industrial goods, as peasants will trade the food against industrial consumer goods, inputs (such as fertilizer, pesticides, etc.), building materials, implements, and equipment. Transformation of a subsistence-oriented peasant economy into a market-oriented one, and its simultaneous modernization, may prove to be one of the most important long-term goals, spaced over several five-year plans.

The three conditions of effective planning just described clearly indicate that, far from being a substitute for effective economic policies, as some would like to believe, to be meaningful planning requires the economic policies leading to its implementation to be embodied in it. The lesser the scope for direct action of the State through the public sector, the more difficult it becomes to frame an integrated and consistent set of policies covering both the public and the private sectors. An important question which arises in this connexion in mixed economies is the "degree of boldness" of the policies the government is willing to propose.

This being the general setting of long-term planning in a mixed underdeveloped economy, we turn now to the question of planning procedure. We shall be more particularly concerned with the applicability of the method evolved by M. Kalecki in the context of Polish planning, which was generalized in his theory of growth of a socialist economy.[15] Of course, the transfer, pure and simple, of this method is ruled out because of the deep differences between mixed and socialist economies, which were already referred to. But we believe that the logic of Kalecki's approach remains valid for the case we are dealing with, though some additional issues must be taken care of. We shall, therefore, briefly describe the method, introducing at the same time the modifications necessary to adapt it to the case of mixed economies.

[15] See M. Kalecki, *Selected Essays, op. cit.*

(a) The plan[16] is to be constructed by an iterative method. Several rounds of successive approximations will be necessary to arrive at its final version. For the sake of simplicity we shall describe below only one round.

(b) We begin by choosing, on the basis of past performance and general knowledge of the economy, a hypothetic rate of overall growth and set out to investigate the consequences of such an assumption. This rate should not be entirely unrealistic; on the other hand, it should be rather high in order to expose all the bottlenecks bound to arise if it were actually kept as a goal.

(c) The first macroeconomic test of acceptability of this rate is that of the distribution of income it entails between productive investment and increase in inventories, on the one hand, and consumption at large, on the other, subdivided into personal consumption, collective consumption, and social investment. We arrive at a broad estimate of the relative share of productive investment in the national income (i) necessary to sustain the proposed rate of growth r, by multiplying r by a hypothetical capital–output ratio estimated on the basis of past performance, general knowledge of the economy, and cross-country comparisons.[17] The coefficient i should be corrected for the normal increase in inventories.

Obviously, the higher the i, the lower the relative share of consumption in the national income $(1-i)$. In a socialist economy with a fairly egalitarian distribution of income, an increase in i means

[16] Preferably, as we shall see, a few variants of the plan differing in assumptions about the degree of boldness of the government policies with respect to income distribution and institutional action upon agriculture, as well as the prospects of foreign trade.

[17] Kalecki's formula for the rate of growth reads as follows:

$$r = \frac{1}{k} i - a + u$$

where $r =$ rate of growth
   $k =$ capital–output ratio
   $i =$ relative share of productive investment in the national income
   $a =$ parameter of amortization
   $u =$ coefficient of improvements leading to a better utilization of the existing capacities of production

At this level of approximation we can abstract, however, from a and u, or for the sake of consistency assume that a and u are approximately equal and with opposite signs so that they cancel each other out.

for the large masses of population a sacrifice in terms of the rate of growth of consumption in the initial years of the plan for the sake of quicker growth of future consumption. In a mixed economy, however, characterized by inequalities in the social distribution of income, it is possible to conceive a strategy of growth which accommodates a high i with a reasonable rate of increase of consumption of broad masses, at the expense of the rate of growth of the consumption of higher-income brackets.[18] This may require, however, a complete overhauling of the fiscal system and, in particular, the imposition of heavy excise duties on luxuries, strongly progressive taxes on sumptuary houses and private cars according to their size, etc., as well as improving the collection of direct income taxes.

To turn back to our test: in a socialist economy it consists of deciding whether i is politically acceptable in a given country and at a given point of her history; in a mixed economy the alternative "more jam today or more jam tomorrow" loses its sharpness, but it is necessary, in compensation, to assess which income and fiscal policies would meet the double test of efficiency and social purposiveness and, then, to decide whether they are politically feasible, i.e. whether they are not too bold for the government concerned. In particular, it is necessary to devise a fiscal system which will not permit tax evasion. Although theoretically direct progressive taxes are the most equitable, in practice they may be evaded by rich people. That is why heavy indirect taxes should be imposed on luxuries, as already mentioned.

If i turns out to be too high, it is necessary to scale down the initial r and to repeat the exercise. We shall assume, however, that i is found acceptable.

(d) The next step then will consist of making a projection of the likely pattern of demand for consumer, investment, and intermediate goods, taking into consideration, on the one hand, the assumptions made at the previous stage about the splitting of income into personal consumption, collective consumption, social investment, increase in inventories, and investment and, on the other, the existing industrial capacities at the beginning of the plan, as well as projects under imple-

---

[18] An alternative way of putting the problem is that of curbing the rate of growth of consumption of luxuries which are mainly consumed by rich people, while keeping a high rate of growth for the essentials mainly consumed by the poor strata of population.

mentation. As for the personal consumption, the choices with respect to essentials are pretty obvious—their consumption should be stepped up as quickly as possible in the case of developing countries.

Therefore, "non-essentials", in particular "luxuries", should be sacrificed, in the sense that at least their consumption should grow at a much lower rate and that they should be taxed instead of "essentials". Of course, the projection of the likely commodity pattern of personal consumption of non-essentials in particular will not be entirely free from certain more or less arbitrary decisions, even though past trends in consumption, elasticities of demand, cross-country comparisons, and biological standards of nutrition should all be used. We do not dispose, as yet, of adequate tools to optimize the pattern of consumption.[19]

A further useful distinction will be that between "demand-determined industries", where we are entirely free to choose the rate of growth of output according to our needs, and "supply-determined industries", which for different reasons (e.g. limited natural endowments, organizational and technological problems, lack of skills,[20] danger of starting too many new projects at the same time, etc.) cannot develop beyond a certain rate. We shall, of course, start by examining the supply-determined industries and check to what extent they meet the home demand and still allow for exports. The balance between the necessary imports and the exports from supply-determined industries will be covered by export surpluses from demand-determined industries. Knowing broadly the industrial structure of the national income we can proceed with a closer analysis of investment pattern and an examination of the balance of payments.

(e) Total investment will include projects turning out goods or marketable services for the home market, foreign-trade-oriented projects (which either promote exports or substitute imports) and social projects (hospitals, schools, etc.) which, however, were computed above as part of broad consumption. Considerable attention should be given to the

---

[19] The situation is thus distinct from foreign trade and from the choice of techniques. In both these cases tools leading to optimal solutions exist.

[20] The situation in most developing countries is characterized by an overabundance of unqualified labour and an acute lack of qualified manpower, often aggravated by unemployment among the educated, who did not secure, however, the kind of education which makes them fit for the vacant jobs.

choice of proper techniques, in such a way as to get the fullest possible utilization of the abundant resource, i.e. labour, and, at the same time, full utilization of the scarce resource, i.e. capital. This requires, in general, a policy aiming at the lowest possible overall marginal capital–output ratio, subject, however, to the following qualifications:

(i) The choice of techniques follows that of the investment pattern and several important projects will require, as a rule, highly capital-intensive techniques because alternative techniques do not exist at all. Moreover, in certain cases capital-intensive techniques may be chosen because they require only a handful of highly qualified people, which is easier to secure than a larger amount of workers with intermediate skills.

(ii) The policy of maximizing employment with a given amount of investment is tantamount to seeking such techniques which, though very primitive, frequently imply an excessively high capital–output ratio; that is why our emphasis is on a moderate capital–output ratio with an acceptable productivity and, as a result, a not too high capital intensity.[21]

(iii) Labour-intensive techniques of the pick-and-shovel variety applicable in public works cannot be used on too great a scale, because of the constraint of limited food availabilities which prevent excessive increase of employment at planned real wages and of organizational difficulties, as well as of the excessively long gestation period of such investment.

As investment in modern processing industries, such as chemicals, basic steel, iron, etc., will be, perforce, biased towards capital-intensive techniques, it should be compensated by the selection of labour-intensive

---

[21] Let this be:

$$k = \frac{\text{capital}}{\text{output}}, \text{ i.e. capital–output ratio}$$

$$i = \frac{\text{capital}}{\text{labour}}, \text{ i.e. capital–labour ratio}$$

$$p = \frac{\text{output}}{\text{labour}}, \text{ i.e. productivity}$$

The following identity relates these three magnitudes: $pk = i$.

methods in public works, construction, transport, agriculture,[22] and the promotion of viable small-scale industries, characterized by moderate capital intensity. Considerable attention should be thus paid to the so-called "intermediate techniques", to the borrowing of techniques which are no longer applied in advanced industrial countries, and to the fostering of research in the field of capital-saving techniques. The example of the Vietnamese Democratic Republic points to the huge unexpected reserves which can be put into use in an underdeveloped economy with surplus labour, provided enough attention is given to labour-intensive techniques and decentralization of industrial activities, while food is rationed. This example is all the more significant because war conditions compel the Vietnamese to go to extremes. It is in a sense a "limiting case".

Moreover, special attention should be given to such problems as utilization and modernization of existing capacities, improving the supply of certain raw materials by investing in equipment, which reduces their input per unit of final product, rather than opening, for example, new mines and reducing expenditure on unnecessary "shells" of industrial equipment.

Investment should not be spread over an excessive number of individual projects; lack of concentration is likely to create organizational and technical problems, which will result in unnecessary extension of gestation periods and eventually a wasteful increase in the capital–output ratio.

Criteria of evaluation of projects, used to compare alternative methods of production, should be, of course, biased against the wasteful substitution of capital for labour. This means that the notional cost of capital should be high (or the "recoupment period", incorporated in the formula for the evaluation of the investment efficiency, low).

If we except the rather unusual case of the limited supply of labour in a developing country (in which case the recoupment period should be fixed in such a way as to guarantee full employment), the factor

[22] Institutional reforms may release, as we already know, unutilized reserves existing in peasant agriculture, permitting, at least for quite a considerable period of time, a considerable progress with relatively little or no external investment. On the other hand, sheer imitation has led several underdeveloped countries to waste resources in mechanization of agriculture, in cases where such an investment was not justified on agrotechnical grounds.

limiting the volume of employment at planned real wages will be the availability of food—the main "wage good" and counterpart of wages. If employment exceeds the limit set out by the supply of food, inflation will follow and real wages will drop below the planned level. The recoupment period should be chosen, therefore, in such a way as to seize all the employment opportunities subject to the above-mentioned constraint.

Such criteria only serve to compare alternative methods of production of a given output.

The situation is, however, different with respect to foreign-trade-oriented investment where, as we have already mentioned, the use value is of no importance at all.[23] We are only concerned with the amount of foreign currency earned through additional exports or saved through additional import substitution. We can thus range all the projects, whether export-oriented or import-substituting, according to their increasing cost per unit of foreign currency earned or saved and select the best choices from the list.

(f) Theoretically it should always be possible to balance foreign trade or to achieve an export surplus to compensate for the negative balance of invisibles, if such is the case. But moving from the top to the bottom of the list of foreign-trade-oriented projects means selecting projects with an ever-higher capital–output ratio.[24] What we gain, therefore, on the side of the balance-of-payments position is offset by an increase in the relative share of investment in the national income. There is a point beyond which the operation becomes self-defeating. Thus the consideration of the balance-of-payments position becomes the second macroeconomic test of the feasibility of the hypothetical rate of growth. Let us emphasize once more that this test does not apply just to foreign

[23] More exactly it is irrelevant as far as exports are concerned, because for import substitution the only condition which should be fulfilled is that it should fall within the range of goods which must be supplied according to the plan, whether from home production or from imports.

[24] Of course, the whole calculation is based on expectations with respect to the situation on world markets. It may prove too pessimistic if conditions change favourably and terms of trade improve. But the opposite may also happen and upset the whole plan. Hence the importance of long-term agreements and contracts. Such agreements and contracts may be used also to increase foreign trade operations above the level necessary to finance unavoidable imports and to reap additional advantages from the international division of labour.

trade. The balance-of-payments difficulties reflect also all the internal tensions of the economy. In particular, the worse the expected performance of food agriculture (the main supply-determined industry), the bigger the strain on imports.

If the proposed rate of overall growth leads to difficulties in the balance of payments which cannot be overcome, even taking into consideration the likely availability of foreign credits, the rate of growth must be scaled down and the whole exercise should start again. Of course, in the second round full use will be made of all the information collected during the first round with respect to different aspects of the economy and its bottlenecks, sectoral capital–output ratios, available techniques, and even main characteristics of the major projects. The second round should, therefore, lead to a better, if not definitive, variant.

It would seem that the method summarized above has for the developing countries several advantages, as compared with more sophisticated methods. We list those which seem to us the most relevant:

(a) First of all, this method can be mastered by practice and does not need a staff with exceptionally high qualifications.

(b) All the difficulties and bottlenecks are identified and political choices made explicit. Even though stepping up of investment is usually possible in mixed economies without sacrificing the popular consumption—so long as a policy of redistribution of social income is politically viable—difficulties of an organizational and technical nature, limitations on account of natural endowments, and the foreign trade position are likely to arise. The method permits us to discuss them one by one and to engage in the necessary dialogue with the politicians and the public in a manner and a language which make the problems understandable.

The above remarks should not be understood as an implicit rejection of mathematical methods in planning. We believe that such methods can be used with great advantage to solve all the partial problems where it is possible to establish a homogeneous goal function. In particular, it applies to the choice of techniques and to the optimization of foreign trade. As for comprehensive models of overall optimization of the economy, their use, at present, is at best confined in actual planning to sensibility tests, quick testing of alternative options at initial stages of discussion, testing of the internal consistency of the plan after its elaboration, and, last but not least, training of the planning staff. None of these applications, however, is a substitute for "pedestrian" planning, which constitutes for the developing countries the prime necessity, at least at the present stage.

(c) Macroeconomic planning is integrated here with planning at the branch level and with major individual projects, and the necessary link between planning proper and anticipated consideration of implementation difficulties is maintained.

(d) The method does not pretend to find the *optimum optimorum*, but simply to illuminate various choices and to reduce waste by "variant thinking" at all levels. In particular, such variant thinking applies to the following:

  (i) Choice of the overall strategy of growth, with particular reference to the degree of boldness of the policies of the government with respect to income distribution, agrarian policies, etc., and their impact on the rate of growth of the economy and of the popular consumption.

  (ii) Choice of the pattern of consumption.

  (iii) Optimization of techniques to be incorporated in actual projects.

  (iv) Optimization of foreign trade operations.

Explicit consideration of variants and alternatives at different stages of planning and levels of the economy should reduce the scope for wrong investment and management decisions, although the best method by itself cannot eliminate the possibility of such decisions if it is not being properly applied. Hence the importance of administrative and organizational aspects of planning. In particular, an independent agency to screen the major projects with respect to the choice of techniques should be incorporated into the planning machinery. It is all the more important in mixed economies, where the choice of suitable techniques has particular relevance to the acuteness of the employment problem, and, at the same time, is very difficult to carry out because a substantial part of investment is carried out by the private sector.

To sum up, let us emphasize once more that long-term planning in mixed economies presents several additional difficulties, as compared with planning in a socialist economy. Even if the three minimum conditions for effective planning are fulfilled, we must build into the plan such strategic variables as the degree of boldness of fiscal and income policies, as well as agrarian policies, and always bear in mind that the private sector can be induced or prevented from doing certain things, but it will not be certain whether the inducement will actually work. All this increases still more the already considerable margin of uncertainty inherent to long-term planning and widens the scope for variant thinking. Two conclusions should be drawn from this. On the one hand, the time horizon should not be extended beyond fifteen years; on the other, whenever possible at least two full-fledged variants of the plan should be presented: the low and absolutely realistic and the high, somewhat more optimistic hypothesis, differing by clearly specified assumptions with respect to political variables.[25] With all these qualifications, the logical approach outlined above seems to offer a suitable line of approach to long-term planning in mixed economies.

[25] Further variants can be built differing from the previous ones by assumptions with respect to the behaviour of exogenous variables, such as, for example, the terms of trade. The two problems should not be mixed up, however, in order to make clear the link between the choice of policies pursued by the government and the rate of growth of the income and of the popular consumption, which is in the long run the supreme criterion of evaluation of economic performance in a mixed economy.

CHAPTER 2

Industrial Development Strategy (1971)*

Development strategy

The term "development strategy" is now commonly used to denote the fundamentals underlying the operational approach to the process of long-term development. Emphasis is on rationale rather than on operational details. Thus, the strategy is more general than a long-term plan or programme in two senses:

(a) It outlines the system to be set up in order to obtain the development objectives and hence logically precedes the plan.

(b) It leaves aside the quantitative details, concentrating on fundamental ratios and sequences.

Even so, to be practically useful, the development strategy will indicate, at least roughly, the pace and the path (the broad commodity pattern scheduled over time) of the desired process of development.

Since, in an absolutely free market, there is practically no strategy to promote the process of growth other than recognizing profit as the major aim and regulator of economic activity, it follows logically that the emphasis in the strategy should be put on governmental policies.[1] All governmental policies must be tested for their consistency (coherence, completeness, and beneficial effect), allowing for the actual environmental conditions, society's desired objectives, and how bold the government is willing to be in intervening in economic affairs. Such tests will at times show the need for policy changes.

* Paper written with Kazimierz Laski.
[1] Assisting the free-market forces by means of various Government policies is admittedly a strategy, though a weak one because it gives little guarantee of achieving definite objectives in a given time-span.

19

The framing of a strategy is an exercise almost identical in its structure to long-term planning. First, it is necessary to identify the conditions for economic development, particularly the weak spots and bottlenecks, on the one hand, and underutilized resources, on the other. Then, the general objectives of society must be clarified, for later they should be the criteria by which alternative programmes of action, i.e. sets of goals, are compared. Finally, ways of relating means to objectives, i.e. new policies, must be conceived. At the strategy-framing stage, we are primarily interested in evolving a framework or system to be used for solving the developmental problems, identifying areas for decision and action, and identifying means for such action.

The strategist, therefore, has more freedom to use imagination than the planner. He is less bound by figures, as the quantitative details will be worked out during the later planning stage. Lacking precise quantitative targets, the strategist cannot produce optimal solutions but endeavours to provide the planner with a global framework within which he can work out sectoral optimizations to incorporate in the plan.[2] Briefly, strategy-framing is to long-term planning what systems analysis is to operational research.

If the above view is accepted, it follows that strategy and planning are complementary. Strategy-framing cannot replace planning, for a strategy without a plan, or at least a general programme, is meaningless. Nor can planning be thought of solely as a detailed quantification by the planner of a previously worked out strategy. Nevertheless, to be most effective, planning should proceed within a carefully evolved strategic framework.

The choice of a strategy is as much an exercise in "variant thinking" as planning itself, and meaningful variants of strategy can be conceived only on the basis of extensive information of the kind required by planners. The strategist must be continually fed with information by the planner. On the other hand, he should keep the planner informed

[2] Strict optimization of development plans does not appear to be practical, since plans are, by definition, multipurpose, while mathematical methods of optimization are based either on a single goal function or on a strict hierarchy of goals. Theoretically, it is always possible to optimize by assigning different weights to different goals, but the choice of weights is itself an arbitrary procedure. Sectoral optimizations, however, appear to be quite practical and useful.

on the general direction of his thought, long before the best strategy takes final shape. As a matter of fact, the feedbacks between strategy-framing and plan-making are so many, particularly when both are considered as a continuous process, that perhaps the best solution would be to provide a single team with the hats of both strategists and long-term planners. The planners would put on their strategist hats when they discuss the inner logic of their approach to fundamental decisions likely to commit several generations[3] or of their approach to the invariants (mostly of an institutional nature) which they may wish to build into the social economic structure during a period spanning several normal plan periods.[4]

The development strategy should be continuously reviewed to the extent possible, i.e. to the extent to which the processes set out by previous action can be modified by new, more appropriate action. Strategists and planners will always be, to some extent, prisoners of prior strategy and plans, but this dependence should not be overstated.

Overall development and industrial development strategy

The place of industrialization in the overall development strategy of a country should be carefully examined.

Neither a development strategy nor a development plan is an arithmetical sum of sectoral strategies or plans. It is impossible to frame a sectoral strategy without referring to the economy as a whole, but it would be meaningless to try to set out the intersectoral relations, as embodied in the overall strategy of development, without an intimate knowledge of the problems and possibilities of each sector. Indeed, the pace and pattern of growth of the industrial sector are likely to influence heavily the whole development strategy of a developing country, even though the sector may account for only a small part

---

[3] Such as the opening of virgin lands, the building of new towns, or the development of industries requiring large capital investment.

[4] In mixed economies, where the public and the private sectors coexist, the government may wish to commit itself for a period of several years with respect to the areas which are to be left to private initiative and those which are to become the government's responsibility in order to create a suitable climate for private investment.

of the national product for many years to come. The relative share of manufacturing industries in GNP is not a good index to use to illustrate their role in a country's economic development. Using as criteria the rates of growth, levels of and changes in productivity, diversification of the output mix, introduction of new techniques, and new forms of management, the industrial sector appears to be leading the process of economic development in nearly every case. This is why most developing countries want rapid industrialization.

How rapid should this industrial growth be? Should priority be given to it over all other goals? In the past, the reply to these questions was often formulated in excessively simple and extreme terms, according to whether the speaker was a partisan of industry or agriculture in the debate over their rival claims. The advocates of structural change were all for industrialization. Meanwhile, development through agriculture was being defended with two arguments: the common-sense observation that industrial workers had to eat and the expected comparative advantage of many developing countries if they specialized further in export-oriented crop agriculture. It was easy to object that this expectation was based on two questionable assumptions:

(a) The inflexibility of the international division of labour.

(b) The high elasticity of export markets for agricultural crops produced by developing countries.

Thus, both sides were sometimes right and sometimes wrong. Simplified one-pronged strategies rarely suit actual cases; at best they serve to illustrate the limits within which economic development will fall. All of the reasonably good strategies—except for a few exceptionally short-lived ones—fall in between. The dichotomic formulation "either . . . or" must be discarded in favour of a changing mix of proportions, varying from country to country and over time. The creation of dogmas that favour one economic sector or another is ill-advised, although there is agreement that manufacturing industries are likely to be one of the prime forces of economic growth in the great majority of developing countries.

The same reservations apply to all such dichotomic discussions on lower levels of strategy-framing and planning, including export promotion *versus* import substitution, cash crop *versus* subsistence agriculture, and heavy *versus* light industries. In all of these instances, the need is to vary proportions intelligently rather than to proceed by exclusions. Of course, some sectors (or subsectors or single industries) will be given priority and may accordingly receive the lion's share of investment. These will then be the dynamic industries, which is tantamount to saying that, in a given context and time span, they will develop at a quicker rate than the rest of the economy. But this priority cannot be derived from the character of an industry nor from a regression analysis of the development pattern of a number of countries, though such an analysis may be useful as one element among many in the discussion on relative size of various sectors and subsectors. The priority must instead be established for each individual country on the basis of an extensive analysis of all the relevant information and an examination of various alternatives. In some cases, these may conform to the actual experience of other countries, but as a rule they will differ in a number of significant features.

To summarize, no *a priori* assumptions can be made about the exact place of industrialization in the overall development strategy of developing countries. This is a matter of crucial importance indeed, and one which must be treated in the context of each country's actual experience. Nor is it profitable to discuss whether growth should be balanced or unbalanced, as these alternatives are actually only two different ways of looking at the shape of things, rather than two distinct approaches. To the extent that growth is a discrete process, proceeding by leaps, there are bound to be certain generators of growth, possibly different for each country and period—sectors which not only grow at a quicker rate than other sectors of the economy but also have the germinative property of creating external effects conducive to accelerated growth in other parts of the economy. Paying special attention to them is likely to result in unbalanced growth. However, as the main purpose of planning is to avoid waste of resources owing to underutilization of existing and newly created facilities, a planner always looks for a balanced growth path, even when he includes in his plan some growth generators. His plan will be good only to the extent to which he correctly evaluates the working of his growth generators and provides for a distribution of resources that will not tend to waste the germinative power they inject into the economy.

Conditions for industrial development

The urgency of problems faced by the developing countries stems, in large part, from the fact that, due to unusual demographic pressures, they need to industrialize at a much quicker pace than that achieved in the past by more advanced countries. The developing countries are confronted with additional difficulties, among which are the considerably higher capital–labour ratios now prevailing in most industries, the growing complexity of modern techniques, and the unfavourable impact on them of the international division of labour. These disadvantages more than offset the possible benefits reserved to latecomers who supposedly can omit some stages of technological development. As matters now stand, even after a considerable leap forward in industrialization, a developing country can hardly expect to enter world markets for industrial goods, although the lack of access to these markets does not solely come from a lack of competitiveness. If this were the only obstacle, it could probably be overcome by a policy of subsidies for exports. In the long run, however, there is no reason to believe that developing countries will suffer from a comparative disadvantage in industrial production as long as such activity is well planned, i.e. adapted to the local conditions and availability of resources. The more a particular type of production depends on human skills, the less reason there is to believe that people living in one particular country are more fit for it than those in another; they may be better trained or better equipped, but such differences can be overcome. The last century provides many historical examples in support of this proposition.

This optimism about the long run (which boils down to a reaffirmation of the basic equality of all groups of human beings with respect to their potentialities) should not be understood, however, as an invitation to indulge in adventurous planning that is out of touch with the hard realities of the present day. The quest for industrial development strategy should start with a sober assessment of the available resources and their limitations.

Natural resources

As manufacturing consists of making articles from raw materials extracted from nature or grown by man, the possession of plentiful supplies of such materials constitutes an invitation to enter the field of processing industries, particularly where these raw materials are bulky as well as cheap, thus making transport costs high in relation to their value. In practice, however, we see many exceptions to this rule of thumb. Oil producers export the bulk of their output in the form of raw petroleum, while Japan manages to produce steel at competitive prices, even though it is compelled to import the necessary raw materials over great distances. If the case of the oil-producing countries can be explained by the pressure of vested foreign interests, solidly entrenched and backed by big powers, no such reason can be invoked to explain why Sweden, for example, finds it profitable to export iron ore.

These examples are used to emphasize the need to undertake a careful economic analysis whenever the apparently obvious case for exploiting a country's natural resources arises. Mineral riches do not necessarily make a country rich; access to them may require costly investment, characterized by a "lumpiness" of the capital expenditure involved and long gestation periods. As for processing industries based on locally produced raw materials, they may not enjoy an internal market of reasonable size. Furthermore, access to foreign markets often depends not so much on the competitiveness of the articles produced as on the policies followed by the major industrial countries and powerful oligopolies. Briefly, no easy optimism can be derived from the mere identification of large mineral deposits, forestry resources, or similar natural resources.

In spite of the need to guard against early overoptimism, there will normally be plenty of opportunities to start or expand industries based on locally produced raw materials and to specialize eventually in some of them. This calls for a careful surveying of domestic resources and a concentration of scientific and technological research on the best way to utilize them. Whenever possible, the strategy for industrial development should specify one or more industries that are expected to become leaders in the economy. All forward and backward linkages of such industries should be carefully investigated, as it may prove rewarding to pursue the idea of an industrial complex organized around each of them.

As for export-oriented industries based on exportable raw material, their development should normally be rewarding; it should pay a country to increase the value-added incorporated in its exports. But two qualifications must be noted. One is the problem of access to foreign markets. This problem can often be solved by developing an appropriate foreign trade strategy, consisting of long-term export agreements. It may be possible to negotiate such agreements in return for granting similar import contracts. The developing countries have hardly started to explore such fields of mutual co-operation. The second problem is that of vertical integration. An investigation should always be made whether it is more profitable to enter all stages of production, from extraction to the distribution of the final product, or to enter only certain areas. The time scheduling of the whole operation is an important matter.

Human resources

Only the broad outlines of an inquiry into this complex subject can be indicated here. A full treatment comprises an assessment of the impact of the sociopolitical organization on the working of the economy and studies of the social stratification, the demography, and some more specific questions dealing with the labour force and manpower availability. In other words, it calls for a global institutional approach.

Perhaps the most delicate task in framing development strategy is dealing with wholesale changes in the economic behaviour of the various strata of the population. How can social change, commonly called modernization, be brought about? To what extent does it constitute a prerequisite to, or an outcome of, industrialization? Under what circumstances is the implementation of industrial development programmes most likely to catch the popular imagination and so gain active support? What place should be assigned to the national government? What institutions should be created, or supported, or discriminated against? The strategist must have an intimate knowledge, based on extensive interdisciplinary research, of what goes on at the grass roots. It is permissible to doubt whether he is always aware of this important dimension of his task.

The labour force and manpower situation are more commonly reviewed. Broadly speaking, an investigation is likely to highlight the following aspects:

(a) An overabundance of unskilled labour, coupled with acute short-ages of qualified manpower, aggravated by a wasteful distribution of skills (too many lawyers and holders of diplomas in the humanities, but very few scientists, engineers, or technicians and hardly any inter-mediate-level skilled manpower).

(b) Urbanization without sufficient accompanying industrialization, owing to the migration from outlying villages, where living conditions are miserable, of people attracted by the mirage of job opportunities in towns[5].

(c) Social stratification very different from past experience in Europe and the United States, with relatively few industrial workers enjoying a privileged position compared to the large but poor rural population and those urban wage earners who have not managed to get stable employment in the modern sector of the economy.

Taken as a whole, the human resources situation imposes severe con-straints on the strategy of development. Some economists and politicians tend to argue that an overabundant supply of unskilled labour is a boon, as it can be used for labour-intensive investment projects. Unfor-tunately, there are limitations to such operations; even workers who perform the very simplest of tasks must be fed, clothed, and housed, and therefore the ability to satisfy these essential needs sets an upper limit on mass mobilization of labour. One should also be aware of the very difficult organizational problems involved, as well as of the relatively restricted scope of investment activity of the pick-and-shovel type. Thus, investment schemes based on labour-intensive methods will continue to find a place in industrial development strategy, but they will seldom, by themselves, provide the possibility for a big leap forward.

Supply of technology

The supply of technology is a severely limiting factor. As a rule, developing countries live by direct transfers of techniques used in more advanced countries, and often they are not equipped even to adapt

[5] In some towns of the Third World, the construction of each new plant adds to the host of unemployed as the newcomers from villages, attracted by the possibility of employment, far exceed the number of jobs created.

such techniques. Original local research is scarce and its results are seldom developed into workable production techniques. This dependent condition makes the developing countries vulnerable to all sorts of pressures. They must buy on a seller's market, mitigated to some extent by international competition. Many transfers of technology are ill-conceived or simply redundant, not necessarily through the action of a vested interest; often it is due to lack of imagination on the part of foreign technicians from developed countries who are used to completely different environmental conditions and factor ratios and so are naturally inclined simply to duplicate solutions already existing in their own countries. Thus, mimicry of modern techniques takes the place of invention. On the other hand, developing countries must rely for years on a dual industrial structure, owing to the employment implications if their cottage industries were destroyed. For this reason, the traditional techniques should definitely be improved wherever it is even marginally feasible to do so, i.e. whenever they do not result in a level of productivity below the acceptable minimum having regard to the postulated level of real wages.

Markets

The size of the market is of paramount importance in making decisions about the introduction of new industries. The indivisibilities and economies of scale affect especially the modern steel, petrochemical, and automobile industries. However, for many industries the minimum viable size of plant continues to be relatively small and, in those countries where transport costs are high, local industries enjoy a kind of protection on this account.

The size of the market depends roughly on the country's total population and its *per capita* income. This approach can be misleading, however, to the extent that it does not take into account the distribution of income by social or economic classes. If, in a country of 100 million people, 1 per cent of the population enjoys an average annual income of about $6,500, 9 per cent about $800, 40 per cent about $300, and 50 per cent about $125,[6] the average *per capita* income of more than $300 indicates little about the demand for different kinds of commodities.

[6] This is roughly the estimated income distribution in Brazil; many other developing countries have a similarly uneven distribution of incomes.

In fact, the top 1 per cent can afford many luxuries, the next 9 per cent have already crossed the income threshold which permits them to purchase durables, but the poorer half of the population can hardly spend more than a few dollars a year on very simple manufactured goods. Thus, there is a very differentiated picture of the demand for various types of goods. There is a relatively small market of relatively well-to-do people for luxuries, a larger market for less-expensive durables (easy to overestimate, owing to the existence of deferred demand arising from import difficulties), and a deceptively small market for mass-consumption industrial goods, including those produced by traditional techniques. Expansion of this last market depends on bold policies of support for peasant agriculture which, at the same time, would increase the food supply for additional industrial workers.

An industrial development strategy should not be based wholly on market considerations. In the interests of long-term social and economic development, the rate of expansion of industries turning out luxuries has to be restricted in order to permit the allocation of scarce resources, such as capital goods, foreign exchange, and skills, to other projects with higher social priority. The application of this social policy on the supply side needs to be co-ordinated with an income and fiscal policy directed towards a corresponding restraint of the growth of demand for luxuries.

The opposite approach is required for essentials. The income policy should aim at increasing the demand for them, and the income elasticities of demand should be carefully respected.

Thus far, only the domestic market has been considered. But whenever the minimum viable size of production exceeds the domestic demand, the question of access to foreign markets arises. Here the basic problem is not usually competitive prices, for it is often possible to subsidize exports if this is the only obstacle;[7] rather, it is a problem of organizational and political obstacles. Whenever the world market has an oligo-

---

[7] The case for such subsidies can be argued along the following lines. In an import-sensitive economy, what matters most is to obtain additional foreign currency, even if the real marginal domestic cost of a unit of foreign currency earned is higher than the exchange rate. How far this line should be pursued is a matter for political decision. Of course, there will be no problem as long as the average domestic cost of a unit of foreign currency does not exceed the official exchange rate or if export subsidies on some goods are paid out of export duties imposed on other goods which enjoy a comparative advantage in the world market.

polistic structure and big vested interests are involved, a newcomer has little chance to break through. This problem can be dealt with only through imaginative trade policies and active entry into markets that are not entirely dominated by such interests.

When comparing the prospective demand with the production possibilities, it may be useful to divide all industries into two groups:

(a) So-called supply-determined industries, where rates of growth are limited by the availability of natural resources or by technical or organizational ceilings.

(b) Demand-determined industries, where it should be possible to expand output as the markets grow.

When rates of growth become sufficiently high, all industries are supply-determined, and therefore the concept has only a relative meaning in the context of a given rate of growth. It does help to clarify, however, the importance of the market size for each industry considered and to identify potential export surpluses and supply shortages to be covered by imports.

Capacity to import and foreign aid

All deficits in supply—whether of raw materials, intermediate goods, capital equipment, consumer goods, management know-how, or skilled manpower—can be made up by imports, as long as the country has sufficient import capacity. Thus, there is a fundamental need for the strategist to make a sober and realistic assessment of the country's present and future position in the international division of labour, as well as of the foreign resources available on conditions considered acceptable in the country's long-term interest. His conclusions drawn from such an assessment may weigh heavily on the rate of industrial development he proposes, depending on whether or not the country can expect a sizable yearly expansion of its traditional exports at reasonable prices.

It may be desirable to resort to foreign resources when an irreducible trade gap appears likely. On the other hand, a savings gap may be taken care of by proper fiscal and income policies.[8] But the strategist

---

[8] Looked at *ex post*, the two gaps are equal.

should make sure that the growing indebtedness and the non-economic obligations which often accompany foreign aid do not restrict still more his freedom of choosing a development strategy. The policies regarding the inflow of foreign resources should be geared to the implementation of the chosen strategy, but in practice the strategy quite often is made to conform with projects that are offered as a package within the framework of foreign assistance.

When considering resort to foreign resources, it is necessary to take into account all inflows and outflows of resources. The inflow of foreign capital must be weighed against payments to be made abroad in order to service foreign debt and foreign direct investment. Technical assistance received from outside should be weighed against the brain drain of young talents to other countries.

Evaluation criteria

In order to ensure that a strategy of industrial development will make the fullest possible use of available resources, it is necessary to clarify the objectives of society. Industrialization is not an aim in itself, but a means to achieve economic progress and social welfare.

It is a matter for philosophical reflection whether all societies have the same concept of progress. Nevertheless, it appears likely that the same concept of material well-being permeates the ideas pursued by the overwhelming majority of men. Thus, common consent is assumed with regard to the desirability of achieving more output per worker, more jobs, higher productivity, higher wages,[9] a greater variety of goods available at economical prices to the common man, and a fairly equal distribution of wealth geographically. Furthermore, it is assumed that people like to feel that the economy is continuously on the move and that they can expect a steady and continuous improvement in their standard of living. They derive less satisfaction from occasional forward

---

[9] Economic well-being cannot be measured exactly, but the least imperfect quantitative approximation to such a measurement is consumption *per capita* for different income brackets. Higher output without increases in consumption and higher productivity without increases in real wages may help to build a better future (if they do not simply add to the wealth of the rich), but they do not increase the current living standards of the majority.

leaps followed by stagnation. This means that resources must be husbanded so as not to exhaust them. In particular, the most precious
resource, foreign exchange, should be continuously replenished and
therefore industrialization should promote exports and import substitution.

The development objectives that are chosen will evidently differ in
the degree to which they can be measured. Gross output and value
added per worker can be measured fairly well. The number of jobs
created is a definite figure, and it should be possible to define adequately
the ultimate goal in this respect. Full employment, based on an average
minimum productivity, can be calculated from demographic and sociological data about the labour force. Output-mix can be described in
detail, as can the rate of exhaustion of natural resources (corrected
for possible new discoveries). The impact of new industries on the
balance of payments can be estimated, and it is even possible to work
out balance-of-payments criteria to aid in the selection of new projects.
The export-oriented or import-substitution industries will be chosen
that are rated most desirable in terms of net domestic cost per unit
of foreign exchange earned or saved.[10] It is more difficult to work out
a dynamic picture of interindustry relations and to find ways of taking
into consideration the complementary nature of certain industries.
Moreover, germinative power and the modernization effect are phenomena that undoubtedly exist and must be taken into account, but
they defy the imagination when it comes to finding suitable quantitative
indices for them.

Unfortunately, the various objectives involved are not all consistent.
Pareto-optimal situations (in which it is possible to maximize each
goal up to a certain point without negatively affecting the pursuit of
the other goals) seldom occur when the goals consist of reasonably
high overall rates of growth. For lower rates of development, a strategy
is not necessary. In many aspects, the objectives are even contradictory.
For instance, with a limited amount of investment resources it is impossible to maximize employment and productivity per worker simultaneously. Whenever the desire for a better geographical balance in

---

[10] It should again be emphasized that no sharp conflict should arise between export
promotion and import substitution.

the distribution of industries results in the selection of an underdeveloped site for a new plant, the decision must be paid for in terms of added construction costs and additional operating costs resulting from the lack of supporting external facilities available in more developed parts of the country.

There is usually constant opposition between short- and long-term objectives. A strategist must decide whether, to use Joan Robinson's expression, he prefers "more jam today or more jam tomorrow". More investment today means less current consumption but higher levels of future consumption, as well as higher long-term rates of growth. In contrast, allowing more consumption in the short run means slowing down the long-term rate of growth. This is, of course, a political decision to be taken when framing the overall development strategy. But at the level of industrial development strategy, decisions must also be made about problems of a similar nature. For example, the import-substitution opportunities yielding the best results in the short run are likely to be exhausted after some time, and the long-term interest requires that the more difficult import-substitution industries manufacturing intermediate and capital goods should also be developed at an early stage. Investment in industrial infrastructure, because of its indivisibilities and long gestation periods, must be planned with a much longer time horizon than industrial projects themselves. But how long should this time horizon be and how much capital should be immobilized in infrastructure? The anticipated modernization effect may prompt the strategist to advocate the early implantation of some industries, which even though their operation is non-economic will be judged useful because they disseminate technological knowledge in a population hitherto completely innocent of modern technology.

The foregoing examples highlight the fundamental importance of time-scheduling in strategy-making and point to the need to make compromises between different objectives. This is the Achilles' heel of economics—a fundamental inability to add different sorts of utility and hence to pass from vectorial to scalar calculus when dealing with a multiplicity of objectives. It is possible formally to give weights to each objective and then to maximize their sum, discounting future utilities at their present value. But there is such a considerable degree of arbitrariness involved in using one particular set of weights and discount rates rather than another that less formal and more direct ways of arbitrating between the different objectives are to be preferred. Such an approach may look pedestrian, but it has the advantage of not concealing the political decisions and the arbitrary choices involved. Regardless of the particular method used, deliberate varying of the objectives-mix and of its distribution over time gives rise to alternative strategies, one of which will be chosen.

Setting strategic goals

Once the general economic objectives are established, they must be translated into specific strategic goals, capable of being realized with the country's existing resources and the proposed policies. For convenience, the policies proper will be discussed later. It should be made clear, however, that the choice of policies will definitely affect the setting of goals and, for all practical purposes, the two operations—goal-setting and matching of goals with policies—should be conducted simultaneously, allowing for feedbacks in both directions.

One procedure for setting strategic goals, which particularly emphasizes the areas for decision-making, is graphically summarized in Figure 2.1. Here objectives are translated into goals by setting them against the resources and constraints that are objectively imposed upon the process of growth. The consideration of different policies, which will ultimately determine how many resources are effectively mobilized, will be discussed later.

The goals will normally take the form of an output-mix, varying over time in conformity with the approximate growth rates foreseen for each industry.[11] The relative rates of growth of different industries will have to be chosen, taking into consideration the interindustry relations and the postulated complementarities. Strategies may vary in this respect between the following two extremes:

(a) The implantation of integrated industrial complexes, self-sufficient from the extraction of raw material to the production of final goods, including the manufacture of the necessary machinery. This autarkical

---

[11] The output-mix becomes more and more diversified through the addition of new industries.

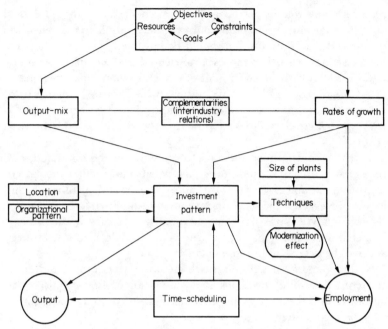

Fig. 2.1   Procedure for setting strategic goals

industrialization pattern is particularly tempting for huge, almost continent-wide countries with severe balance-of-payments difficulties.

(b) Geographically scattered construction of selected industries which are well served by the country's natural endowments or potential markets. This is a frequent industrialization pattern for countries that have no difficulties with their balance of payments.

The output-mix will reflect the strategist's expectations about the prospective demand and certain of the goals he chooses to be built into his scheme. It will be a compromise involving a rather extensive and laborious exercise of allocating the available resources to the production of goods that fit into the assumed pattern of demand and can be produced at a reasonable cost. In other words, the strategist will try to identify those industries which are likely to yield the highest returns in terms of satisfaction of some of the goals pursued. This exercise requires many rounds or repetitions, as good results can be reached only by trial and error, on account of the multiplicity of objectives pursued. Partial optimization should be possible, however, as already mentioned, by selecting the export-oriented and import-substituting industries that earn or save a unit of foreign exchange at a reasonable net domestic cost. Other considerations which affect in one way or another the output-mix include the complementarities between industries and external facilities, germinative power, and modernization effect.

Given the output-mix and rates of growth, on the one hand, and the existing capacities, on the other, it is possible to visualize the pattern of investments and arrive at a first approximation of their time-scheduling. However, this time-scheduling should be submitted to an additional rigorous analysis as it is of paramount importance for the whole strategy. In fact, it constitutes a major part of any industrial development strategy and will be described in more detail later on.

At this point, it is possible to enrich the strategy with three additional elements. First of all, decisions about the location of new projects will introduce into the strategy measures to fulfil the objective of reducing regional inequalities.

Second, it is possible at this stage to choose an organizational pattern for the industries and, in particular, to decide how the responsibilities will be distributed between the public, private, and mixed sectors. It should also be possible, through the organizational pattern, to implement some of the social objectives of the overall development strategy, such as a new pattern of income distribution.

Finally, there is a very important element in strategy-framing—selection of techniques. Given the volume of the investment, the number of jobs created will depend on the capital intensity of the techniques employed. In many cases, the only available technique is capital intensive—hence the importance of not making unnecessary use of capital-intensive techniques in those areas where a wide spectrum of techniques exists, as, for example, in construction. This criterion also applies when deciding the size of new plants and, more particularly, the place accorded in the industrial development strategy to small-scale industries which may be necessary to preserve and protect the employment potential of cottage industries. As for modern small-scale industries, they may offer various advantages that will offset their higher production costs, as compared with big plants where full economies of scale are achieved. Moreover, they may offer more scope for regional decentralization and stand a better chance of attracting small and medium-sized savings and managerial talents, which cannot cope with big, modern industries but are good enough for smaller units such as family businesses. A special case is that of modern production units which are quite small in terms of the capital and labour employed, but are so narrowly specialized that they reap all the economies of scale; they often make ancillary engineering products. Of course, such plants represent an ideal solution, except for the knotty organizational problems they create at the level of interindustry co-operation. Large industries can rely on such ancillary units only if they are sure that they will not be compelled to slow down production owing to the lack of some part ordered from an ancillary unit. This problem can be solved by keeping large stocks, but this usually involves a serious increase in the capital–output ratios, owing to the increase in working capital requirements.

The pressure of unemployment, both overt and disguised, is likely to be so great that the strategist will be tempted to bias his output-mix towards labour-intensive industries, chiefly the modern labour-intensive industries like electronics. A note of warning should be sounded here. Though there should be feedbacks between the selection of techniques and that of an output-mix, one should be aware of the existence of important limitations, such as the size and accessibility of the market. As a rule, considerations of the output-mix should take priority over those of the selection of techniques.

Time-scheduling

As previously mentioned, time-scheduling provides a new dimension to the framing of industrial development strategy. In fact, the same goals can be pursued by different time solutions, based on different sequences for the implantation of new industries and expansion of existing ones. Freedom of decision is restricted, of course, by considerations of crude complementarity. There is no point in setting up a steel mill, meant to use local inputs, five years before opening the local iron ore and coal mines intended to supply the mill, or five years prior to linking the mines to the steel mill by appropriate transport facilities. But many more considerations are involved, particularly in the initial stages of industrialization, when external facilities, production capacities, and investment possibilities are relatively restricted.

Should one start by concentrating on the infrastructure, hoping (as many experts did in the late forties and as some partisans of the theory of growth poles still do) that investment in manufacturing industries will automatically follow? Or should the strategist start, instead, by concentrating on import-substituting consumer goods industries, contenting himself with a more modest investment in infrastructure?

In Figures 2.2 to 2.5, interindustry relations are shown schematically in the simplest terms. Industry is subdivided into five sectors as follows:

M_1 = sector of machines to produce machines and intermediate goods
M_2 = sector of machines to produce consumer goods
R = sector of raw materials and intermediate goods
C_1 = sector of essential consumer goods
C_2 = sector of non-essential consumer goods

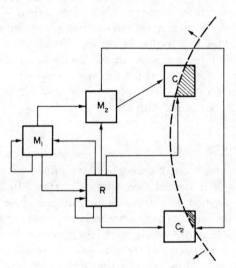

FIG. 2.2   Development through import substitution: emphasis on sectors yielding rapid results

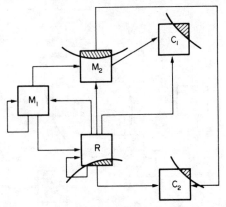

FIG. 2.3 Development through import substitution: mixed strategy involving sectors yielding both rapid and long-term results

The results of concentrating on import-substitution investments are likely to be spectacular in the beginning, but the possibility will be exhausted after some time (see Figure 2.2). Industrialization starts in this case in C_1 and C_2 industries. A hypertrophy of C_2 may retard the development of the remaining sectors (the case of perverse growth). Furthermore, the real net import substitution may be much less than the apparent gross substitution, especially if we take into account the

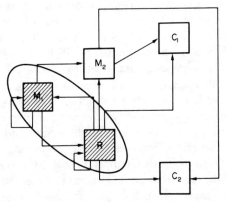

FIG. 2.4 Development by establishing a self-sufficient heavy-industry complex

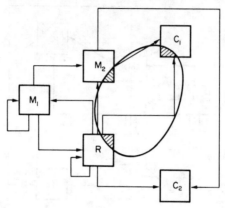

Fɪɢ. 2.5   Development by exploiting forward and backward industrial linkages

additional imports in the form of equipment and material inputs and
the additional payments abroad incurred by the industries in the form
of royalties, technical services, and dividends to foreign capital.

In addition to import substitution of consumer goods, import substitution can also be undertaken with respect to industry inputs and equipment, but the gestation periods in these branches of production are
long (or at least longer than in consumer industries), considerable knowledge is required and, in many cases, the minimum necessary investment
is very high. Thus, a long-term investment strategy oriented towards
import substitution should contain an element of early preparation
of this more difficult import-substitution phase (see Figure 2.3). The
future advantages of such an approach will have to be paid for by
an initial period of aggravated balance-of-trade difficulties during which
some essential consumer goods will have to be imported, since some
of the investment is to be diverted towards those projects which do
not produce consumer goods and which have longer gestation periods.

Obviously, the balance between the immediate and the long-term
import-substitution effects requires careful consideration. Some strategists believe that under such circumstances it pays to go through an
initial period of hardship in order to implant complete production complexes, from raw materials to final goods. These complexes would be
established in mining, steel, and other basic metals, as well as in capital

goods industries. But such a short-cut towards self-sufficiency in capital goods and inputs can at most be taken only by exceptionally large countries which are richly endowed with natural resources and which are prepared to undergo whatever self-imposed austerity in consumption may result from adverse conditions in foreign trade or in their political or military affairs.

A complete industrial complex may, however, still prove to be desirable in certain specific industrial fields in a particular developing country (see Figure 2.4). It may often constitute a suitable approach to an integrated industrial development programme, based on complementarities on a regional, national, or multinational scale. Such a programme may not exhaust all the industrial possibilities of the country, but may well give a definite purpose to a particular sector. For example, a country with abundant resources of marine life may well consider an integrated industrial programme which would exploit all the backward and forward linkages of fishing—from canning, food processing, and chemical factories at one end to the construction of boats and boat engines at the other (see Figure 2.5).

The degree of technological complexity of the different industries involved may offer one primary criterion for determining the sequence of implementation. The impact of an industry on the foreign exchange position may offer another important criterion; it may be used to determine the industries for import substitution and the delicate question of the right moment to start the right export-oriented industries. The choice and the timing will depend on the country's natural endowments, available skills, and foreign market prospects. The risks involved may be greatly reduced through an imaginative foreign trade policy seeking, whenever possible, long-term arrangements and contracts with other countries[12] and sectoral division of labour on an international basis.

One final aspect of time-scheduling needs to be explored. Suppose a decision is made to invest a certain amount in a given industry over five years. It may happen that there would be a choice between investing in one large project, with a relatively long gestation period, or five smaller ones, which have higher capital–output ratios but shorter ges-

---

[12] A practical solution might be to enter into bilateral long-term contracts so as to guarantee to each partner outlets for some newly manufactured products in a given branch of industry.

tation periods. The total investment over time would be the same, the capacities installed in the first case bigger than in the second, but the productive effects of the second alternative would be felt earlier (not considering the added possible advantage of locating the five factories in five different regions). It may prove advisable to adopt the second alternative in certain cases. The two solutions are compared in Figure 2.6. In the first case, investment would go on for five years before production starts. The total investment would be five units and the output would also be five units per year, starting from the sixth year. In the second case, total investment outlays would also be five, but production would start in the second year. Maximum yearly output, from the sixth year, would be only $3\frac{1}{3}$ but, between years 2 and 5, the factories would produce cumulatively $6\frac{2}{3}$, which might be of considerable importance in the context of balance-of-payments or other difficulties.

It should be noted that none of the foregoing considerations are intended to substitute for the detailed time-scheduling needed at the implementation stage, when some type of network analysis may be needed.

Matching goals with policies

The setting of goals and the time-scheduling are now complete. The strategy will essentially take the shape of an investment pattern scheduled over time. The following areas for decision-making have been considered: choice of output-mix, choice of relative and absolute rates of growth, geographical location, choice of an organizational pattern, selection of techniques, and the size-mix of industries. The expected results will materialize in increases in output, in new jobs, and in the social change brought about by the modernization effect which, for the sake of simplicity, was represented as arising mainly from the introduction of new production and management techniques. To achieve these results, however, effective policies must be evolved and used to mobilize the country's resources and use them rationally.

It should be made clear from the very outset that a whole spectrum of policies is usually possible. These may vary significantly in their degree of boldness, as well as in their effectiveness. Their effectiveness

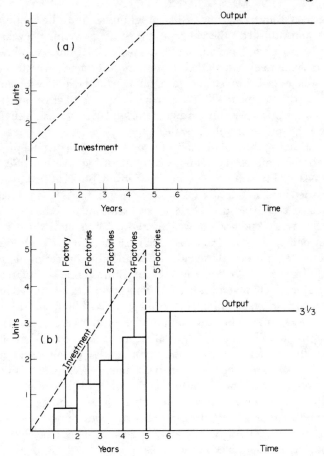

Fig. 2.6 Balancing the length of the project gestation period with the capital–output ratio: (a) single-factory project over five years with a capital–output ratio of 1.0; (b) five smaller factories built at annual intervals, each with a capital–output ratio of 1.5

in a mixed economy should normally increase with the participation of the public sector, which can be specifically geared to the implementation of the strategy, whereas the private sector can, at best, be induced and persuaded to join in a given programme. On the other hand, policies are likely to become relatively ineffective when overambitious goals are set. Similarly, policies, like programmes, must be continuously revised and adjusted; therefore, at the strategy-framing level, there should be more emphasis on identifying which instruments will be used than on trying to give them their final shape. Of course, overall development policies will influence to a great extent the policy choices for industrial development. This is particularly true of measures aimed at the mobilization of resources and of the kind of relationship envisaged between the public and the private sectors.

In considering the mobilization of resources, several distinct problems arise. First, it is necessary to find ways of financing investment at large, and industrial investment in particular. Second, physical resources must be provided in a suitable mix and at the proper time. As for the financing problem, it comprises the whole set of fiscal and income policies, as well as the price policy followed by the public sector. Such policies will normally pursue several aims which are more or less contradictory. For example, in order to increase the financial resources of the public sector, it is necessary to increase taxes. In contrast, one way of inducing private investors to invest consists of giving them special tax reductions, coupled with special credit facilities for projects of high social priority. In such cases, arbitration and compromise solutions are necessary.

As to the mobilization of physical resources, it seems advisable not to leave the matter entirely to the free interplay of market forces. As a rule, a reasonably speedy industrialization process will require the imposition of some type of control on foreign trade in order to ensure that the best use is made of the available foreign exchange. The direct physical allocation of certain scarce capital goods should not be completely ruled out, though rationing, in general, is not beleived to be a viable measure in mixed economies.

Third, there is the problem of mobilizing human resources, in particular the problem of promoting labour-intensive investment and public works within the narrow limits imposed by the availability of food, by organizational difficulties, and by the restricted scope of projects of the pick-and-shovel variety. In addition, there is the problem of releasing the dormant initiative of the people and of creating a mood of participation and interest in the strategy and in the subsequent plans. Unfortunately, however, a precise knowledge of social engineering methods conducive to arousing such an attitude is lacking, and experience to date is of a rather negative nature. Mere propaganda will not do.

Specific policies supporting industrialization may include:

(a) A statement setting out the spheres of influence of the public and private sectors. This is desirable in order to avoid uncertainties which often paralyse the initiative of private entrepreneurs.

(b) The organization of special financial institutions to give selective support to investors who take up projects falling within the programme priorities.

(c) The provision of technical assistance to industries.

(d) Schemes combining fiscal advantages, credit availability, and technical facilities in order to attract industrial investment to a given region or area.

(e) The granting of protection to infant industries by means of tariffs, import restrictions, and, if necessary, subsidies to exporters.

(f) The protection of cottage industries through tax concessions and, if need be, subsidies.

In the selection of techniques, there is little chance of influencing private entrepreneurs except by controlling the introduction of manufacturing and trying, whenever possible, to build into fiscal and credit policies incentives to save on equipment.[13] This illustrates the importance of making proper choices in the public sector, on the one hand, and, on the other, of co-ordinating industrial development strategy with policies of research and development on manufacturing techniques. The latter aspect has often been neglected. A vigorous, government-supported programme of research, centred on the specific problems of the country concerned and ultimately leading to the invention of new, original techniques better suited to local factors, factor ratios, and social environment, should be capable of making a significant contribution to the effectiveness of future investment in industry. A carefully

---

[13] No case is yet known in which such a policy has actually been used. But, in contrast, many existing schemes of support to industrialization which are intended to create jobs have proved to be self-defeating because the opportunity cost of capital for the entrepreneur fortunate enough to get government support becomes so low that it encourages him instead to import the most capital-intensive techniques, particularly as this helps him avoid the troubles that occasionally arise with a large labour force.

framed educational programme, paying special attention to vocational and technical training, should have a similar effect.

Conclusion

In this chapter, two major ways of building alternative strategies have been presented. The first is by varying the goals-mix; the second is by varying the intensity of the policies adopted. A third implicit way is by comparing different paths or, more specifically, different sequences of obtaining approximately the same results after a given time span. The framing of strategy is thus typically an exercise in "variant thinking". The purpose of the exercise is to acquire a better knowledge of the particularly sensitive decision areas and of possible means of intervention.

Under these circumstances, the number of possible viable strategies of industrialization is so large and depends to such an extent on the particular conditions of each country that a rigid typology of strategies cannot be established which would be meaningful for the strategist. Nevertheless, his ability to frame useful strategy can be improved considerably by a deep comparative analysis of the actual experience of different countries. After all, economics is the study of economies.

Such an analysis would seem to constitute a valuable task to be performed with the assistance of international organizations, not for the purpose of undertaking yet another academic exercise, but rather to assist planners and development strategists. It would give them a sober, critical appraisal of the industrialization path followed by selected countries, chosen in such a way as to vary the initial conditions as well as the policies followed. Such a procedure would constitute the least imperfect approximation obtainable through an empirical investigation such as natural scientists conduct in their laboratories.

CHAPTER 3

Development Planning and Policies for Increasing Domestic Resources for Investment—with Special Reference to Latin America (1968)

General considerations

The post-war development of the Latin American economies offers a puzzling picture. Rates of growth have not been too bad on the whole, though to a great extent nullified by the population explosion: 5 per cent per year for the continent taken as a whole from 1950 to 1955, 4.7 per cent for the next five years, and 4.6 per cent from 1960 to 1965 (note the decreasing trend, while the rate of population growth has increased from an average of 2.7 per cent per year from 1950 to 1955 to 2.9 per cent in 1963).[1] In any event, many Latin American countries have fared much better than their Asian and African counterparts. Industrialization has made such considerable progress that, in 1963, 23.4 per cent of the gross social product was generated by manufacturing industry and another 3 per cent by construction, while the relative share of agriculture was 21 per cent only and that of mining, 5.1 per cent. Admittedly, industrialization has not brought with it sweeping changes in the pattern of employment. An ECLA study has pointed out the fact that workers in manufacturing industries today do not represent a proportion substantially higher than in 1925! Actually, their relative share in the employment roll was 14.3 per cent in 1960 as compared with 13.7 per cent thirty-five years earlier. It is true, however, that employment in factories went up from 3.5 to 7.5 per cent, while in artisan-type workshops it decreased from 10.2

[1] All data, unless otherwise stated, are taken from ECLA publications.

to 6.8 per cent. At the same time, employment in construction rose from 1.6 to 4.9 per cent.[2]

Several Latin American countries could claim considerable success in achieving import substitution over a wide range of products (though not necessarily those which should enjoy the highest priority, so that the process quickly reached a stalemate); but, at the same time, this process of growth, to a large extent unplanned, produced serious distortions in the economy and increased still more the enormous social disparities between a minority of rich and vast masses of poor people. Inflation, with all its evil effects on the standards of living of wage and salary earners, has become the scourge of almost all the Latin American countries and is bound to persist as long as the present imbalance between the insufficient growth rates of agriculture and those of the non-agricultural sectors of the economy persists, and is aggravated by an uncontrolled and uncontrollable exodus of the poverty-stricken rural populations towards the urban areas. To this we should add foreign trade difficulties, to some extent beyond the control of the Latin American countries, but intensified by a lack of suitable policies for import control and the planning of foreign-trade-oriented industries (including export promotion and import substitution) and, above all, for the proper control of the operations of foreign-owned enterprises.

Several ECLA studies have assembled impressive evidence of both the successes and the deficiencies of the growth process in Latin America.[3] If the prevailing mood today is somewhat pessimistic and the emphasis is rather on the shortcomings and the dangers looming ahead, it is because in terms of land resources–men ratios the situation of Latin America is, on the whole, much more favourable than that of other less-developed regions of the world. The reasons for the present impasse must lie, therefore, primarily in the social organization, under-

[2] "Structural changes in employment within the context of Latin America's economic development", *Econ. Bull. for Latin Am.*, **X,** no. 2, October 1965, pp. 163–187.

[3] Of course, the record is different for each country concerned and, needless to say, sweeping generalizations on Latin America as a whole should be avoided as much as possible. One realizes this on looking at the figures for national income per head, first in different countries and then in different regions of each country. The range of national income per head in cross-country comparisons extends from 1 to 7 (Bolivia and Argentina) and interregional disparities in a country like Brazil are of the same order or magnitude (Piaui and Sao Paulo).

stood here in the broadest sense of the term. This is a matter for bitter reflexion in the short run, and for considerable optimism in the longer perspective, as human societies should be able ultimately to overcome obstacles created by man.

In the Latin America of today there is a growing awareness of the goals to be pursued. "Development ideology" has spread throughout the continent and finds supporters among representatives of different social classes and political factions, though their agreement may not go beyond concurrence in aims stated in the most general terms. It is also more and more widely understood that—to quote the opening statement of a study by the Chilean economist Osvaldo Sunkel—"development, viewed in proper historical perspective, appears in the last analysis to be a process of transformation of structures and institutions, economic, social, political and cultural. . .". This necessarily implies changing traditionally accepted situations and, therefore, challenging vested interests both at the internal and at the international level.[4]

The sensitive areas for action are easy to identify. The following four seem to be the most important:

(a) Redistribution of social income, leading to a higher volume of productive investment and, at the same time, to better standards of living for the working people, at the expense of superfluous (and conspicuous) consumption on the part of the moneyed élite.

(b) Land reforms achieving the double purpose of increasing agricultural output and improving the lot of the impoverished peasants (who will thus become prospective buyers of industrial goods).

(c) Tightening of controls on foreign trade operations and capital movements, with the aim of getting more income from a given volume of exports,[5] and making the best use of the existing capacity to import.

(d) Channeling of the development process through a plan, which would indicate not only goals but match them with means and suitable policies guaranteeing their implementation. A plan which does not spell out the implementation policies is but a "pseudo-plan", to use

---

[4] O. Sunkel, "Politica nacional de desarrollo y dependencia externa", *Estudios Int.* (Santiago, Chile), no. 1, April 1967, p. 43.

[5] Even with given terms of trade, computed in the traditional way, a country can get more from a given volume of exports if a ceiling is placed on the profits subsequently made by foreign-owned exporting firms and expatriated.

Cz. Bobrowski's terminology, and here I should like to subscribe emphatically to the following statement made by the United Nations Committee on Development Planning: "Planning viewed as a social technique is not a substitute for development policy. This truism, however, seems to be widely forgotten. There is a tendency to assume that planning could supersede or even replace the framing of sound policies from economic and social development. Nothing could be further from the truth, and any notion that difficult policy decisions can be evaded by recourse to development planning should be promptly dismissed."[6]

To be operational, planning must deal with the social and institutional conditions for development. Planning without a policy framework, to borrow an expression from D. R. Gadgil, becomes an exercise on paper, which is by no means innocuous, however, as it helps to create false hopes and dangerous illusions.

The crux of the matter is, therefore, implementation, which starts at the very moment of plan-framing. Implementation and planning are but two sides of the same process. All this is nowadays more or less agreed upon among planners and has been discussed in the light of Latin American experiences.[7] The range of policies and measures which could instil dynamism into Latin American planning is also known. Thus, the problem lies in the sphere of decision-making, largely of a political nature. This makes the outside economist's task easier; he can claim that his responsibility is marginal. On the other hand, he is bound to be repetitive and to restate much that seems obvious. Aware of this weakness of my position, I shall, nevertheless, try to analyse once more the Latin American process of growth in order to substantiate a few policy recommendations, which—without being necessarily new—need to be driven home.

The trap of "perverse growth"

An underdeveloped economy is essentially a supply-limited economy, although lack of effective demand and idle capacities may arise in

---

[6] *United Nations, Committee for Development Planning: Report on the Second Session (10–20 April 1967)*, E/4362, p. 2.

[7] See, in particular, the papers presented at the second session of the Committee for Development Planning by the Centre for Development Planning, Projections and Policies and the ECLA secretariat.

respect of certain categories of goods, as we shall see later in this chapter. The growth rate of the economy, and, still more important, of popular consumption, thus depends on optimum use of scarce resources, i.e. on the fullest use of existing production capacities for socially meaningful purposes. This implies not only ensuring that capacity does not lie idle but also preventing social waste, which takes the form of diverting scarce resources into production of goods and services to satisfy the rapidly growing superfluous consumption of the élite so that bottlenecks appear if the growth rate of other sectors of the economy is stepped up. It is important to realize that all the sectors of the economy compete for the scarce resources, but their expansion does not have the same effects on the long-term growth potential of the economy. For the purpose of this argument, let us divide the national economy into the following four sectors:

Sector M, turning out investment goods.

Sector R, turning out raw materials and intermediate goods.

Sector E, turning out basic consumer goods and services, including staple food, called here "essentials".[8]

Sector L, turning out "non-essential" consumer goods, called here "luxuries", although this is stretching the meaning a little.

Each sector may sell a part of its ouput abroad; conversely, available supplies of each category of goods may be increased by imports.

Intersectoral flows, including foreign trade operations, are indicated in Figure 3.1. It is perfectly clear that the two sectors turning out consumer goods compete for raw materials and intermediate goods *R,* investment goods *M,* and the capacity to import *T;* therefore, other things being equal, the growth rate of one can be achieved only at the expense of the other. Now, their function in the process of growth is completely different. Expansion of *E* is a *sine qua non* for a non-inflationary rise in employment and in the standards of living of the working population. In so far as expansion of *L* largely serves the selfish interests

---

[8] The definition of "essentials" and "non-essentials" must be established for each country and stage of development on the basis of the study of consumption patterns. A certain measure of arbitrariness cannot be eliminated altogether from such an exercise, but the concept remains valid and very useful for planning.

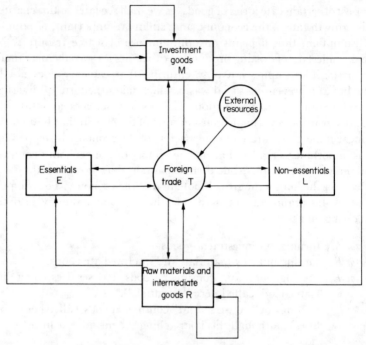

FIG. 3.1   Flows of goods and utilization of the capacity to import

of an élite,[9] it does not contribute to the long-term growth process, which depends on the available flows on *M* and *R*, matched by a proper supply of *E*—the main counterpart of wages. On the contrary, a hypertrophy of *L* is likely to endanger long-term development prospects, because *L* is competing not only with *E* but also with *M* and *R* for the utilization of *M*, *R*, and *T*. Growth will not be arrested immediately, however, and during a certain period of years expansion of *L* is bound to be reflected in indices which show an increase in national income, creating a mood of euphoria. This is precisely the trap of "perverse growth". Conventional indices point to progress and an industries boom. Inflation—the first symptom of perverse growth—is

[9] I am simplifying the problem for clarity's sake by not making a further distinction between *L* goods, which are consumed by a relatively large number of people, and "luxuries" in the narrow sense of the term.

dismissed lightly as a "growing pain" and then dealt with by means of completely inappropriate monetary measures which overlook its primary source, i.e. the imbalance between the slow expansion of production of staple foods and the rapid increase of the urban population and of employment in the L sector. The next phase is only too well known. Growth comes to a stop, but not inflation, and an inflationary deflation ensues.[10]

My analysis can be somewhat refined in several ways, but without affecting its substance:

(a) We must take into consideration not only the direct flows of M, R and T to L, but also the indirect flows (M to produce R for use as an input in L, etc.)

(b) We may deal in the same manner with the problem of utilization of qualified manpower and managerial skills in short supply (see Figure 3.2), including the inflow of foreign technicians and what has been called the "brain drain".

(c) The same approach also holds good for an analysis no longer in physical but in financial terms (see Figure 3.3), "savings" being the scarce resource (subject to further qualifications to be stated later).

(d) In so far as available supplies of E (which constitute the main counterpart of wages) limit the overall volume of employment on the assumption of a given wage-level and non-inflationary growth, E may also be dealt with as a scarce resource, for which workers employed in all sectors of the economy compete (see Figure 3.4). It is immediately clear how greatly a large increase of employment in L services endangers the prospect of growth.

The problem of effective demand

It is now necessary to qualify our basic assumption that a mixed developing economy is supply-determined only and does not suffer from a lack of effective demand in any way. We shall, therefore, look at

[10] See, for example, an article on Argentina by E. Eshag and R. Thorp, published in the *Bull. of the Oxford Inst. of Econ. and Statist.*, no. 1, 1965. Developments in Brazil have shown that inflationary growth can proceed, resulting in growing inequality in income distribution with all its adverse effects.

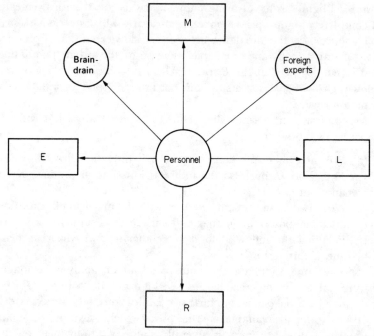

Fig. 3.2   Utilization of skilled personnel

the problem of the lopsided development of the Latin American econ-omies from the side of demand for consumer goods.

The demand function for staple food (F), for non-durable and semi-durable consumer goods other than staple food (I), and for durable goods (D)[11] for different levels of personal income are represented sche-matically in Figure 3.5.

Let us explain the shape of the curves. Demand for staple food (F) is high even at very low levels of income, and rises steadily to point A, where income elasticity for food is equal to $I)$. It continues to increase up to a maximum at point B and is stabilized shortly afterwards at a level lower than the maximum, corresponding to a diet which

[11] We are not using here the previous classification into essentials and non-essentials; all F goods are, however, essentials and practically all D goods non-essentials, while I goods should be partly allocated to E and partly to L.

is socially considered to be optimum, though medical opinion may not be altogether in agreement.

Demand for other non-durable and semi-durable consumer goods (*I*), in which we include higher grades of processed foodstuffs and a wide range of industrial articles from textiles and shoes to radio sets, appears at a very low level of income and rises as income rises. The elasticity of demand for these goods is likely to be particularly high at income levels between *B'* and *C'* because expenditure on staple foods has already decreased and the level of income at which it becomes possible to purchase durables has not yet been reached.

Demand for durables (*D*), defined here in a rather restrictive sense to include mainly houses, motorcars, and household appliances, makes its appearance only at a relatively high level of income *C'*. Elasticity of demand is fairly high between *C'* and *D'* (taken here as a point of relative saturation). The pressure of expenditure on durables is likely

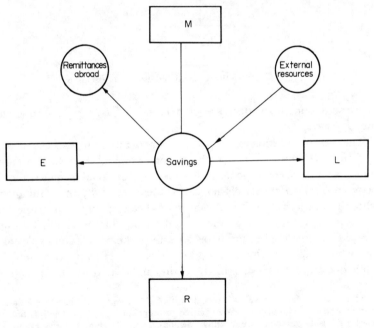

Fig. 3.3   Allocation of savings

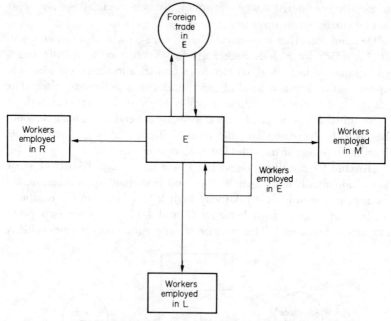

Fig. 3.4   Utilization of available supplies of essentials

to cause a temporary decrease of demand for I goods as shown in the (I) curve.

The present situation in many Latin American countries is characterized by the coexistence of very large population strata, which by any standards are extremely poor and have levels of personal income situated between C' and P' probably not far to the right of A', and a minority whose incomes exceed R and who have been mainly responsible for the former buoyant state on the market for durables.[12] The first group is rapidly increasing in number as a result of the population explosion, and which explains why demand for F goods is growing very quickly while demand for I goods (chiefly textiles and similar goods) is lagging

---

[12] I am careful not to make RR' coincide with CC' to signify that the upper stratum of the intermediate group is already engaged in purchasing durables. The question of how far this is the result of an unhealthy "demonstration effect" need not be examined here.

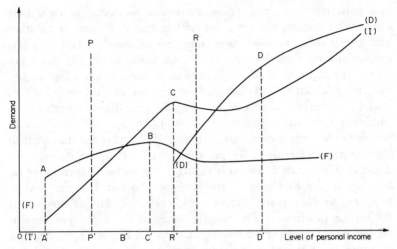

Fɪɢ. 3.5   Demand for *F, I,* and *D* goods

behind. As for the demand for durables, it is reflected principally in the scope of the income distribution curve. After all, according to estimates 19 per cent of total personal incomes in Latin America accrues to the top 2 per cent in the income scale and another 14 per cent to the next 3 per cent, while the half of the population in the lower income bracket receives a bare 16 per cent of the total. This gives an average income of only 120 dollars per head for the lower half, compared with 3,500 dollars for the top 2 per cent and 1,750 dollars for the next 3 per cent.[13]

To substantiate my argument a little more, we shall now briefly consider the estimates of individual consumption contained in another ECLA study.[14] They are not strictly comparable to my scheme, owing to slight differences in the classification of goods, but they fully support my conclusions. In round figures, the lower income half of the Latin American population spent less than 130 dollars per head on personal consumption in 1960, of which about 75 per cent went to purchase

[13] *The Economic Development of Latin America in the Post-war Period*, United Nations Publication, Sales no. 64.II.G.6.

[14] ECLA, *The Process of Industrial Development in Latin America*, United Nations Publication, Sales no. 66.II.G.4, p. 126.

food and another 12 per cent was spent on services, leaving a bare 7 dollars for textiles, footwear, and clothes, and 10 dollars for all other industrial goods, including beverages and tobacco! Needless to say, expenditure on durables was nil. On the other hand, the top 5 per cent of the population (about 10 million persons) could afford a consumption of about 2,000 dollars per head per year, distributed as follows: food, 14 per cent; textiles, footwear, and clothing, 10 per cent; durables, 14.25 per cent; other industrial goods, 16.75 per cent; services, 45 per cent. Their expenditure on durables slightly exceeded that on food and accounted for about 74 per cent of the aggregate demand for durables. (In reality it was still higher if we include expenditure on housing; in the ECLA study the latter was included in the services category, which explains the very high relative share of services in the total expenditure.) The relative share of the top 5 per cent in the income scale and of the lower 50 per cent in the aggregate demand for other categories of goods were, respectively, as follows: food, 9.5 and 32 per cent; textiles, footwear, and clothing, 33 and 11.5 per cent; other industrial goods, 39 and less than 12 per cent.

The picture is clear. The prospect of further expansion of production of *I* goods depends on the access of broader population strata to higher income levels.

The same applies *a fortiori* to *D* goods, though two qualifications must be made here:

(a) Projections of demand for *D* goods are more complicated because it is necessary, on the one hand, to make a proper assessment of deferred demand in the initial stages of production on account of import restrictions and, on the other, to make assumptions about the likely rate of renewal of these goods. It is quite likely that demand for *D* goods will slacken even in the highest income brackets of the Latin American population in years to come.

(b) For reasons of social justice and as a result of income redistribution measures, demand for several *D* goods could (and in this writer's opinion should) be stabilized or even drastically cut back for quite a long time. It is possible to conceive, theoretically, of a society that enjoys much higher average incomes per head than is the case in Latin America at present, with a fairly equitable pattern of income distribution, so as to reduce the number of people in the D goods consuming bracket.[15] More generally, the present pattern of consumption in advanced industrial countries, though exerting an undeniable attraction on people in both socialist and developing countries, need not be taken either as a model or as a true picture of the shape of things to come. The affluent societies of tomorrow might wish to pay considerably more attention to public services, thus redressing·the balance between privately consumed goods and publicly rendered services, so conspicuously absent at present in Western industrialized society.[16]

In any case, there does not seem to be much scope for further growth of industrial output in Latin America by means of expansion of industries producing D goods even if the present extremely slanted and socially inequitable distribution of income were to prevail. It could still be argued that lack of measures leading to a redistribution of social income and the ensuing expansion of demand for I goods would sooner or later affect the earnings of those sections of the upper strata concerned with the production of I goods, thus reducing their expenditure on D goods. A serious recession, affecting the whole manufacturing sector, might well follow.

The demand for F goods is likely to grow at a relatively fast rate in any set of circumstances, short of an economic and social disaster leading to further deterioration in the standards of consumption of the poorer people. Even assuming that per capita incomes remain constant (a very harsh assumption indeed!), demand would still grow *pari passu* with the population increase, i.e. in Latin America at about 3 per cent per year, thereby imposing a tremendous burden on agriculture. In fact, the following equation is approximately true:

$$f = p + ey$$

[15] Of course, thresholds for each category of D goods are different and vary as a function of price and preference (i.e. utility and fashion). A refrigerator is likely to be purchased before a motorcycle and, at any rate, before a car, while an air-conditioner, though much cheaper than a car, will come much later.

[16] I am following here J.K. Galbraith's argument on this subject (see his book *The Affluent Society*, New York, 1958) to stress that this view is shared also by people who are not suspected of a leaning towards socialism.

Where f = rate of growth of demand for F goods
         p = rate of population increase
         e = income elasticity of demand for F goods
         y = growth rate of personal per capita income

Thus, wherever y is positive, f exceeds p. As, roughly speaking, the overall income elasticity of demand for food in Latin America can be estimated to be 0.5 at least,[17] every 1 per cent increment in personal per capita income produces an increase of 0.5 per cent in the demand for F goods on top of the 3 per cent annual increase in this demand, assessed on the basis of the population increase and the assumption that per capita income would remain steady. Under the circumstances, demand for food is likely to exceed supply in most Latin American countries, even if it is assumed that a much more vigorous effort will be made on the production side. Hence inflationary pressures, with all their regressive effects as far as income distribution is concerned, are likely to persist. By hitting urban workers and salary earners, inflation limits the market for I goods still more. Insofar as price increases of F goods accrue to intermediaries and landlords, and not to peasants and agricultural workers (this seems to be the rule, with few exceptions), they are not translated into an additional demand for I goods. The only beneficiaries, as far as the market is concerned, are the producers of D goods, purchased by landlords and merchants, and to a smaller extent producers of M and R goods for agriculture. The result is that the foundation on which the disproportionate expansion of industries producing D goods rests, becomes even more precarious.

The above analysis of demand leads to the conclusion that the development plans should pay most attention to the following three tasks:

(a) Expansion of agricultural output, and more specifically of the production of F goods.

(b) Broadening of the market for I goods (of course, the achievement of point (a), if carried out properly, would to a great extent solve

[17] According to FAO estimates (*Agricultural Products—Projections in 1970*, Rome, 1962), the income elasticity for aggregate food in terms of prices paid to the farmer was 0.58 in Mexico in 1958. Needless to say, the elasticity coefficients vary according to the category of goods and to the income bracket. There are, moreover, significant differences from country to country and between urban and rural populations. For a fuller study of this problem see Chapter 4.

the second problem automatically, as farmers would then spend more on *I* goods).

(c) Curbing further expansion of the industries turning out *D* goods.

Thus, our picture of a supply-determined developing economy needs to be qualified, as far as the demand for *I* goods is concerned. Nevertheless, the basic development problem consists in improving the utilization of scarce goods in such a way as to increase the long-term growth potential.

Market allocation of investment versus effective planning

At this stage it may be asked *why* development in many Latin American countries has been lopsided and ultimately proved to conform to the "perverse growth" pattern. In my opinion the reasons lie essentially in the dominant role played by the market as far as investment allocation is concerned.

Some Latin American economists and many politicians continue to believe that the profit criterion is a sound one, and that whenever an investment proves profitable and bankable it conforms *ipso facto* to the social benefit criterion. Our whole analysis leads to a diametrically opposite conclusion: a sound investment policy must be based on investment goals established in the plan on the basis of considerations which have nothing to do with the rate of profit of the individual enterprise. Once the priorities have been chosen, it is possible to adjust credit and fiscal policies (including the granting of subsidies in some justified cases, e.g. to some lines of export production) in such a way so as to attract private capital to investment which is in harmony with the plan. At the same time, it is necessary to prevent private investment in projects that are regarded as undesirable, irrespective of the rate of profit they may yield. There can be no accelerated growth without a policy of austerity (Lange used to say in this connexion that a developing economy is a war economy). And austerity must start with curbs on investment leading to further expansion of the *L* sector. In other words, it is necessary, on the one hand, to prevent excessive growth of demand for *L* goods, mostly by means of proper fiscal measures (both higher direct taxes on the rich and much higher, indirect, progressive, *ad valorem* taxes and duties on *L* goods are required). On the other hand, there is no need to be afraid that the demand for some "luxuries" will be altogether unsatisfied. The income elasticities of demand should be rigorously respected only as far as *E* goods are concerned.

Now, it is possible to argue that in countries with a slanted distribution of social income aggravated by inflation profit rates are particularly high in the *L* sector, which, therefore, attracts a sizable part of the savings available for investment, both private and public.[18]

Two types of investment within the *L* sector are likely to be preferred: construction of luxury dwellings[19] and the establishment of import-substituting industries turning out semi-durables and durables ranging from home appliances to motorcars. Because of balance-of-payments difficulties, these import-substituting industries enjoy the safest type of protection, namely drastic and effective import restrictions on goods similar to those produced at home. The public for whom they produce—small in number but rich—is ready to pay almost any price for "prestige goods" and, therefore, profit rates may skyrocket, even though production costs are extremely high owing to inefficiency and lack of economies of scale. In point of fact, none of the supposed advantages of free competition materializes as the market is imperfect.[20] In the limiting case (such as the motorcar industry in several Latin American countries), competition leads to splitting of the market among several producers who, in spite of producing in highly uneconomic conditions, make huge profits, since they operate as an oligopoly and fix sales prices practically at will.[21] This explains why private industries can be profitable even though their capacities are severely underutilized.

[18] In so far as the latter consists in financing the private sector or providing it with a transport and power infrastructure and/or with raw materials and intermediate goods for production.

[19] Construction accounts for a substantial share (almost half) of total investment in Latin America. In Central America the relevant percentage is still higher, exceeding 60 per cent. There are good reasons for believing that this heavy share of construction in total investment is due to the construction boom in luxury dwellings.

[20] Imperfection of the market including the capital and labour markets, is a feature of all the developing mixed economies. That is why the neo-classical growth models, which assume a perfect market and full mobility of factors of production, do not reflect the realities of life.

[21] For this reason, lack of profits in public enterprises should not be taken as a proof that they are more inefficient than prosperous private business, without closely investigating the operating costs and price policies of both.

Thus, allocation of investment through the market is bound to intensify the lopsided development of the economy; while in the pre-industrial phase this lopsidedness resulted from heavy concentration of investment in export production (often a single product of plantations or mines), the emphasis has now shifted to the L sector, creating a further new imbalance. Regional imbalances are also likely to increase, as industrial investment will tend to concentrate in areas where it can enjoy external economies.

The undesirable effects of growth through the market have been magnified in many Latin American countries by a policy of undiscriminating support for industrialization and import substitution, mostly when it took the form of imports of machinery and equipment financed by an inflow of foreign capital. I am not against industrialization, of course, and I believe that the only viable strategy for the majority of developing countries consists precisely in promoting import substitution;[22] but in order to achieve it over a long period of years, it is absolutely necessary to choose investment priorities carefully so as to prevent an abrupt termination of the phase of easy import substitution carried out mostly in the L and E sectors. In this connexion, I should like to re-emphasize the importance of rapid development from the standpoint of long-term strategy. Import substitution of a considerable range of L goods is a waste of resources, as consumption of these goods should be deferred altogether. Investment in industries turning out luxury goods proper should be prevented instead of encouraged, whatever credit facilities may be offered to finance the imports of necessary equipment.[23] At the same time the possibilities of achieving at least some measure of import substitution in M and R goods, to say nothing of agricultural E goods, should be carefully explored. Import substitution in M and R goods is more difficult to achieve and may require

---

[22] See on this point the author's book *Foreign Trade and Economic Development of Underdeveloped Countries*, Bombay, 1965, partly reproduced in *Obstáculos al Desarrollo y Planificación*, Mexico, 1967. See on this point R. Prebisch, *Towards a Dynamic Development Policy for Latin America* United Nations Publications, Sales no. 64.II.G.4.

[23] An altogether different problem is that of frequent overestimation of import-substitution effects. If one takes into account the import requirements of the import-substituting industries and the outflow of foreign currency in the form of royalties, expatriated profits, payments for technical services, etc., the net import-substitution effects may prove negligible.

heavy investment, but, in compensation, in an expanding economy there are unlimited possibilities of providing substitutes for potential imports of M and R goods. While going ahead with import substitution of many I goods and some D goods, belonging both to "essentials" and the lower range of "non-essentials", I would prevent the dissipation of resources on premature or altogether superfluous investment in the production of many other L goods and services and use them to promote an earlier and more rapid expansion of M and R industries[24] and the creation of additional capacity to turn out E goods and services (including low-cost housing). Of course, the pattern of investment should be harmonized in such a way as to make the best use of the existing resources and to avoid as much as possible the emergence of bottlenecks, on the one hand, and idle capacity, on the other. In other words, I believe that effective planning could have prevented many Latin American countries from falling into the trap of "perverse growth".

Minimum conditions for effective planning

What, then, are the minimum conditions for effective planning in a "mixed economy", i.e. in an economy where a dynamic but usually small public sector coexists with a large private sector (modern and traditional)?

In my opinion they are three. To plan effectively, i.e. to be able simultaneously to set realistic targets and to define policies for implementation which have a fair probability of success, it is necessary to establish direct controls on the investment process and on foreign trade operations, as well as to control the price level indirectly by means of appropriate agricultural policies. Let us discuss briefly each of these conditions.

CONTROL OF INVESTMENT

It follows from my considerations on perverse growth that policies for accelerated long-term growth cannot consist in simply maximizing

---

[24] Of course, both the pattern and the sequence of development of M and R industries should be very carefully studied, taking into consideration the natural resources of the country, its position in the international division of labour, its availabilities of capital and skills, and also the size of the market. As a rule, however, even in small and poor countries there should be room for some engineering industries, if for no other reason than to prepare for future industrialization and to train manpower.

investment. Undesirable investment, i.e. investment in projects enjoying no priority from the social point of view and not provided for in the plan, hampers the long-term growth process and should be prevented. As far as this writer knows, the only practical means to this end is to subject private investment[25] to licensing by the competent authorities, taking into consideration at least the selected line of production and the proposed location of the new plant. In the case of major projects, the proposed technology should also be screened by a competent panel of experts for the purpose of choosing the best from the range of available technologies, having in view such parameters as the capital–output ratio and the amount of imported material used in the construction of the plant and in the production process. Licensing should also be extended to investment in housing, which could easily be achieved by enlarging the scope of the existing controls of projects from the technical and town-planning points of view.

The imposition of direct controls on private investment should go hand in hand with active policies aimed at attracting private capital into projects enjoying high social priority and fitting into the plan. A whole range of well-known fiscal, credit, and administrative measures is called for. They should be applied in a selective and elastic way so as to ensure that the highest priority enjoyed by the project the greater the benefits granted, thus discouraging undesirable investment.[26] In spite of all these incentives, private capital may not be attracted to the investment opportunities provided for in the plan, and instead of accelerated growth, recession of the type well known in developed industrial economies would follow. The State must be ready, therefore, to supplement private investment and to finance and/or carry out the projects which are necessary for the success of the plan but do not attract the private investor. The bigger the relative share of the public savings in total

[25] Small investment, however, should be exempted from licensing, in order to avoid cumbersome administrative procedures, whenever it is likely to have little impact on the national economy.

[26] And thus reduce the number of cases in which the licensing authorities must refuse applications for investment permits. Such cases would arise normally only in some industries producing D goods and in luxury housing, which top the list of investment opportunities from the point of view of prospective profits and, at the same time, have the lowest social priorities.

savings[27] and of the public sector in the national economy, the easier this task becomes. This is so, because the public sector may be geared to the implementation of the plan, while the private sector primarily seeks to maximize the profits of private enterprise.

CONTROL OF FOREIGN TRADE

Foreign currency is the joker in the planning game, as it is always possible to make up for shortfalls in local production by additional imports. It is no wonder, therefore, that for the great majority of developing countries foreign currency becomes the scarcest resource, whenever attempts are being made to accelerate the rate of growth of the economy, and ultimately the barrier of foreign trade imposes a ceiling on the overall rate of growth. In these circumstances, State intervention in the operation of foreign trade becomes necessary in order to guarantee the best utilization of the existing import capacity, in accordance with the plan priorities, and also to maximize real income from exports.

The minimum tools required to carry out the first task are either some type of import licensing or the operation of a multiple exchange rate system, complemented by the screening of import prices, to avoid at least the most flagrant cases of overpricing and the ensuing outflow of resources. Direct participation of the public sector in foreign trade operations may also be called for. The scope of the controls and the administrative solutions adopted are subjects for specific decisions, which will vary depending, on the one hand, on how far interventionist policies are pursued and, on the other, on the peculiar conditions of each country, the commodity and the geographical pattern of its imports, etc. In order not to go into detailed discussion of these problems, we shall confine ourselves to three observations of a more general nature.

(a) There is lack of consistency, in my opinion, between the efforts pursued by the developing countries at the international level with the aim of producing a fair measure of intervention in world markets

---

[27] The government can also invest, without imbalancing the economy, up to the amount of privately held savings. In countries where there is hoarding of jewellery, gold, or foreign currency, it is an important consideration, although the complicating factor is its repercussions on the balance of payments.

and the widespread belief in the supposed advantage of relying on the free play of market forces in each country's foreign trade. The latter idea dies hard, although its falsity has been proved by bitter experience in so many developing countries.

(b) The argument concerning the inefficiency of the administrative services set up to control imports in many countries is valid, in fact, but the conclusion usually drawn from it that in some circumstances controls should be abolished altogether is a *non sequitur*. What is needed is to work out measures to simplify and rationalize the procedures employed, and to keep opportunities for corruption down to a minimum rather than to throw out the baby with the bath water.

(c) One important way of improving the performance of import control services is to abandon simplified and erroneous criteria, such as undiscriminating support for all imports of machinery without considering whether the investment they will sustain is desirable or undesirable, whether they will promote import substitution of high social priority, or whether they will contribute to further expansion of the L sector. Priorities, as far as imports are concerned, can be worked out rationally only in the context of an overall plan, and there should be no prejudice against maintenance of imports as such.

Let us turn now to the second task, that of maximizing real income from exports. It implies, on the one hand, the tightening of controls on the operation of foreign-owned firms in order to reduce the profits expatriated under the different headings of the balance of payments (income from capital, technical services, royalties, licences, etc.) and/or through underpricing of exports and overpricing of imports required for export production.

On the other hand, some system of subsidizing selected exports, combined with export duties on other more profitable commodities, should be devised, in order to raise the volume of exports to the desirable level. It is, of course, always possible to push ahead with additional exports, which, however, require an ever-increasing amount of subsidies, offsetting the advantage of additional earnings in foreign currency. How far one should go in terms of marginal net domestic cost per unit of foreign currency earned is a matter for a delicate and important decision to be taken by the planning authorities and should periodically be reviewed in the light of possible shifts in the terms of trade.[28] The decision will depend therefore, on the cost (and the physical possibility) of stepping up production of import substitutes.

INDIRECT CONTROL OF THE PRICE LINE

As stated above, I consider that the process of growth should be non-inflationary as a matter not only of economic expediency but above all of social equity. It is, therefore, imperative to maintain a stable price line for the domestic production of E goods, all the more so since the impact of negative shifts in external terms of trade cannot be eliminated altogether. I do not believe, however, that this goal can be achieved by administrative measures, except for the rather unrealistic case of a comprehensive and smoothly working distribution system ensured by rationing, with no parallel black market. The only other alternative consists, therefore, in dynamic agricultural policies, able to ensure an elastic supply of basic E goods, combined with measures aimed at reducing the pressure of demand for E goods on the part of people employed in the I sector by curbing the rate of expansion of employment in this sector. These policies should, at the same time, promote the structural transformation of traditional agriculture and of outdated production systems with a view to improving the lot of the poorer sections of the rural population and to fostering the expansion of output in such a way as to balance the supply of marketable surpluses[29] with the demand for them. As active agricultural policy should, therefore, be built into the plan, this is also a condition of effective planning itself.

[28] A similar argument holds true for the choice of foreign-trade-oriented investment, embodied in the plan, i.e. of export-promoting and import-substituting projects. The gains in terms of additional exports or import substitution must be paid for by a growing volume of investment distributed among the possible projects, ranged according to their increasing capital–output ratio.

[29] Self-consumption of the farmers should be deducted on both sides of the equation. It is likely to grow more than proportionately in the first stages of transformation of traditional agriculture, as the first natural reaction of people who are undernourished is to eat more whenever such a possibility arises. No matter how this is likely to complicate the problem of supply to urban centres, it should be welcomed as a first step towards the attainment of an important social goal.

Policies for accelerated growth

I can now indicate a few more specific policies which could, in my opinion, step up the mobilization of domestic resources for accelerated growth. I shall deal first with policies aimed at improving the economic performance of Latin American countries by means of a better utilization of existing resources, and then discuss ways of increasing, on the one hand, the volume of savings and, on the other, the marketable surplus of E goods. In the final analysis, this is what sets a limit to the expansion of non-agricultural employment and thus, together with the availabilities of foreign currency to finance the import content of the investment process,[30] imposes a physical constraint on the financing of accelerated growth.

SQUEEZING MORE FROM THE AVAILABLE RESOURCES

Contrary to a widespread belief, the relative share of gross domestic savings in the gross domestic product of many Latin American countries is quite high. From 1963 to 1965 it averaged over 20 per cent in Peru and Venezuela, and ranged from 15 to 19.9 per cent in Argentina, Brazil, Colombia, Jamaica, Nicaragua, Panama, Trinidad, and Tobago.[31] Actual savings may have been even higher, if account is taken of non-monetary investment, which in some countries assumes considerable proportions.[32] Nevertheless, they do not sustain very high rates of growth, the most extreme case being that of Argentina. The high overall capital–output ratios in many Latin American countries reflect an undesirable pattern of investment heavily biased towards prestige construction, both public and private, and perhaps an excessive concentration on infrastructural projects[33] and an unnecessary

---

[30] Deficiencies in the supply of E goods could be made good, of course, by additional imports, but this would correspondingly reduce the availabilities of foreign currency to import equipment.

[31] See UNCTAD, *The Mobilization of Internal Resources by the Developing Countries*, TD/B/C.3/28, 26 January 1967, p.16.

[32] I refer here, in particular, to bringing new land under cultivation with hardly any capital outlay.

[33] This happens frequently as a consequence of a peculiar development philosophy, evolved in the post-war years by the IBRD and still shared by some governments, according to which public money, both local and foreign, should be invested exclusively in infrastructure, leaving the directly productive investment to private initiative. When the supply of public funds is abundant, too much investment may be earmarked for infrastructure.

reliance on capital-intensive technologies (building and construction in general are again involved here). The latter point was very strongly emphasized at the Symposium on Industrial Development in Latin America, held in Santiago in March 1966.[34] While in some fields the only technology available is capital intensive, there are others. Careful choice should be made from the whole range of technologies which have been used at some other time by other countries, taking into consideration above all the relative local costs of capital and labour. There is also the need to stimulate original technological research, on the one hand, to solve problems which do not occur in other more industrialized countries and, on the other, to promote labour-intensive technical progress.

Lack of active policies with respect to the choice of technologies is closely linked with the conspicuous absence of employment targets in Latin American planning.[35]

Measures aimed at decreasing the overall capital–output ratio should be accompanied by a stricter enforcement of controls on foreign trade and operations of foreign capital (including more radical and effective measures to prevent the outflow of Latin American capital) so as to squeeze more resources for development from the existing volume of trade.

INCREASING SAVINGS BY MEANS OF INCOME REDISTRIBUTION

In nearly all the Latin American countries the volume of domestic savings can be substantially increased by means of a redistribution of social income. Stepping up of investment should go *pari passu* with a substantial increase in the incomes of the poorer strata of the population. The argument often adduced that in a poor country the relative share of savings cannot be increased without depressing still more the already low levels of living does not hold good in a society characterized by marked inequalities of income. To illustrate my point, I shall compare

[34] See United Nations, *Industrial Development, Latin America; Report of the Symposium*, New York, 1966, p. 41.
[35] See the paper on experience and problems in the implementation of development plans submitted by ECLA to the Committee for Development Planning, E/AC.54/L.13, 9 March 1967, p. 25.

two hypothetical patterns for an economy with the following initial distribution of income:

Consumption of the élite (upper 10 per cent of the population)

$$C_e = 40 \text{ per cent}$$

Popular consumption (90 per cent of the population)

$$C_p = 50 \text{ per cent}$$

Investment $= 10 \text{ per cent}$

We assume throughout the exercise a constant captial–output ratio equal to 2.5.

Hypothesis A features a steady growth at 4 per cent per year with a constant distribution of income (see Table 3.1). Hypothesis B, starting with the same initial position, assumes that the relative share C_p remains constant throughout the whole period considered, while C_e increases for the first five years at one-quarter of the overall growth rate and, thereafter, at the rate of growth of the economy (see Table 3.2). The "gains" resulting from a lower rate of growth of C_e compared with that of the economy as a whole are transferred to I. As the capital–output ratio remains constant (2.5 as in the previous hypothesis), the rate of growth is stepped up and exceeds 6.5 per cent in the sixth year (t_6), to be stabilized thereafter.

The results are compared in Figure 3.6 (a) to (d). Under hypothesis B, C_p rises from the very beginning and in the year t_{10}, C_p (and the national income Y) exceeds the level attained under hypothesis A by almost 19 per cent and increases at a rate exceeding that of hypothesis A by 62.5 per cent. The volume of investment in the year t_{10} is almost twice as high under hypothesis B than under hypothesis A and the only casualty is C_e, which, however, in the year t_{10} is practically the same under both hypotheses and grows thereafter at a much quicker rate under hypothesis B. It should be pointed out also that there is a constant increase in C_e.

The redistribution of income featured in hypothesis B consists in increasing the relative share of investment from the initial 10 per cent to over 16 per cent at the expense of the relative share of C_e. As the

TABLE 3.1

Hypothesis A: Growth of the economy with no changes in the income distribution and a capital–output ratio of 2.5 (Rate of growth r = 4 per cent)

	t_0	t_1	t_2	t_3	t_4	t_5	t_6	t_7	t_8	t_9	t_{10}
National income Y	100	104	108.2	112.5	117.0	121.7	126.5	131.6	136.9	142.4	148.1
Popular consumption C_p	50	52	54.1	56.2	58.5	60.8	63.3	65.8	68.4	71.2	74.0
Consumption of the élite C_e	40	41.6	43.3	45.0	46.8	48.7	50.6	52.6	54.8	57.0	59.3
Investment I	10	10.4	10.8	11.2	11.7	12.2	12.6	13.2	13.7	14.2	14.8
Rate of growth r		4	4	4	4	4	4	4	4	4	4

TABLE 3.2

Hypothesis B: Growth of the economy with changes in the income distribution and a capital–output ratio of 2.5 (r increases from 4 per cent in t_1 to over 6.5 per cent in t_6 and thereafter stabilizes)

	t_0	t_1	t_2	t_3	t_4	t_5	t_6	t_7	t_8	t_9	t_{10}
National income Y	100	104	108.6	114.0	120.2	127.5	136.0	145.0	154.4	164.4	175.1
Popular consumption C_p	50	52	54.3	57.0	60.1	63.7	68.0	72.5	77.2	82.2	87.5
Consumption of the élite C_e	40	40.4	40.8	41.3	41.9	42.5	45.9	48.9	52.1	55.5	59.1
Investment I	10	11.6	13.4	15.6	18.2	21.2	22.1	23.6	25.1	26.7	28.5
Rate of growth r		4	4.38	4.95	5.48	6.04	6.5	6.5	6.5	6.5	6.5

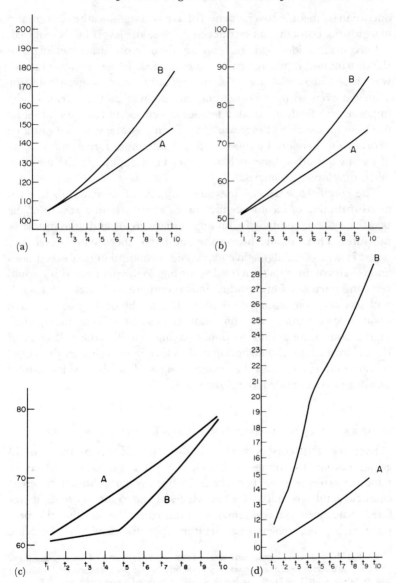

FIG. 3.6   Growth of (a) national income Y, (b) popular consumption C_p, (c) consumption of the élite C_e, and (d) investment I

operation is scheduled over a period of five years against the background of a growing economy, no sacrifice in the absolute level of C_e is required.

Of course, bolder policies bringing about more drastic changes in the distribution of income could be envisaged. However, my example was chosen in such a way to show that substantial progress could be achieved even without postulating far-reaching political reforms, by imposing relatively mild and temporary curbs, not on the absolute level but on the rate of increase of C_e. Such a strategy as that outlined here should therefore be considered as a minimum target, but in spite of its obvious advantages it has not yet been applied in the majority of the developing countries.

The specific operational measures capable of bringing about such a redistribution of income should consist essentially in a reform of the taxation system, combined with appropriate credit and administrative measures. There should be, on the one hand, incentives to save and invest instead of indulging in conspicuous consumption (tax exemptions and rebates on income reinvested according to the plan priorities would serve this purpose). On the other, indirect progressive taxes[36] on I goods and services, comprising the bulk of C_e, should be imposed in such a way as to discourage such consumption, in so far as it continues, while at the same time adding to public saving. Finally, the collection of direct income taxes should be imposed on such items as luxury dwellings, private motorcars, and other external signs of wealth, which cannot be altogether concealed as can income.[37]

SOME REMARKS ON COMPREHENSIVE AGRICULTURAL POLICIES

Even the most cursory systematic discussion of this problem would go far beyond the limits of this chapter. It is necessary to bear in mind the extreme diversity of the evils affecting agriculture in different countries, and even in different provinces of one country. I shall, therefore, limit myself to a few remarks prompted by the fact that the aims pursued by comprehensive agricultural policies should be the same

---

[36] What I have in mind is progressive excise taxes, whereby articles of mass consumption (E goods) are either exempted or taxed only lightly, while taxes on luxuries are heavy and proportional to how far the article concerned is deemed a non-essential.

[37] I shall deal with the land tax in the section devoted to agricultural policies.

in all developing countries, namely they should lead to a substantial improvement in the level of living of the rural population while at the same time ensuring an elastic supply of agricultural *E* goods to urban areas. A natural outcome of such a situation would be an expansion of the internal market for industrial *E* goods and for inputs and agricultural requisites.[38]

The issue boils down to encouraging the farmer to increase his marketable production and assisting him to do so by providing appropriate technical advice and supplies of inputs. At first sight it would seem that in inflation-ridden economies price increases should provide a strong incentive to farmers.[39] This is not so in practice, however. Price incentives do not reach the tiller of the soil, for they are intercepted by intermediaries[40] who, far from being interested in increasing the supply of *E* goods, reap additional profits from speculation and invest a substantial portion of their earnings in the expansion of stocks. No wonder, therefore, that a large number of small-holders confine themselves to subsistence agriculture, the more so since they are frequently compelled to do what amounts to forced labour in different forms on the estate to which they are attached.

Owners of larger estates find it more profitable to specialize in traditional export crops, heavily financed and subsidized by the State. As they are both producers and rural intermediaries with respect to some *E* goods for the domestic market, they may deliberately organize their production so that there are shortages, from which they reap high profits. In such circumstances, a comprehensive agricultural policy should comprise four sets of measures:

[38] I am convinced that the advantages reaped by industry from such an integration of domestic economies would far exceed all the possible gains from international integration, even on the most favourable (and unrealistic) assumptions about the pace of progress in international co-operation. Although I am well aware of the fact that a few industries cannot achieve economies of scale within national boundaries, I believe that too many easy generalizations have been made and that the whole issue of foreign markets has been played up as a move to divert attention from the politically explosive issue of internal markets and land reform.

[39] Elasticity of the food consumer price index with regard to the cost of living in the years 1952/53 and 1963/64 has fallen in several Latin American countries in the range of 1.10 to 1.20.

[40] I am not interested here with what share accrues to rural intermediaries and how much goes to urban traders.

(a) Changes in the land tenure system and ownership pattern so as to free small-holders from exploitation by landlords and give them permanent ownership of land.

(b) Introduction of a strongly progressive land tax which would compel owners of larger estates either to sell large tracts of land or to increase their output substantially, with the double advantage of improving the supply and increasing public revenue.

(c) Drastic intervention in the marketing of E goods, preferably by offering advantageous minimum prices to the producer, signing with him contracts in advance, and setting up an efficient State trading agency, so as substantially to reduce the profits now reaped by the intermediaries, be they rural merchants, landowners directly engaged in trade, or big commercial firms (frequently foreign-owned). Measures of support for traditional export crops should at the same time be revised to prevent the expansion of low-quality output which finds no outlets abroad but which is nevertheless profitable because State agencies purchase the unsold surplus at handsome prices.

(d) Credit policies and technical assistance should be overhauled so as to ensure that they are of benefit to more than a small minority of big farmers.

If all these measures are perseveringly applied, they should be a shot in the arm to ailing agriculture and give it growth rates which would result in both a substantial increase in rural consumption of agricultural goods and a considerably increased supply of such goods to the urban markets.

I should like to close this chapter by stating that, in my opinion, the so-called "savings gap" does not constitute an obstacle to accelerated growth, as it can always be made up for by appropriate income redistribution measures, at least within the range of growth rates, which can be seriously considered as feasible. The difficulties are more likely to appear in the area of the supply of agricultural E goods (the real counterpart to wages and incomes) and/or in that of the "imports gap", which will still persist even after the best use has been made of all reasonable measures of export promotion and import substitution.[41] Suitable mea-

---

[41] I assume that all the possibilities of entering into long-term arrangements with parties abroad have been explored.

sures for mobilizing domestic resources are likely to reduce the reliance of the growth process on imports, however;[42] that is to say, it will be possible to maximize the overall rate of non-inflationary growth with a given capacity to import, if such measures are introduced.

[42] In this context let me emphasize, once more, the connexion between foreign trade and agricultural policies. Development of domestic food production in many countries provides the most important source of actual and potential import substitution. Self-sufficiency in food need not, however, be sought without exploring the possibilities of agricultural specialization linked with international trade.

CHAPTER 4

Levels of Satiety and Rates of Growth (1966)

In his essay on *Problems of Financing Economic Development in a Mixed Economy*,[1] Professor M. Kalecki used the following equation of the rate of growth of demand for necessities:

$$c_n = q + e(r - q) \qquad (1)$$

where
c_n = rate of growth of demand for necessities
r = rate of growth of the economy and rate of growth of total consumption, if we assume the share of consumption in the national income to be constant
e = income elasticity of demand for necessities
q = rate of increase of the population
(No price fluctuations are foreseen.)

The same relation holds true for food alone, which accounts for the bulk of consumption in less-developed countries:

$$c_f = q + e(r - q) \qquad (2)$$

where c_f denotes the rate of growth of demand for food.

If we discard foreign trade and movements of stocks, and agree to deal only with the part or population which purchases its food on the market and to equate the food production with the marketed surplus,[2] the rate of growth of food output and of food consumption become identical. Let us denote the maximum rate of growth of the agricultural output by

---

[1] See *Essays on Planning and Economic Development*, vol. II, Warsaw, 1965, reprinted in *Selected Essays on the Economic Growth of the Socialist and the Mixed Economy*, Cambridge University Press, 1972, pp. 145–161, and in *Essays on Developing Economies*, The Harvester Press, England, and Humanities Press, Inc., U.S.A., 1976, pp. 98–115.

[2] This is, of course, a far-fetched simplification. We shall discuss the problem later on.

a_{max} and the rate of growth per capita of the national income and of consumption for sake of simplicity by y $(y = r - q)$.

From (2) we get the following maximum rate of growth without inflation of national economy y_{max}, warranted by the maximum rate of growth of agricultural output a_{max},

$$y_{max} = \frac{1}{e}(a_{max} - q) \qquad (3)$$

Let us observe that to have any growth of per capita income and consumption at all the rate of expansion of agricultural output must be higher than the rate of increase of population. Though this condition is not always fulfilled in developing countries, I shall assume throughout this chapter that $a_{max} > q$, and shall introduce the symbols a_q to denote the rate of growth of agricultural output per capita and a_{qmax} to denote the maximum rate of growth of this output. Equation (3) reads, therefore, as follows:

$$y_{max} = \frac{1}{e} a_{qmax} \qquad (3')$$

The higher the income elasticity of demand, the lower the maximum rate of growth of national income, warranted by the performance of the agricultural sector. Figure 4.1 illustrates the point. We have $OQ = q$, $OA = a_{max}$, and, of course, $QA = a_{qmax}$.

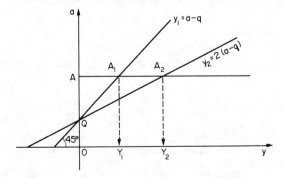

FIG. 4.1

For the curve y_1, in which $e = 1$, we get $y_{1\max} = a_{q\max}$. Graphically $y_{1\max} = OY_1 = AA_1 = AQ$, as y_1 makes an angle of 45 degrees with both axis and it passes through point Q.

For the curve y_2, in which $e = 0.5$, we get $y_{2\max} = 2a_{q\max}$. Thus, in the latter case, the economy develops twice as fast as in the former (in per capita terms), with the same agricultural output. Were the income elasticity of demand for food to decrease to zero, the rate of growth of the economy would become independent of the rate of growth of agricultural output, given $a \geqslant q$.

In these conditions, knowledge of the behaviour of e, both in the long and in the short run, acquires considerable importance for the planner dealing with the less-developed economies. I propose to explore the problem in the subsequent sections of this chapter.

The income elasticity of demand is a function both of the level of income and of the rate of its change, the latter being particularly important in the short run. We can write

$$e = f(Y, y) \tag{4}$$

In this section we shall discuss the behaviour pattern of e in the long run, discarding for the moment the influence of y.

Ever since Engel's pioneering studies, two propositions have usually been enunciated:

(a) The income elasticity of demand for foodstuffs decreases with the growth of income.

(b) The share of food in total expenditure decreases with the growth of income, and, therefore, the income elasticity of demand for food must be lower than unity.[3]

For the second proposition empirical evidence and theoretical research combine to show that it holds true only after a certain level of

---

[3] By definition

$$e = \frac{\Delta A/A}{\Delta Y/Y} = \frac{\Delta A}{A}\frac{Y}{\Delta Y} = \frac{\Delta A}{\Delta Y}\frac{Y}{A} = \frac{\Delta A/\Delta Y}{A/Y}$$

where $\Delta A/\Delta Y$ corresponds to the keynesian marginal propensity to consume food and A/Y stands for the average share of expenses on food in total expenditure. If $e = 1$, A/Y remains constant, it grows when the marginal expenditure on food is higher than it used to be, i.e. when $e > 1$, and it decreases when the consumer devotes to food purchases a lower portion of the increment of his income than he used to do with his previous income, i.e., when $e < 1$.

prosperity has been achieved. The usual shape of Engel's curve does not fit the case of extremely poor countries, regions, or sections of population, which actually show an income elasticity of demand higher than unity and, therefore, spend a higher proportion of their total income on food when they are better off.

The following data support this view.

In the United States the share of food in consumption expenditure for households with a yearly net income below 1,000 dollars is 33.2 per cent, while in the bracket between 1,000 and 2,000 dollars it goes up to 35.2 per cent. In the next group (earning from 2 to 3 thousand dollars) food still makes up 33.9 per cent of total expenditure, i.e. more than in the lowest bracket.

We obtain the same picture for agricultural labourers in India (data from 1950 to 1951). In the lowest group, with a yearly expenditure per consumption unit of less than 50 rupees, as much as 83.6 per cent of total income is spent on food. It increases to 85.5 per cent for the 50–100 rupee and 100–160 rupee brackets. Even for those earning more than 350 rupees the share of food in total expenditure (84.5 per cent) exceeds that of the lowest bracket.

Statistics on wage earners in Djakarta, in 1957, and on urban wage earners in Japan, in 1960,[4] show the same pattern: the lowest groups live on a very miserable diet, because they must cover certain unavoidable extra food expenses, such as rent, taxes, interest for loans, etc., from their meager incomes. Every increase in money income is translated almost exclusively into food purchases and at times the income elasticity may exceed unity.

Indirect evidence for the fact that the income elasticity for food (mostly for homegrown food) exceeds unity among poor peasants in poor countries comes from the study of the variations of marketed surplus. This surplus may actually dwindle when prices increase, because peasants sell the least they can. The phenomenon is well known from the economic history of feudalism.[5] On the other hand, the marketed surplus as a percentage of the gross value of output decreases when we move from small holdings to medium ones, and increases again when we pass to big

---

[4] See Appendix.

[5] Compare W. Kula, *ThéorieÉconomique du Système Féodal—Pour un Modèle de l'Économie Polonaise XVIe–XVIIIe siècles* (translated from Polish), Mouton, Paris–La Haye, 1970.

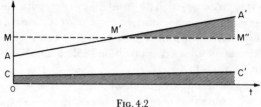

FIG. 4.2

agricultural enterprises.[6] Instead of speaking of marketed surplus in the case of depressed, small holdings, we should really speak of forced commercialization and consumed surplus. The "genuine" marketed surplus appears only at a higher level of agricultural income. That is why many "grow-more-food" campaigns fail to achieve their main purpose, i.e. the increase of the marketed surplus, although they contribute to the betterment of the peasant's standard of living, which is by all means a desired and commendable goal in itself. Figure 4.2 illustrates the point. AA' denotes the rise of output over time, CC' shows the level of minimum commercialization, $MM'M''$ stands for the level of satisfactory consumption, after a deduction for forced commercialization, and the area $M'M''A'$ for the genuine marketed surplus.

The data on the countries reproduced in Table 4.1 are less revealing, because nation-wide averages conceal social and regional disparities in incomes, as well as the differences between rural and urban patterns of consumption. The problem is complicated furthermore by the differences between income elasticities for marketed and home-grown supplies of food[7] to which I referred above. They still show, however, that in many countries income elasticities for food are quite high, especially in Asia. On the other hand, they confirm that a broad inverse correlation exists between the level of income and the income elasticity for food.

---

[6] According to the calculations of D. Narain from the Delhi Institute of Economic Growth, in India, marketed surplus as a percentage of the gross value of output is as high as 20.7 per cent in holdings below 5 acres, a minimum of 9.7 per cent in holdings between 10 and 15 acres and returning to 20.4 per cent in holdings from 20–25 acres.

[7] In India, where only 25 to 30 per cent of the food grain production is marketed, the income elasticity of home-produced foods has been estimated at unity (N. V. Sovani, "Food problem and economic development in underdeveloped countries", in *Paths to Economic Growth*, ed. by A. Datta, Delhi, 1962, p. 70).

The picture is more accurate if instead of considering income elasticities for aggregate food demand, as shown in column 3 of Table 4.1, we single out elasticities for grains (column 5) and consider the income elasticity of aggregate demand in terms of calories and of animal proteins (columns 4 and 6 of Table 4.1).[8]

Let us note that countries of a relatively low level of income per capita reach a stage when the income elasticity of demand for grains becomes negative, while only a few countries in the world have attained absolute satiety in terms of calories (the income elasticity for calories = 0), though the same countries did not arrive at a level guaranteeing full satisfaction of potential needs in terms of animal proteins (the income elasticity for animal proteins is 0.14 in Oceania).[9]

On the basis of the data contained in Table 4.1 it is possible to distinguish the following four critical levels of satiety for purposes of classification only:

Level I, the borderline between hunger and subnutrition (the income elasticity for aggregate food in terms of prices becomes less than unity). This is a level which all the countries covered by international statistics have surpassed by now, although it should be noted that the income elasticity for food in Pakistan runs as high as 0.96. The income elasticity in terms of retail prices is probably still higher.

Level II, the relative satiety in terms of calories, achieved by an increase in cereal consumption which passes the maximum (the income elasticity for cereals is at that point equal to zero). This is the level reached by Mexico and, not long ago, by Japan.

Level III, the absolute satiety in terms of calories (the income elasticity for calories decreases to zero). This level has been surpassed by Oceania and North America and is about to be reached by the most advanced countries of Western Europe.

---

[8] The coefficients of income elasticity for calories are lower than those of income elasticity for aggregate food in terms of prices, because the unit value of each calorie goes up when the incomes are increasing (in other words, the quality of food improves).

[9] We are speaking, of course, of national average, which may conceal a wide difference between an overfed minority and an undernourished section of population.

TABLE 4.1

Country or region	Gross National Product per capita in 1958 (converted in dollars according to parities of purchasing power)	Coefficients of income elasticity for aggregate food in terms of prices paid to the farmer	Coefficients of income elasticity for calories (in quantity)	Coefficients of income elasticity for cereals (in quantity)	Coefficients of income elasticity for animal proteins (in quantity)	Consumption of calories per head per day (average for 1957 to 1959)	Consumption of cereals per head in kilogrammes per year (average for 1957 to 1959)	Consumption of starchy roots per head in kilogrammes per year (average for 1957 to 1959)	Consumption of animal proteins per head in grammes per day (average for 1957 to 1959)
1	2	3	4	5	6	7	8	9	10
North America	2,190	0.16	−0.03	−0.5	0.23	3,118	67	48	66
Oceania	1,570	0.10	−0.06	−0.5	0.14	3,250	87	55	62
European Economic Community (EEC)	1,285	0.47	0.10	−0.3	0.57	2,850	109	103	41
Mediterranean Europe (Greece, Portugal, Spain, Yugoslavia)	575	0.55	0.18	−0.3	0.90	2,655	141	91	23

84

Japan	917 (613)	0.58	0.20	−0.17	0.94	2,220	153	66	16.6
Argentine and Uruguay	825	0.17	0.04	−0.3	0.22	3,100	118	82	65.2
Mexico	535 (415)	0.58	0.30	0.0	0.81	2,420	147	10	16.0
Middle East (excluding Egypt and Turkey)	260	0.79	0.57	0.3	1.21	2,144	140	11	12.0
North Africa	315	0.64	0.37	0.2	1.08	2,603	188	10	13.1
Rest of Africa (excluding Republic of South Africa)	210	0.64	0.39	0.4	1.08	2,356	35	397	10.0
Asia and Far East (excluding Japan)	165	0.89	0.62	0.5	1.49	1,980	133	33	7.0
Ceylon	240	0.78	0.49	0.35	1.46	1,970	125	22	6.2
India	150	0.89	0.64	0.5	1.57	1,950	133	11	6.0
Indonesia	175	0.79	0.54	0.5	1.23	2,079	117.1	159	5.4
Pakistan	145	0.96	0.68	0.5	1.62	1,950	149	6	7.6

Source: FAO, *Produits Agricoles—Projections pour 1970*, Rome, 1962. The estimates of GNP, arrived at by the FAO experts seem too high, mostly in the case of Japan and Mexico. I indicated in brackets the estimates of P. Rosenstein-Rodan, published in the *Review of Economics and Statistics*, 1961. Coefficients of the income elasticity for calories and for animal protein refer to the caloric content and animal protein content of the aggregate demand for food and not to selected commodities, as in the case of grain.

Level IV, the absolute satiety in terms of quantity and quality, expressed by the fact that the income elasticity for animal proteins becomes equal to zero.[10] No country has reached this stage as yet, but Colin Clark tried to give a quantitative expression of the asymptote to which the curve of human consumption of food tends. His estimate is 114 IU per capita per year, at farm value.[11]

The relevant parameters for each critical level are shown in Table 4.2. It goes without saying that these parameters are but a rough approximation and only indicate a broad order of magnitude. Discrepancies between them and the actual performance of diverse countries should be expected due to differences in the pattern of consumption, independent of the level of income,[12] historical circumstances, etc.

Figure 4.3, reproduced from the FAO study already quoted shows the correlation between the different income-elasticity coefficients and the level of income, converted into dollars on the basis of parities of purchasing power. The four critical levels delimit five zones (we shall call them zones *A, B, C, D, E*). Each zone poses specific problems of food supply.

In *zone A* (below the level I), the income elasticity for food is higher than 1 and the share of food in total consumption expenditure may be as high as 0.8. In such circumstances the rate of supply of food practically sets a ceiling to the overall rate of growth. If, furthermore, the rate of supply of food does not exceed the rate of population growth, the country (viz. region) is doomed to stagnation, if there is no recourse to foreign trade and/or to inflation.

The agricultural barrier acts with unparalleled intensity,[13] although

[10] The income elasticity of aggregate demand for food may still be positive at that moment, on account of certain luxury items, which, however, do not weigh heavily on the aggregate demand for food. For example, the income elasticity for cocoa is about 0.1 in North America and Oceania, but the income elasticity for coffee runs as high as 1 in Oceania, while it is 0.6 in Canada and 0.3 in the United States.

[11] Colin Clark, *The Conditions of Economic Progress*, 3rd ed., London, 1957, p. 445.

[12] Let me mention, for example, the unusually high consumption of meat in Argentine and Uruguay, on the one hand, and the vegetarian diet of Hindus on the other.

[13] My case is unrealistic to the extent to which I do not take into account the existence of subsistence economy, based on self-consumption. We have seen, however, that the income elasticity for home-grown food is even higher than the elasticity coefficient of the demand for marketed surplus.

TABLE 4.2 *Critical levels of satiety*

Levels	Income elasticity for aggregate food in terms of prices paid to the farmers	Income elasticity for cereals	Income elasticity for calories	Income elasticity for animal proteins	GNP per head in "real" dollars	Consumption of cereals (kilogrammes per head per year)	Consumption of starchy roots (kilogrammes per head per year)	Consumption of animal proteins (grammes per head per day)	Daily intake of calories per head
1	2	3	4	5	6	7	8	9	10
I	1	0.9–0.7	0.8	>1.5	<100	50–150	10–150	5	<2,000
II	0.6	0	0.3	1–0.8	400–600	150	10–100	15–20	2,200–2,400
III	0.4	−0.3	0	0.3–0.1	1,500	100	50–100	50	3,200
IV	about 0	strongly negative	negative	0	about 3,000	60–70	about 50	70–80	3,200

87

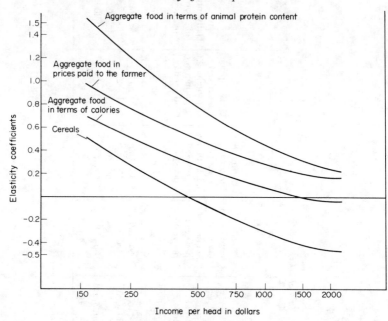

FIG. 4.3   Income elasticities and levels of income

the demand for food expresses itself mainly in terms of cereals, while
starchy roots supplement the diet.[14]

In *zone B* (between levels I and II), the income elasticity for food decreases considerably, but it still runs high and the share of food in the
total expenditure frequently exceeds 50 per cent (in India it varies
between 60 and 70 per cent). The consumption of cereals per capita continues to increase. At the same time important substitutions take place
between roots and cereals, as well as between cereals of lower and
higher grade.[15] A serious problem is posed by products of animal origin

[14] The level of consumption of roots depends very much on specific consumption
patterns of a given country. It is extremely high in Africa, where, as a compensation, consumption of cereals is the lowest in the world.

[15] According to estimates of the Indian Statistical Organization the income elasticity for
wheat—still a "luxury" product in India—is over 1.5 in rural areas and over 0.8 in urban
areas, while the aggregate income elasticity for cereals is much lower (0.63 and 0.32). For
rice it is 0.65 and less than 0.3.

(the per capita intake of protein increases 3 to 4 times). On the whole the agricultural barrier is still very intense and if we take into account the complications involved in expanding the supply of animal products, it may be as intense as in zone *A*, despite the decrease of the overall coefficient of the income elasticity for food.

In *zone C* the supply of grain ceases to be a problem, assuming it was tackled successfully, while the country was still moving through zone *B*. The only difficulty is the trebling of daily per capita intake of animal proteins.

In *zone D* the agricultural problem ceases to act as a barrier, the more so because the share of food in total consumption expenditure has been reduced considerably. The decrease of domestic consumption of cereals may even create surpluses for export, or agricultural production may be decreased.

In *zone E* the rate of supply of food only needs to equal the rate of growth of population.

On the whole, a paradoxical picture emerges: Adam Smith was certainly right in saying that "the desire for food is limited in every man by the narrow capacity of the human stomach". In terms of calories, members of well-to-do communities eat less than double the daily intake of the starving populations of Asia. But in terms of animal proteins the difference is fifteenfold, and it certainly takes a very long time to reach the level of satiety, both in terms of calories and of quality. What is more, the richer a country, the less intensive is the barrier of agriculture. This barrier vanishes at the very moment when a country, thanks to its general development and, more particularly, to industrialization, can overcome it. But in the initial stages of development, when it most needs to increase the rate of growth, no suitable conditions exist to cope with the task: institutional obstacles, and the necessity of investing for a number of years before a steady rise of agriculture productivity is achieved, face the developing countries with the dilemma of either going through a radical transformation of agrarian relations or giving up ambitious rates of growth.[16]

For the planner, it is extremely important to know how the income elasticities will change over time. For a full assessment of the situation,

---

[16] I abstract here from foreign credits and exclude the possibility of inflationary growth.

he should know the income elasticities for basic commodities by broad sections of population (at least separable sets of figures should be provided for rural and urban areas). Then he should evaluate the increase of population not dependent on home-produced food (migration from rural areas to towns), the rate of growth of their personal incomes, and the rate of supply of marketed surplus. As a first approximation, we shall deal with overall income elasticities for food.

Professor Kalecki, in the paper already quoted, assumed the income-elasticity coefficients to be stable over a period of five years or so (the period of medium-term planning). Such an assumption is reasonable, but it should not be extended to long-term planning (10 to 20 years). Though we have established five zones and we know, by and large, what the behaviour of income-elasticity coefficients is in each zone, it is quite risky to apply the figures arrived at to any single country,[17] the more so because we have to assume a rate of overall growth in order to know how long it will take to reach a given level of income per capita.

For the sake of illustration, we have computed the compound rate of change in income elasticity on the assumption of a 3 per cent per capita rate of growth of income per year. The results are given in Table 4.3.

The rate of change, on the whole, is higher in the last two intervals, where the whole matter is of much less importance than in the lower ones. A welcome, though not unexpected, result is the relatively rapid decrease of income elasticity for cereals in the third interval.[18]

In projections over a period of 12 years, the FAO experts have used inverse logarithmic functions with decreasing coefficients of elasticity. Table 4.4 compares their projections of annual rates of growth of demand agricultural products (the lower hypothesis) with the rate of growth of agricultural production in the fifties and the potential demand, calculated on the assumption of constant elasticities. With the exception of Japan, which has a high rate of growth and is going through a phase of rapid transformation of consumption pattern, the differences between columns 4 and 5 do not exceed 0.1 per cent, which, in the case of less

[17] Studies of behaviour of income elasticities in the long run face the usual limitations: lack of long time series, risks involved in international comparisons or in substituting the scale of incomes of different strata of population (family budgets) for the time series.

[18] The difference may be significant even in terms of a five-year plan, the more so because the income of Japan has been overestimated and, therefore, the time span between Latin America and Japan is shorter than indicated in the table.

Table 4.3

Country or region	GNP per head in "real" dollars	Time necessary to catch the level of income of next region in years	Average annual rate of decrease of income elasticity for food	Number of years necessary for a decrease by 0.1	Average annual rate of decrease of income elasticity for cereals	Number of years necessary for a decrease by 0.1	Average annual rate of decrease of income elasticity for calories	Number of years necessary for a decrease by 0.1	Average annual rate of decrease of income elasticity or animal proteins	Number of years necessary for a decrease by 0.1
1	2	3	4	5	6	7	8	9	10	11
Asia (without Japan)	165	16	1.3%	8	3%	5	1.8%	8	1.1%	11
Near East and Africa	260	22	0.6%	22	1.1%	44	1.0%	22	1.2%	5
Latin America	500	20	0	—	6.0%	6	1.4%	20	0.6%	20
Japan	910	11	1.5%	11	5.3%	8	3.8%	11	2.6%	4
EEC	1285	18	2.9%	5	2.9%	9	4.7%	14	2.7%	5
North America	2190									

TABLE 4.4

Country or region	Projected rate of growth of GNP (1958 to 1970)	Projected rate of growth of GNP per capita	Projected rate of growth of demand for food	Projected rate of growth of demand for food on assumption of constant elasticities	Past rate of growth of agricultural production (in the fifties)
1	2	3	4	5	6
Asia and Far East	3.6	1.3	3.4	3.5	2.9
Middle East and Africa	4.0	1.5	3.5	3.6	2.1
Latin America	4.7	2.0	3.7	3.9	3.8
Japan	6.0	5.3	2.9	3.9	4.6
EEC	4.7	3.9	1.8	2.7	2.8
North America	3.1	1.3	1.9	2.0	1.9

developed countries, is within the statistical margin of error. But if one looks at the gap between estimates of growth of demand for food, set in column 4 (arrived at on the basis of a very conservative rate of overall development), and the actual rates of growth of agricultural produce, every tenth of a per cent acquires significance.

Let us turn now to the influence of the rate of growth of income y on the short-term behaviour of the income elasticity for food. We shall discuss three problems:

(a) The difference between intensive and extensive growth of income.
(b) The impact of the speed of the growth process.
(c) The consequences of steady or erratic growth.

The same increment of national income ΔY may be obtained by increased productivity with no additional employment (intensive growth) or by enlarging the roll of working people (extensive growth). All other conditions being equal,[19] extensive growth in an underdeveloped economy will cause a bigger pressure on the food supply than intensive

---

[19] We assume in particular that no changes take place in the distribution of income between social classes, i.e. that the share of wages remains constant.

growth,[20] except in drastic situations, when each employed worker has a large number of dependants and their standard of living is so depressed that all additional income is used for additional purchases of staple foods. It is clear, therefore, that the overall income elasticity for food will be less in the case of intensive growth. To look at the same problem from another angle, the overall elasticity for food is a weighted average of elasticities of different groups of population, classified according to income. Extensive growth means increasing the number of wage earners in the lower brackets with higher income elasticities for food, and therefore increasing the weight of these brackets, while intensive growth means shifting people from lower to higher brackets.

If we abandon the field of economics proper and move to that of social psychology, we can make the following observations on the behaviour of consumers in periods of intensive growth: the mood of optimism creates conditions for the working of the "demonstration effect"; if people expect incomes to continue rising, they start to save for durable consumer goods[21] and the income elasticity for food drops below the "normal" level. On the contrary, a slow and imperceptible rise in incomes reflects itself in the substitution process and/or in increased purchases of non-durable consumer goods, mainly food.

The most important question, however, is that of erratic changes in levels of income, both in positive and negative directions.

As a rule, poor populations try to maintain the standard of nutrition, even if their income shrinks. They do it by sacrificing other extra food consumptions to the outmost limit and, if necessary, by making substitutions for lower grade cheaper food articles.[22] That is to say, when personal income is decreasing the demand for food becomes highly inelastic and the income-elasticity coefficient shrinks to zero or remains very low (big decreases of income cause small decreases in the demand for food). In such circumstances, the total consumption over a period of n years, in

---

[20] Compare W. Herer, *Rolnictwo a Rozwój Gospodarki Narodowej*, Warsaw, 1962, p. 187: "A zloty spent on increasing employment goes more to purchase agricultural consumer goods than the zloty spent on the increase of average wages".

[21] A bicycle, a sewing machine, or a cheap radio.

[22] An extreme case of it is the so-called "Griffen paradox" observed in Ireland: consumption of bread increased after an increase in prices, because to keep up with the previous consumption of bread people had to renounce richer food and, therefore, compensate by eating extra rations of bread.

which an average rate of growth y has been achieved, will be higher if this average conceals ups and downs than in the case of steady growth. In an underdeveloped predominantly agricultural country, a fall in total income usually is a consequence of bad crops. This adds to the drama of the situation. The demand for the marketed surplus of food is at least at the level of the previous year,[23] but food is in short supply, and the extraction of marketed surplus from villages quite frequently reduces the peasants to starvation. The stage is set for violent inflationary pressures in the town and social unrest throughout the country.

Up to now, we have assumed a non-inflationary process of growth. It is necessary to examine now the case when food is in short supply compared with the effective demand. Let y_n be the rate of growth of nominal income per capita. We shall assume that the rate of effective supply of agricultural goods a_r is less than the required one:

$$a_r < a_n = ey_n + q \tag{5}$$

Let it be

$$a_n - a_r = d$$

and let us assume, for the sake of simplicity, that $q = 0$.

The prices will obviously rise until

$$d = -pf \tag{6}$$

p being the percentual price rise and f the price elasticity of the demand for food (f being negative $-pf > 0$). The rate of growth of real income y_r will be

$$y_r = y_n - pA \tag{7}$$

where A is the share of the food in total expenditure. Since I am only discussing the short run, I will not take the repercussions of p on the other prices into account. For that very reason my argument does not deal with incomes of intermediaries which come from the increase in prices. Nor will I examine, at this stage, the possible shift in employment

---

[23] Quite frequently a fall in agricultural products coincides with a rise of monetary incomes of urban populations, not to speak of the acceleration of the peasant exodus to towns in periods of acute shortage of food supplies because they abandon famine-ridden villages.

induced by the price movements and their effects. Let us assume that $y_n > pA$, that is to say, $0 < y_r < y_n$.

If we now return to equation (3), and assume that $a_n - d$ is the maximum rate of supply of food, we can write

$$y_{\max} = \frac{1}{e}(a_n - d) \tag{8}$$

Let us compare equations (7) and (8). We find that $y_{\max}$ will be equal to y_r if the following condition holds true:

$$y_n - pA = \frac{1}{e}(a_n - d) \tag{9}$$

and after substitution of a_n and d, and simplifications:

$$A = \frac{-f}{e} \tag{10}$$

or $\qquad\qquad\qquad\qquad eA = -f \qquad\qquad\qquad\qquad\qquad (10')$

Of course, if $eA > -f$, then $y_{\max} > y_r$, and if $eA < -f$, then $y_{\max} < y_r$.[24] In other words, if $eA > -f$ and food is in short supply relative to the prospective rise of income, it is better to restrain the rate of growth of nominal incomes than to restore the equilibrium on the market by increasing prices because the final effect on the income will be worse: the rate of growth of real income y_r will be less than $y_{\max}$ compatible with a given rate of increase of food supply. In both cases real consumption of food will grow by 3 per cent. But the shift from other consumption will be less in the first case.[25] The above description implies a situation where the benefits of rising food prices accrue to intermediaries, and not to the tillers. Such a redistribution of income may increase the demand for

[24] In the short run we get a rate of real growth higher than the maximum rate of non-inflationary growth warranted by a given level of food supply.

[25] The following description by N. V. Sovani seems to apply to the case discussed in this section, namely an increase of real wages through a combination of rapid increase in nominal incomes and price increases which partly offset it: "The primacy of demand for foodgrains over all other demands leads to a peculiar situation in which a sharp rise in foodgrain prices sucks up so much of the increased total demand and the residual total demand for other commodities and services smaller than previously results in a situation of slack demand conditions in those markets" (N. V. Sovani, *Analysis of Inflation in Underdeveloped Economies, Changing India. Essays in Honour of Professor D. R. Gadgil,* Bombay, 1961, p. 304).

luxury goods (unless the increase of luxury consumption is restricted by proper taxation, as assumed in Professor Kalecki's paper), but the decreased demand for non-agricultural essentials by working people, who have to pay more for food, is not compensated by a rising demand for industrial goods by agriculturists. In the long run, therefore, we are likely to get a shift of employment from the production of essentials to that of non-essentials. An alternative assumption might be that of hoarding the additional savings by intermediaries. This would lead, on the one hand to inflation, due to the lack of a proper supply of food, and, on the other hand, it would lead to a reduction of employment in the consumer goods industries due to a lack of effective demand. The increasing unemployment would in turn decrease the effective demand for food. But at this stage I should definitely introduce further assumptions about the rate of investment, taxation, etc. However, as this would complicate my case, I prefer to stick to the short run.

Now, it is necessary to interpret the formal condition $eA > -f$. It occurs in practice only for goods for which e is high, f low, and which account for a considerable part of total consumption. This is precisely the case of foodgrains in an underdeveloped country.[26] The disproportionate reactions of prices of grain in short supply were observed about three hundred years ago by Geoffrey King. I believe that the formal condition analysed above permits a more satisfactory interpretation of the so-called King effect. We know by empirical evidence, furthermore, that price policies, used in less-developed countries to equilibrate the food market, as a rule prove to be self-defeating: to offset the demand in excess it is necessary to raise the prices to such an extent that the real incomes begin to stagnate or to fall; inflation ensues with undesirable flows of incomes from working people to capitalists and traders and the full set of well-known adverse effects, of which the overall rate of growth is usually the last victim.

The short-term fluctuations, described in this section, are not as relevant for medium- or long-term planning as for the framing of economic policies.

While limitations imposed on the process of growth by the agricultural barrier should be duly accounted for, we should not adopt an attitude of

[26] This is probably the only important instance of a rather unusual combination of e, f, and A (or its equivalent).

resignation. A slightly more optimistic view is warranted, if the following circumstances are taken into account:

(a) Untapped possibilities of rapid increase of agricultural output exist in many less-developed countries; the real barrier, here, is the institutional one.

(b) Rational utilization of the capacity to import may help us to ease the grip on the agricultural barrier.

(c) Policies of redistribution of national income, though mainly directed at limiting or banning—whatever the political case may be—the luxury consumption of the upper classes, would also justify a lower rate of growth of popular consumption than that of the national income, if such a redistribution steps up the share of investments enjoying high social priority.

Moreover, certain specific policies may be recommended (apart from rationing which requires certain smoothly working institutional arrangements), namely:

(a) Manipulations of relative prices, aimed at inducing desirable substitutions among similar goods.

(b) Price and credit policies, aimed at inducing desirable changes in patterns of consumption, favouring, for example, a shift of the purchasing power of some clerks and workers, who are relatively better off, from higher grades of food to durable consumer goods,[27] thus reducing the effective income-elasticity coefficient for higher grade foods.

(c) Resorting to planned shortages of selected goods while simultaneously increasing the supply of others (some kind of forced substitution). Of course, such a policy involves many grave risks—including that of creating a black market—and planners should not abuse it, nor apply it for too long a period. But certain experiences would point to the possibility of patching up the situation if selected goods which do not weigh heavily on total consumption are in short supply by a fraction of 5 per cent or so of the total demand and, therefore, occasional defaults of supply occur here and there at irregular intervals.[28]

[27] For example, by selling bicycles on 24 monthly instalments, payable by deduction from salaries and wages, with no interest or only a symbolic one.
[28] People will be queueing and buying perhaps more that they actually need, but organized speculation will not be rewarded in such a case.

(d) Some price increases on selected goods may be made, especially if they do not significantly affect the general price level and do not weigh on the "basket" of popular consumption.

It goes without saying that policies (c) and (d) should not be considered a virtue but a hard necessity, to be applied in the last instance.

On the whole, there is not much elbow-room left for manoeuvring and the more underdeveloped a country the less the amount of freedom. Still, no opportunity of easing the agricultural bottleneck should be neglected: it is here in overcoming the shortages of supply in food and other necessities (we might call it Kalecki's paradox) that the real problem of financing economic development in a less-developed economy lies.

APPENDIX

Private household consumption expenditure by income level, and percentage distribution by object of expenditure

Continent, country, year coverage, and income or expenditure level	Average total consumption expenditure per household	Percentage distribution of consumption expenditure						
		Food and drinks	Housing		Furniture and utensils	Clothing		Miscellaneous
			Rent	Fuel and light		Clothes and utensils	Personal effects	
	1	2	3	4	5	6	7	8
United States, 1950, urban, all types of household, yearly net money income per household (in $)								
Up to 1,000	1,333	33.2	17.9	7.2	4.2	5.5	0.5	31.5
1,000– 2,000	1,822	35.2	15.2	5.9	4.8	8.2	0.8	29.9
2,000– 3,000	2,784	33.9	12.5	4.7	6.2	9.1	1.0	32.6
3,000– 4,000	3,654	32.0	11.2	4.2	6.5	9.6	1.0	35.5
4,000– 5,000	4,571	30.2	10.6	3.9	7.2	10.0	1.2	35.9
5,000– 6,000	5,423	29.3	9.9	3.6	7.0	10.7	1.2	38.3
6,000– 7,000	6,262	28.1	9.9	3.3	6.9	10.9	1.4	35.5
7,500–10,000	7,439	27.6	9.5	3.2	6.1	11.2	1.7	40.7
10,000 and over	11,869	22.3	9.7	2.5	7.6	10.9	1.9	45.1
India, 1950 to 1951, rural, agricultural labourers, yearly expenditure per consumption unit (in rupees)	1	2	3	4	5 + 6 + 7			8
Up to 50	219.00	83.6	0.5	1.8	6.8			7.3
51–100	343.00	85.5	0.6	1.2	6.0			6.7

99

Continent, country, year coverage, and income or expenditure level	Average total consumption expenditure per household	Food and drinks	Housing			Clothing		Miscellaneous
			Rent	Fuel and light	Furniture and utensils	Clothes and utensils	Personal effects	
	1	2	3	4	5	6	7	8
101–150	440.00	85.5	0.7	1.2		6.3		6.3
151–200	528.00	84.9	0.8	1.1		6.6		6.6
201–250	584.00	85.2	1.2	1.0		6.0		6.6
251–300	628.00	84.3	1.6	1.1		5.9		7.1
301–350	644.00	83.7	1.7	1.1		6.2		7.3
351 and over	700.00	84.5	1.5	1.0		6.3		6.7
	1	2	3 + 4 + 5			6	7 + 8	
Indonesia, 1957, wage earners, Djakarta, monthly income per household (in rupiahs)								
Up to 199	190.04	65.4	13.6			11.4	9.6	
200– 299	287.46	68.3	14.0			6.5	11.2	
300– 399	378.51	66.7	12.1			7.6	13.6	
400– 499	460.49	65.0	11.6			8.4	15.0	
500– 599	537.20	67.8	8.4			7.7	16.1	
600– 699	681.76	63.6	10.4			9.3	16.7	
700– 799	748.97	63.6	10.6			8.5	17.3	
800– 899	833.45	63.1	10.4			8.1	18.4	
900– 999	910.08	61.1	10.1			10.1	18.7	
1,000–1,099	1,034.72	58.6	9.3			13.1	19.0	
1,100–1,499	1,146.35	61.9	8.5			4.6	25.0	
1,500 and over	1,781.81	52.9	14.0			9.6	23.6	

	Average total consumption expenditure per household	Percentage distribution of consumption expenditure						
		Food and drinks	Housing			Clothing		Miscel-laneous
Continent, country, year coverage, and income or expenditure level			Rent	Fuel and light	Furniture and utensils	Clothes and utensils	Personal effects	
	1	2	3	4	5	6	7	8
Japan, 1960, urban wage and salary earners, monthly money income per household (in yens)								
Up to 4,999	18,802	47.8	3.7	5.4	4.4	5.8	2.9	30.0
5,000– 9,999	12,777	53.5	4.3	6.0	2.1	5.1	2.5	26.5
10,000–14,999	14,417	52.2	6.4	5.6	1.7	5.4	2.6	26.1
15,000–19,999	17,774	48.2	6.2	5.4	3.7	6.0	2.6	27.9
20,000–24,999	21,368	46.2	5.4	5.2	4.4	6.2	2.9	29.7
25,000–29,999	24,800	44.5	5.1	5.2	3.7	6.5	3.2	31.8
30,000–34,999	28,782	41.8	4.8	5.0	4.4	7.1	3.4	33.5
35,000–39,999	31,772	40.5	4.4	5.0	3.9	7.1	3.5	35.7
40,000–44,999	35,040	38.9	4.2	4.9	4.3	7.5	3.7	36.5
45,000–49,999	38,112	37.4	4.2	4.9	5.0	7.6	3.8	37.1
50,000–59,999	42,790	35.5	4.5	4.9	4.4	7.9	3.9	38.9
60,000–69,999	49,318	32.9	4.6	4.6	4.6	8.1	3.9	41.3
70,000–79,999	52,701	31.3	3.8	4.5	5.0	9.0	4.3	42.1
80,000–89,999	57,184	30.4	4.3	4.7	6.6	9.2	4.1	40.7
90,000–99,999	62,862	28.4	4.9	4.3	5.9	8.8	4.4	43.3
100,000 and over	76,741	24.6	4.2	3.7	5.8	9.2	4.6	47.9

Source: UN, *Compendium of Social Statistical*, 1963.

CHAPTER 5

The Significance of the Foreign Trade Sector and the Strategy of Foreign Trade Planning (1967)

Introduction

Theoretical studies and empirical evidence both point to the critical importance of foreign trade in the drafting of a strategy for accelerated economic development.

The commodity pattern of production in a developing economy is relatively undifferentiated, while the pattern of demand is much more varied. Under the circumstances, the adjustment of the supply to the demand must involve operations of foreign trade, through which surpluses of a few commodities are, as a rule, exchanged against a more sophisticated list of goods in short supply in the country considered. This translation of internal sectoral imbalances into additional demand for foreign-made goods is not an evil in itself, provided we can assume that the developing economy will find elastic markets for its traditional exports and will thus be able to sell them in growing quantities and at fair prices. Such an assumption, however, does not hold true today for the majority of developing countries. On the one hand, the possibilities of increasing the output of food and of traditional exports are quite frequently limited. And, on the other, the proceedings of the United Nations Conference on Trade and Development, as well as the perusal of the impressive set of studies prepared by the United Nations Secretariat for this occasion, do not leave any illusion about the prospects on the world commodity markets. On the contrary, difficulties of foreign trade are likely to persist for quite a substantial period, whatever the steps taken by the developing countries alone. The majority of developing countries thus belong to the category of "import-sensitive economies", where the insufficient capacity to import acts as a bottleneck, putting a ceiling on the rate of growth of the national economy. This is a circular process: internal imbalances are translated into additional demand for foreign goods, but a feedback develops between foreign trade and the rest of the economy: insufficient imports of capital goods slow down the rate of investments and keep it below the level of potential savings, while insufficient imports of necessities[1] are likely to force the country to choose what seems at the moment to be the lesser evil—a slower rate of growth without inflation or a higher rate of growth with inflation. Either choice is, however, highly unsatisfactory. The emphasis put on foreign trade in our discussions reflects, on the one hand, the gravity of the situation and, on the other, the awareness of the fact that the internal imbalances of the economy *must* be overcome though foreign trade.

In this chapter I shall start with a somewhat more detailed examination of the role of foreign trade in economic development and shall show how the barrier of foreign trade has to be taken into account in perspective planning. A third section will be devoted to planning foreign trade proper, and a fourth one to problems of foreign aid.

The place of foreign trade

I shall begin by analysis with a four-sector model,[2] consisting of the following sectors:

M = sector turning out machines and equipment; construction is also included in this sector

R = sector producing mineral and agricultural raw materials and intermediate goods (including steel, fertilizers, etc.); for certain purposes, it may be useful to include in R the whole production of power, as well as transport

---

[1] Here we see the interplay between the barrier of foreign trade and that of agriculture, hampered in many countries by social and institutional obstacles.

[2] This is a modified version of the four-sector model by Raj-Sen (*Oxf. Econ. Pap.*, February 1961). The sector of consumer goods has been split into two, in conformity with Kalecki's approach. It is not considered necessary, at this stage, to make a distinction between machines to produce machines and raw materials, and machines to produce consumer goods. It will be introduced later.

K_N = sector producing consumer goods classified as "necessities", i.e. the set of goods which in a given country and at a given time constitute the bulk of consumption of working people (including, of course, food)

K_L = sector producing all the remaining consumer goods, called here for the sake of brevity "luxuries" or "non-essentials"

If we agree to include marketable services and housing (with the exception of public administration, defence, and social services provided freely by the State) in the national income, their output will have to be split between K_N and K_L.[3] A dichotomic subdivision will be introduced of R, K_N, and K_L into traditional and modern subsectors (denoted by the subscripts t and m).[4] E will denote the exports and I the imports.

Figure 5.1 shows by means of arrows the likely flows between all these sectors and the foreign markets in a complex, industrial, developed economy. From the diagram the pivotal role of the sector R can immediately be seen, which has the same number of forward links as M. Actually, the lack of proper development of R has proved a major bottleneck in many countries, the more so that the gestation period of investment in R is usually long and the issue is complicated by the "lumpiness" of required capital.

The sector M has no backward links at all, except for the supply of raw materials. The sectors K_N and K_L have no forward links (if exports are excluded).

Let us observe, furthermore, that sectors K_N and K_L compete for supplies of M and R. But while goods turned out by K_N are indispensable to the functioning of the economy as "wage goods", goods K_L perform only a marginal role as "incentive goods", and their bulk is consumed by upper-income groups; under proper institutional conditions this consumption can be kept at a much lower level than the actually prevailing one in the vast majority of developing countries, thus permitting a greater popular consumption with the same level of investment or a

---

[3] A variation on this would be to include in the national income social services provided without charge, accounted at their cost, which is not very satisfactory.

[4] The whole sector M is thus assumed to be "modern". This is not quite exact, because some output of tools and ancillary parts is likely to come from artisan-type workshops, but their relative share in total supplies cannot be very significant.

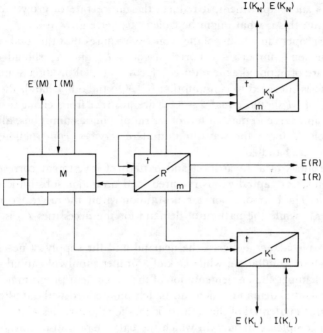

Fig. 5.1

higher level of investment without curtailing the consumption of necessities.[5]

The expansion of K_L, so commonly observed, is a consequence of the great inequalities in the distribution of income. The market mechanism allocated an excessive share of investment to K_L, because wealthy people are willing to pay high prices for luxury goods. While all the other sectors of the economy contribute to its "growth potential" by delivering intermediate goods, final capital goods, and final wage goods, K_L is something of a blind alley. If R and M are in short supply, the growth of K_L slows down the expansion of the remaining sectors and thus, contributing in the short run to the increase of national

[5] In the first case, the imputs R $(\to K_L)$ and the equipment M $(\to K_L)$ are shifted to K_N; in the second case, the displacements within the economy are somewhat more complex and might involve operations of foreign trade.

income and employment, it reduces the future rate of growth of the economy; this is what might be called "perverse growth".

The proper functioning of the economy requires that the total supply (production + imports − exports) of goods K_N and K_L should equal the share of national expenditure Y (gross national product + imports − exports) devoted to consumption (C). On the other hand, the total supply of M should equal $Y - C$, if we abstract from changes in the stocks and agree to make a few other simplifying assumptions, already mentioned, about the way the output of services, construction, and housing are handled.

Of course, to a given level and pattern of investment corresponds a given set of capital goods required, and no major substitutions are possible. There is more room for substitution within the range of commodities K_L, while the pattern of demand for the necessities K_N is fairly rigid.[6]

Lack of balance between the demand and the supply of necessities would lead to inflation, while lack of a proper supply of capital goods would hamper the implementation of the investment programme. The only potential demand which can be left unattended without affecting the growth potential of the country is that for the luxuries K_L.[7]

In a complex economy, in which the balance of transactions on the capital account is equal to zero, total exports and total imports are equal. We can write

$$E(M) + E(R) + E(K_N) + E(K_L) = I(M) + I(R) + I(K_N) + I(K_L)$$

---

[6] This is particularly true of staple foods. For a given rate of increase of per capita personal income y, the rate of growth of supply of necessities should be $a = ey + q$, where e is the income elasticity of demand and q the rate of increase of the population. (See M. Kalecki, "Problems of financing economic development in a mixed economy", in *Essays on Planning and Economic Development*, vol. II, Warsaw, 1965, reprinted in *Selected Essays on the Economic Growth in the Socialist and the Mixed Economy*, Cambridge University Press, 1972, pp. 145–161, and in *Essays on Developing Economies*, The Harvester Press, England, and Humanities Press, Inc., U.S.A., 1976, pp. 98–115. See also ch. 4.

[7] The financial aspects of the growth process are not of primary concern here. It can be said that checks imposed on conspicuous consumption by means of high indirect taxation on luxuries and direct curbs on construction of luxury dwellings will result in forced savings. Even if those private savings are not invested, it is possible for the State to invest to the same amount by means of deficit financing. The real danger is that of the illegal expatriation of local private capital and the consequent worsening of the balance-of-payments position.

But, of course,

$$E(M) \neq I(M)$$
$$E(R) \neq I(R)$$
$$E(K_N) \neq I(K_N)$$
$$E(K_L) \neq I(K_L)$$

Through these inequalities, foreign trade helps to adjust the pattern of the supply to the pattern of the demand on the internal market.

Figure 5.1 refers to a complex economy. A developing economy is likely to be "incomplete", i.e. it will not have all the four sectors, and its pattern of foreign trade is also likely to be simpler.

TABLE 5.1

The stages of development [a]

Structure of the economy	Composition of exports	Composition of imports
1. $K_{Nt} + (R_t) + (K_{Lt})$	$(R_t), (K_{Lt})$	K_{Lm}
2. $K_{Nt} + (R_t) + (K_{Lt})$	$(R_t), (K_{Lt})$	$K_{Lm}, M(\rightarrow K, \rightarrow R)$
3. $K_{Nt} + K_{Nm} + K_{Lm} + R_m$ $+ (R_t) + (K_{Lt})$	$(R_t), (K_{Lt}), R_m$	$K_{Lm}, M(\rightarrow K, \rightarrow R), R_m,$ (K_{Nm})
4. $K_{Nt} + K_{Nm} + K_{Lm} + R_m$ $+ (R_t) + (K_{Lt})$	$(R_t), (K_{Lt}), R_m$	$K_{Lm}, M(\rightarrow K, \rightarrow R, \rightarrow M),$ $R_m, (K_{Nm})$
5. $K_{Nt} + K_{Nm} + K_{Lm} + (K_{Lt})$ $+ R_m + (R_t) + M$	$(R_t), (K_{Lt}), R_m,$ K_L, K_N	M, R, K_N, K_L
6. M, R, K_N, K_L	M, R, K_N, K_L	M, R, K_N, K_L

[a] The sectors (exports, imports) which have been put in brackets do not necessarily exist in a given economy, as they depend on the natural endowments of the country.

Table 5.1 summarizes the stages of development of a non-interventionist economy.[8] Table 5.1 calls for the following comments:

(a) The first stage corresponds to the situation of a backward and stagnant country; exports consist of raw materials produced in the traditional sector and/or consumer luxuries (e.g. coffee or cocoa).

[8] The author has in mind an economy without planning and growing in conditions very akin to those stipulated by Dudley Seers in his purely analytical concept of "normal growth". See D. Seers, "Normal growth and distortions: some techniques and structural analysis", *Oxf. Econ. Pap.*, **16** (1), March 1964, pp. 78–104.

(b) The second stage differs from the first one only by the composition of imports. Machines appear in the import bill.

(c) The imports of capital goods, started in the previous stage, give rise to a differentiation of production and of exports, to which new raw materials are added. On the import list, one new important item is inputs for the recently started industries. If agriculture does not develop satisfactorily, the expansion of industries and the likely urbanization may create a shortage of marketable surplus of necessities, and food will have to be imported.

(d) Stage four differs from the previous one only by the composition of imports: machines to produce machines begin to be imported.

(e) Stage five depicts already a more-developed economy, but the dual structure of production[9] and the lagging behind of the pattern of exports as compared to the structure of production indicate the difficulties which must still be overcome.

(f) Stage six corresponds to Figure 5.1.

Needless to say, Table 5.1 provides a mere illustration of the likely direction of changes; the concrete paths followed by different countries obviously do not conform to a uniform pattern.[10] As a matter of fact, the choice of the strategy of development involves decisions about the timing and the sequence of implantation of the different modern sectors in the national economy. Such decisions will determine to a large extent the future composition of foreign trade and the path of its future transformations. Their implementation will depend, on the other hand, on the feasibility of the targets set for foreign trade. The only reasonable way to handle this interdependence is to construct a long-term, overall plan. The strategy of foreign trade planning cannot be separated from the strategy of planning *tout court*, and, in compensation, problems of foreign trade permeate the whole fabric of the overall plan and influence all its major variables. Before we turn to this problem, it might be useful to complicate somewhat our four-sector model in order to illustrate some problems of import substitution.

---

[9] Here the author has in mind the coexistence of the modern and traditional subsectors, made possible by the differences in wage levels.

[10] For this point see the author's book, *Foreign Trade and Economic Development of Underdeveloped Countries*, Bombay, 1965.

The sector M will be subdivided into two sectors:

M_{M+R} = turning out machines to produce machines and raw materials

M_K = turning out machines to produce consumer goods

In practice, such a subdivision might not work on account of the substitutability of machines and equipment produced in both sectors, but the distinction between M_{M+R} and M_K is relevant from the conceptual point of view. Figure 5.2 illustrates our model.[11]

In theory, it is possible to conceive a developmental path in which foreign trade plays only a subsidiary role in the critical stage of growth. The exercise is illustrated in Figure 5.3, in which uniform time lags are introduced. We shall call them "years", but of course such a denomination is purely symbolic. In the year t_0, equipment is imported for the sector M_{M+R}. Production starts in the year t_1, and in the year t_2 raw materials begin to be extracted with equipment produced in M_{M+R}. Production in the sector M_K starts in t_3, and after four years the final consumer goods reach the market. Further expansion of the production, based entirely on home-made machinery and inputs, becomes possible in the year t_5.

This is obviously an unrealistic case, in which the economy reaches complete autarchy after five "years". It can be observed, however, that in such an economy no production of final goods occurs before the year t_4. It is necessary, therefore, to provide for imports of all the necessary consumer goods from t_0 to t_3.

If, for the sake of simplicity, one assumes consumption to be constant throughout these years and it is agreed to denote by $K_N + K_L$ the yearly consumption and by M_{M+R} the initial imports of equipment for the sector M_{M+R} and the inputs it requires, the total import bill in the period t_0 to t_3 will be $4K_N + 4K_L + M_{M+R} + R_{(M_{M+R})}$. Afterwards, imports will stop altogether.

If, however, instead of equipment for M_{M+R} one agrees to import machinery M_K and some inputs, production of $K_N + K_L$ could be

---

[11] The pivotal role of R becomes still more apparent than in Figure 5.1. M_{M+R}—the sector of machine "mother industries"—has no backward links except for raw materials (which can be extracted, however, with equipment produced by M, so that, in theory, only the imports of inputs necessary to produce the first set of equipment should be provided as an initial fund together with the first "mother machine").

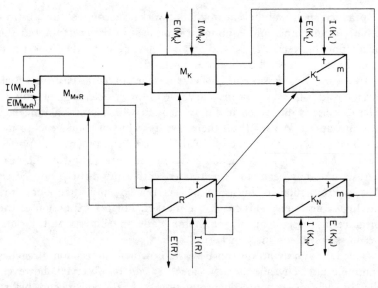

FIG. 5.2

started in the year t_1; but in the subsequent years it would continue to depend on imports of $R(\rightarrow K_N, K_L)$ and M_K.[12] The planner is faced, therefore, with the following choices:

(a) Using the whole import capacity for imports of final consumer goods, i.e. leaving the structure of the economy unaffected[13]

(b) Using part of the import capacity to bring the necessary goods K_N and some K_L and the rest to buy M_{M+R}

(c) Allocating the import capacity between K_N, K_L, M_K, and R

[12] For renovation and expansion.
[13] That is, giving up any development.

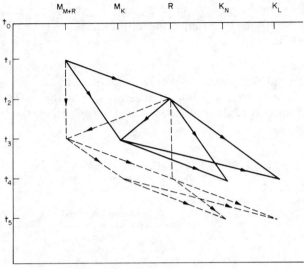

M_{M+R}　　M_K　　R　　K_N　　K_L

t_0
t_1
t_2
t_3
t_4
t_5

Fig. 5.3

The third strategy (c) permits the production of K_N and K_L to start earlier, but it implies a continuous (and growing) dependence on supplies of R and M_K from abroad. Strategy (b), on the contrary, retards the beginnings of industrialization, but aims at the quickest elimination of the dependence on imports.

In actual planning, a strategy containing elements of (b) and (c) is likely to prevail. While no general rules can be drawn, the following remarks seem to hold true:

(a) The smaller a country is the more inadequate becomes strategy (b). A small country could hardly be expected to develop the full spectrum of machine production necessary to a modern economy and to turn out all the intermediate goods, because of the capital cost involved and the diseconomies of scale, to say nothing of the natural endowments. But some production of M_K and even M_{M+R} could well begin, even at a relatively early stage of development.

(b) At the early stages of growth, strategy (c) will be yielding better results, but its potentialities of import substitution will be exhausted within a relatively short period, while imports of R will be growing *pari passu* with the production of K_N and K_L, pressuring the balance of payments. In the long run, elements of strategy (b) have to be incorporated in the plan.

Table 5.2 shows in very general terms the import-substitution potential of the different sectors. Not only the actual but also the potential imports have been taken into consideration. On the other hand, a policy of austerity has been assumed, aimed at a reduction of conspicuous consumption.

TABLE 5.2
Import substitution potential

	Degree of technical difficulty	Gestation period	Potential
M_{M+R}	Great	Medium	Unlimited
M_K	Great	Medium	Great
R	Medium to great[a]	Long	Depends on natural endowments[c]
K_N	Small[b]	Short[b]	Limited
K_L	Small	Short	Very limited[c]

[a] It involves frequently indivisible investments of considerable magnitude (the "lumpiness" of required capital).

[b] As far as industrial consumer goods industries are concerned, the case of agriculture is much more complex and involves institutional reforms.

[c] Technically, there is of course room for import substitution in K_L, as long as K_L is not altogether severely curtailed by a policy of reasonable austerity.

Foreign trade as a barrier to growth

In this section, I propose to show how problems of foreign trade are likely to interfere with the planner's objective of a high rate of overall growth. For this, it is necessary to start with a summary of the procedure employed in the construction of a perspective plan[14]

[14] The method followed is that of successive approximations outlined by M. Kalecki at the United Nations Conference on Science and Technology held in Geneva (first published in *Essays on Planning and Economic Development*, vol. I, Warsaw, 1963, and reprinted in *Essays on Developing Economies*, The Harvester Press, England, and Humanities Press, Inc., U.S.A., 1976, pp. 28–29.

aimed at the selection of the appropriate rate of growth of the national income. I shall proceed by stages.

FIRST STEP

A deliberately high initial rate of growth has been assumed and the consequences of such an assumption have been spelt out with the help of an overall incremental capital–output ratio, assumed on the basis of past experience. We thus have, approximately,[15]

$$D_n = D_0(1 + r)^n$$

On the other hand,

$$r = \frac{i}{k} \text{ , wherefrom we obtain } i = rk$$

$$I_n = iDn$$

$$C_n = (1 - i)D_n$$

where $r =$ assumed rate of growth
$D_0 =$ gross national income in the base year
$n =$ number of years over which the plan extends
$D_n =$ gross national income at the end of the plan
$k =$ incremental capital–output ratio (corrected for the increase in stocks)
$i =$ average share of productive investment (including the increase in stocks)
$I_n =$ productive investment in the year n (including the increase in stocks)
$C_n =$ consumption in the year n, taken in the broadest meaning, i.e. including personal and collective consumption and "non-productive" investments in housing, schools, hospitals, etc.

---

[15] For a more comprehensive formula see M. Kalecki, *Introduction to the Theory of Growth in a Socialist Economy*, in *op. cit.*

SECOND STEP

The above assumption about the distribution of D between C and I is discussed from the point of view of its political acceptability. If one agrees to include services into national income, investment in housing and social services should be added to productive investment I_n. In such a case, one has to decide what share I' of potential consumption, obtained by deducting productive investment I from national income D, should be allocated to "unproductive investment". Consumption C'_n in year n (taken in the narrow meaning of the word) will be

$$C'_n = D_n - (I_n + I'_n)$$

Let us suppose that this distribution proves politically acceptable. (Normally, consumption should grow faster than the population; a still safer minimum condition is that of ensuring at least stable real wages with employment growing at a faster rate than the population.)

THIRD STEP

Now let us check the physical feasibility of the plan. On the basis of the magnitudes C_n, arrived at in the first step and preliminarily accepted in the second step, assumptions can be made about the commodity pattern of required final goods K_N and K_L.

One engages, then, in the study of the industrial structure of the national product with the double purpose of arriving at a more precise estimate of the future balance of trade and the incremental capital–output ratios, which will serve to correct the initial assumption about k.

It is useful to introduce at this stage the distinction between "supply-determined" and "demand-determined" industries. The former have a certain ceiling for their long-run rate of growth for technical and organizational reasons, and even a heavy concentration of capital outlays, therefore, would not help. For practical purposes, one can include in the same category the industries where expansion above a certain ceiling would require a very considerable increase in marginal capital–output ratios. The latter have no such ceilings.

Obviously, one has to assess first the future production of the supply-determined industries and then see how far one should go with the demand-determined industries. Let us denote by K'_N, K'_L, M', and R' the output of the different sectors of the economy, and by K_N, K_L, M, and R the demand arising from the postulated pattern of consumption and investment.[16]

FOURTH STEP

By comparing the two sets of data, one arrives at a first approximation of the import requirements and export surpluses (the positive differences $K'_N - K_N$, $K'_L - K_L$, $R' - R$, $M' - M$ stand for export surpluses and the negative ones for import requirements). Whether the "exportable surpluses" are really marketable, however, still has to be checked. This means that it must be determined whether there are buyers for the quantities offered and what the price behaviour will be if the offer is increased. On the other hand, it is necessary to determine the costs of production and, more particularly, the incremental capital–output ratios in export-oriented industries. The higher the volume of exports, the higher will be the capital–output ratios at the margin, so that one arrives at a point where the advantages arising from further expansion of exports will be more than offset by the increase of k (and, therefore, for a given r of j). Furthermore, a comparison has to be made of the economic advantages of import-substituting *versus* export-promoting investments, since from the point of view of the balance of trade their effect is the same.[17]

The results of this exercise in planning of foreign trade and of export-promoting or import-substituting investment will, in the final analysis, determine the rate of growth to be eventually chosen for the whole economy. If foreign trade cannot be balanced after having taken into consideration the possibilities of "foreign aid" discussed earlier, the assumed rate of growth r will have to be scaled down.

[16] The demand for R is a function of K_N, K'_L, and M'.

[17] *Ceteris paribus*, import substitution might be preferable to export promotion, as it makes the country less dependent on contingencies of world commodity markets—unless, of course, the export-oriented investment is backed by a long-term trade contract. (See the author's paper on "Planning in an import-sensitive economy", submitted to the United Nations Conference on Science and Technology, in *Essays on Planning and Economic Development*, vol. I, Warsaw, 1963.)

From the above considerations it is plain that all the physical tensions and bottlenecks affecting our economy have been given the dimension of foreign trade, reducing thus a multifactor problem to one single factor—foreign trade. One of the most important and delicate phases of perspective planning consists in the detailed evaluation of "foreign currency efficiency" of export-oriented and import-substituting investments, as well as of their impact on k and thus of their maximum sensible size. Of course, the plan must also provide for a rational utilization of the import capacity created.

The discussion will now be concerned with these questions, leaving aside further stages of perspective planning which broadly consist of several successive operations of the same kind, approaching ever closer all the relevant magnitudes, and adjusting each time the whole outline to the changes introduced in the distribution of D between I and C, the commodity pattern of demand and of production, the capital–output ratios, based on the most efficient industrial projects.[18]

Planning foreign trade (some details of the fourth step)

The problem is to arrive at a balanced foreign trade, i.e. to find exports to cover the minimum required imports of R, K_N, M, and K_L.

First, therefore, the minimum level of imports must be evaluated by deciding, at the margin, whether it is better to invest in export-promoting or import-saving industries. Export-promoting or import-substituting industries concern us here only from the point of view of "exchange value" and not of the "use value"; i.e. it is immaterial what particular goods are produced,[19] because the foreign currency earned (or saved) may be used to purchase any required good. That is why all such investments can be compared independent of the branch of economic activity to which they belong, while the efficiency of invest-

---

[18] For a method of assessing this efficiency in socialist planning, see M. Kalecki and M. Rakowski, "Generalized formula of the efficiency of investment", in *Studies on the Theory of Reproduction and Prices*, Warsaw, 1964, pp. 189–201.

[19] Obviously the import substitution must fall into the category of goods really necessary to the economy, which otherwise would have been imported.

ment in industries working exclusively for the domestic market can be analysed only in view of choosing the best project for the production of a given "use value" (determined good).

The formula applied in Poland for this purpose uses two "shadow prices", namely the "recoupment period" (the inverse of the assumed rate of interest plus the rate of depreciation) and the notional exchange rate for imported (or exportable) inputs. The recoupment period is chosen in such a way as to ensure at the same time an optimum capital–output ratio and an optimum labour productivity level for the whole economy, in order to make the best possible use of the available capital and labour.[20]

The price charged for imports should, in theory, be equivalent to the marginal "current efficiency of exports" (the cost in zlotys of a unit of foreign currency), although the term "marginal" is somewhat equivocal because the marginal rates have to be adjusted for different geographical directions, as well as for expectations of future trade, etc. In any case, this "shadow price" should be higher than the average efficiency of exports, in order to introduce an anti-import bias into the plan. (The results of such a policy in Poland can be clearly seen from the following figures: in 1938 exports of machinery and equipment covered 6 per cent of the imports of such items; in 1950, 22.8 per cent; in 1955, 41.8 per cent; and in 1963, 86.5 per cent. In the same year net imports of capital goods amounted merely to 4 per cent of the value of new installed equipment, and gross imports to less than one-third.)

Four lists of export-promoting and import-substituting industries can thus be prepared, subdivided into the categories of "supply-determined" and "demand-determined" and classified according to their decreasing efficiency of investment. The best choices are then selected from the four lists,[21] after having made full provision for the exports

---

[20] These *optima* differ obviously from *maxima* (or *minima*, whichever is the case). With a given volume of investment, output would be maximum with the minimum capital output. But reserves of labour might prove insufficient for such a solution, or other obstacles (such as the lack of wage goods and, more particularly, food) might arise in a densely populated country. Productivity would, in turn, be maximum with highly capital-intensive solutions, but in that case the employment generated would be too small for the existing labour force.

[21] Normally the supply-determined good choices will be used to the utmost.

and the import substitution from the already existing capacities,[22] the necessary adjustments for the price forecasts,[23] etc. Of course, maximum austerity in terms of banning unessential luxury imports is also assumed.

In other words, planning of foreign trade involves two distinct but interconnected operations: the allocation of export-promoting and import-substituting investments (already discussed) and the allocation of the capacity to import. The aim is first to maximize the country's capacity to import through export promotion or to reduce its dependence on imports, whichever will prove more efficient by making the best of the given investment, taking into consideration the manpower which can be employed at the assumed real wages; then the aim is to maximize the rate of growth of the economy with a given import capacity by making the best use of it. The first aspect pertains to the realm of macroeconomic planning, the second to that of operating foreign trade.

This is very far from the traditional approach, which consists in using import elasticities of other similar parameters. From the model presented in the section on the place of foreign trade, as well as from the considerations made in the next two sections, it becomes evident that import coefficients depend on the structure of the economy and on the strategy of development chosen, and, therefore, they cannot be safely estimated either from cross-section studies or from past performance. What is more, their maximum reduction[24] becomes a major goal of the plan. To some extent it is possible to achieve this aim by applying institutional measures and bold policies such as land reform (reduction of dependence on food imports), and launching of labour-intensive investment schemes (reduction of dependence on imports of equipment), and total or partial nationalization of foreign trade (reduction of unnecessary imports, likely to persist even under a tied scheme of government import licensing). In such cases, the "import coefficient"

[22] The opportunity to increase the supply of traditional goods will be examined, keeping in mind the flexibility of prices. Gains accruing from a larger volume of sales must outdo the loss arising from the fall in prices. The utmost attention will be given to new geographical markets for the traditional exports.

[23] A welcome arrangement will consist, from the point of view of the planner, in entering into long-term trade agreements, stipulating the volume of trade and stabilizing, wholly or partially, the prices.

[24] As the maximum utilization of foreign trade opportunities has been assumed, the author is not advocating autarchy, but simply acknowledging a situation characteristic of an "import-sensitive economy".

ceases to be a parameter and becomes a strategic variable, operated through institutional measures.

Another point worth emphasizing is that in our analytical scheme there is no room for the argument about "capital goods *versus* maintenance imports". The whole controversy, which has been raging for some years on this subject, is based on a *malentendu*. Imports of capital goods, as such, are not bad or good. The priorities in the imports' bill and the "strategy of foreign trade" must be established, keeping in mind the whole strategy of development expressed in the plan, while no effective planning can take place without imposing severe controls on foreign trade. The planner will have to work out compromises between long-term and short-term exigencies, accommodating, within a given capacity to import, imports of consumer goods and intermediate goods for immediate use and of machines and equipment for investment projects with different lengths of gestation periods. No exact solution can be provided for such problems, and most probably several viable alternative variants may be drawn, from which one will have to be chosen. The only area for important autonomous decisions in foreign trade is that of selecting the most effective export-oriented or import-substituting projects.

Let us observe finally that any attempt at finding whether foreign trade is profitable or not, in *absolute* terms, is based on a misunderstanding, unless we have a freely convertible currency. Even in the latter case, profits or losses incurred by individual traders in distinct transactions do not give us a guiding line for the reorientation of our foreign trade. To implement the plan, a certain level of exports must be achieved, and the macroeconomic point of view does not at all coincide with the profit motive of the entrepreneur. Subsidies to exporters, together with severe controls of imports, provide a partial solution.

In a planned economy (generally in a country having a governmental monopoly of foreign trade), it might well be considered for all purposes of economic analysis that there are in reality two currencies, the internal and the external, the latter being linked through a fixed coefficient to the dollar or any other convertible currency. Under these circumstances, one asks how many units of internal currency, representing the cost of exports, must be spent to earn one unit of external currency to pay for the imports. Obviously different ratios will be obtained for different goods exportable to different countries. Thus a classification of exports is arrived at according to their decreasing "efficiency" (or increasing costs per unit of external currency earned), but this is a *relative* scale of values and not an absolute one. One might say that it is better to export goods A to the country O, rather than goods B to the country P. But there is no meaning in trying to assess whether these exports are profitable or not in absolute terms.

How far one can move on the list of exports will depend, on the one hand, on the volume of imports that must be paid for and, on the other, on the considerations of the incremental capital–output ratio in the export-promoting industries, which have to be set up if a considerable expansion of exports is to be achieved. At the margin, these capital–output ratios will become so high, and will weigh to such an extent on the average incremental capital–output ratio for the economy, that an attempt to solve the difficulties of foreign trade arising at a very high overall rate of growth r of the economy by means of heavy investment in less and less effective export-promoting industries is likely to prove self-defeating: it becomes wiser to reduce r.[25] For practical purposes, it is possible to fix for every plan a minimum level of efficiency of exports, not to be exceeded unless an adverse shift of the terms of trade occurs. This, in turn, amounts to fixing, under given market conditions and techniques of production, the maximum volume of exports in the plan.

The case for foreign aid

Foreign trade difficulties may impose a ceiling on the rate of growth of the national economy, as was seen in the section on foreign trade as a barrier to growth. At some level r of the rate of growth of the national income, the rate r can be implemented in terms of overall production; however, the commodity pattern of the national product does not correspond to the demand arising from the assumed distribution of income, despite the adjustments between supply and demand performed through operations of foreign trade. In other words, certain

---

[25] For a given i, an increase of k will reduce r; keeping a high r with a high k would mean, therefore, increasing i to over the level warranted by political considerations.

goods from industries determined by demand may be produced in excess of the effective demand, while other goods from industries determined by supply will be in short supply, creating bottlenecks.

Under such circumstances arises the case for "foreign aid"—understood, at this point, as putting at the disposal of the country benefited an additional capacity to import, without requiring repayment over a period of at least five years.[26] Foreign aid will be discussed, therefore, in the context of "foreign trade" rather than in that of insufficient capacity to invest, although it will also add automatically to financial resources.

Let us look at the matter more closely in terms of our four-sector model. Throughout this section, I will deal with hypothetical cases which arise at the stage of plan elaboration and not with adjustments which actually take place through a market mechanism.

The gross national income Y viewed from the supply side is equal to the supply of final goods (and marketed services, if the broader definitions of national incomes are used) $K_N + K_L + M$. The same holds true if imports are included and exports excluded, and one assumes, on the one hand, that total exports and imports are balanced and, on the other, that exports and imports of R are balanced. Thus:

$$C = K_N + K_L$$

where C denotes the consumption in real terms, and

$$I = M$$

where I denotes real investment.[27]

On the demand side, the national income consists of consumption expenditure E and savings S:

$$Y = E_N + E_L + S$$

The distribution of income given is assumed (from practice or from exercises in planning) and all the possibilities of foreign trade already

[26] This definition will be modified later on. However, it should be pointed out now that it excludes foreign direct private investment, which, as far as the capital account is concerned, may never be repaid, but which in compensation imposes, as a rule, a very high and *permanent* burden on the current transactions account in the form of expatriated royalties and profits remitted abroad.

[27] Changes in stocks have been excluded from the argument.

explored. Thus:

$$E_N + E_L + S = K_N + K_L + M$$

and it is assumed that at least two among the following inequalities arise:

$$E_N \neq K_N$$
$$E_L \neq K_L$$
$$S \neq M$$

The case for foreign aid arises at this point, and an analysis of four situations follows.

CASE 1
$$E_N > K_N \quad \text{and} \quad E_L = K_L$$

In this rather infrequent case, obviously $S < M$. Let us denote $E_N - K_N = D$, and let us assume that foreign aid to this amount becomes available and that it will be used for additional imports of K_N.[28] The results may be summarized in the following way:

Initial position		Final position		
Supply	Demand	Supply		Demand
K_N	$E_N = K_N + D$	$K_N + D$	$=$	E_N
K_L	$E_L = K_L$	K_L	$=$	E_L
M	$S = M - D$	M	$=$	$S + D$
Y	Y	$Y + D$		$Y + D$

Foreign aid permitted an increase in the supply of necessities and, at the same time, added to the same extent to savings.[29] Investment

[28] It does not need to be assumed, of course, that the credits available are directly used for imports of K_N. Even if the credits were actually tied to imports of equipment, their utilization would release the corresponding amount of foreign currency, which otherwise would have been spent on imports of capital goods.

[29] This increase in savings finds its counterpart in the growth of the indebtedness of the country benefited by foreign aid, unless aid is administered as a grant.

was carried out at the maximum level permitted by the supply of M and the demand for necessities satisfied, so that no inflationary pressures did occur. Foreign aid was in this case instrumental in raising the relative share of investment i in the total expenditure $Y + D$ to

$$i = \frac{M}{Y + D}$$

Without the inflow of foreign aid, three alternatives were open to the country considered:

(a) Were it to persist in keeping the investment at the level M and the income at the level Y with an unchanged ratio of E_N in the income, it would have achieved an impressive relative share of investment in the national income $i = M/Y$, but the gap between the effective demand for necessities E_N and the supplies K_N would generate an inflationary wave, endangering the whole process of growth.

(b) The other way would consist in reducing the level of investments to $I = K_N(S/E_N) < M$ and the national income to $Y_R = Y(K_N/E_N)$. In this case, some capacities in industries M would be left idle. If additional foreign markets become available, however, foreign aid is no longer necessary. The surplus of goods M is traded against the necessities in short supply.[30] The national income is Y (less than $Y + D$, it is true, but, in compensation, foreign debt does not grow). The rate of investment is S/Y, as foreseen initially in our national income distribution. The opening of additional markets performs a role very similar to that of foreign aid.

(c) If the assumption about the fixed distribution of income is relaxed, a shift of demand could be induced from E_N to S by additional taxation on necessities and the corresponding reduction of real wages. This case is excluded from consideration, however, since it implies a sharp reduction in the standard of living of the workers. A progressive policy would, rather, consist in taxing E_L in such a way as to increase S to the level of M and then trying to use the idle capacities K_L to increase K_N.

---

[30] This surplus, let us repeat, is rather unlikely to occur, except in the case of "tied" aid, which imposes on the aid-receiving country imports of machinery which can be produced at home, thus creating free capacities in some sectors of the machine-building industry.

An attenuated version of case (a) would take place.[31] In some circumstances, additional taxes may be used to finance social services not included in K_N.

CASE 2

$$S > M \qquad E_L = K_L \qquad E_N < K_N$$

Let it be $S - M = D$, and let us again assume that foreign aid will be available to that extent and spent for imports of M. The operation is summarized below:

Initial position		Final position	
Supply	Demand	Supply	Demand
K_N	$E_N = K_N - D$	$K_N \quad =$	$E_N + D$
K_L	$E_L = K_L$	$K_L \quad =$	E_L
M	$S = M + D$	$M + D \quad =$	S
Y	Y	$Y + D$	$Y + D$

Foreign aid permitted an increase in investment to the level warranted by the savings and, at the same time, permitted popular consumption to increase to the level warranted by the productive capacity of K_N. No inflationary pressures are likely to occur. The rate of investment is

$$i = \frac{S}{Y + D}$$

(somewhat lower than the initially assumed $i = s/Y$, but, in compensation, popular consumption is greater than initially assumed at the cost of an increase in foreign indebtedness).

Without taking foreign aid, the country would have to keep its investment at the level $I = M$, consumption would in no instance exceed E_N, and either excess savings D would be invested in stocks of K_N

---

[31] To the extent to which a reduction of E_L would release foreign currency previously allocated for imports of K_L, alternative imports of K_N would certainly be possible.

or the national income would remain at a level lower than Y, unless we agree to change the income distribution and to transfer excess savings $S - M$ to E_N.

Needless to say, the opening of additional foreign markets for exports of K_N to the amount of D would have permitted a balanced growth, with national income Y and $I = S$.

CASE 3

Let us discuss a less hypothetical case. Let it be

$$K_L > E_L \quad \text{and} \quad K_N = E_N$$

Obviously, $M < S$. Let it be $S - M = D$. If foreign aid D becomes available and no policies restricting E_L are foreseen, the operation will take the following form:

Initial position		Final position		
Supply	Demand	Supply		Demand
K_N	$E_N = K_N$	K_N	$=$	E_N
K_L	$E_L = K_L - D$	K_L	$=$	$E_L + D$
M	$S = M + D$	$M + D$	$=$	S
Y	Y	$Y + D$		$Y + D$

In other words, credits available from abroad will be used for imports of machinery, while on the side of demand the additional resources will ultimately increase the consumption of luxuries. If we insist on considering resources available from abroad as savings, we may well say that due to the inflow of foreign capital D, local savings have been reduced to the same amount, e.g. by a reduction of the level of taxation, as compared to that initially assumed.

Were foreign markets available, the excess of K_L should of course be traded to pay for M in short supply, making foreign aid unnecessary, or at least reducing considerably its scope, even on the assumption that owing to low prices obtained the income from the sale abroad of available K_L will not be enough to pay for the necessary volume of M.

In any case, steps should be taken to prevent local savings "released" by the inflow of foreign capital to "land" in E_L. By appropriate taxation, an apparently "unbalanced" growth should rather be promoted with investments equal to $M + D$, consumption of luxuries restricted to $K_L - D$ (thus leaving free capacities D in K_L available for exports at any moment), and popular consumption K_N supplemented by additional social services[32] financed from the "released" savings.[33] (Of course, without foreign aid the "excess" savings D over M should also be used to finance additional social services.)

CASE 4

Let us finally assume, combining the three previous cases, that

$$E_N > K_N \quad \text{and} \quad S > M$$

Of course, $K_L > E_L$. Let it be

$$E_N - K_N = D_1$$
$$S - M = D_2$$
$$D = D_1 + D_2$$

The initial position is as follows:

Supply	Demand
K_N	$E_N = K_N + D_1$
K_L	$E_L = K_L - D$
M	$S = M + D_2$
Y	Y

In this case, foreign aid D should be used to import D_1 worth of K_N and D_2 worth of M, and E_L should be kept by an appropriate taxation

[32] Non-marketable services provided by the government are not included in our national income.

[33] For this point see M. Kalecki, "Problems of financing economic development in a mixed economy", *op. cit.*

at the initial level, thus leaving an idle capacity in K_L equal to D and permitting the government an additional social expenditure to the amount of D.

Of course, new foreign markets for goods K_L turned out by capacities now idle would have the same effect as foreign aid in terms of creating additional capacity to import and generating a higher income (with the significant difference of increasing the gross domestic product and not merely the total expenditure, counterbalanced by a corresponding increase in foreign debt).

What happens if, *ceteris paribus*, E_L is kept at a lower level than initially assumed by means of additional taxation? Foreign currency used to import K_L will be released or additional export possibilities will be created if K_L is home produced, as long as it can find foreign markets. This additional capacity to import will be spent according to the situation, either in additional imports of K_N or M. The same argument holds true for imports of M $(\rightarrow K_L)$, which compete with M $(\rightarrow K_N)$, and for imports of R $(\rightarrow K_L)$.

Creation of additional markets for exports of K_L diverted from the internal market *pari passu* with an appropriate fiscal policy is thus likely to play a role at least equivalent to that of foreign aid, since it will contribute to the same extent to the growth potential of the economy without increasing its foreign debt. Disposable national income will be less than that in the case of the inflow of foreign aid, but investments and popular consumption will be the same.

The argument applies *a fortiori* to sales of accumulated stocks of raw materials and all other commodities which are accounted for in the gross national income, but obviously neither adds to consumption nor to productive investment. Releasing of stocks will mean either increasing consumption or investment, or making "active" a "frozen" share of the national income. Opening of the markets for such sales is therefore foreign aid at its best, although it does not involve inflows of foreign capital.

One reaches the conclusion, therefore, that aid through trade is in many respects equal or superior to inflows of foreign capital, with the purely theoretical exception of foreign grants.[34]

---

[34] Grants usually involve some political conditions and, therefore, cannot be considered on their purely economic merit.

On the other hand, it is not possible to assimilate every inflow of foreign capital to aid. Reservations have been expressed already to the inclusion of foreign direct private investment into this category. Let us now look closer at foreign credits. In the cases discussed above, we assumed a rational utilization of foreign aid D. But mishandling of this additional capacity to import is quite possible and even likely in an economy which does not apply comprehensive planning and strict controls of foreign trade. We might imagine in our second case $(S > M)$ that foreign aid D is dissipated in additional imports of K_L, so that, thanks to additional imports, a shift of income takes place from savings to conspicuous consumption. This eventuality is less hypothetical than it would seem at first sight. The expectation of massive foreign assistance, coupled with sophisms insisting on foreign aid on the grounds of incapacity to raise the level of capital formation in a developing country,[35] makes the wealthy members of the society singularly complacent and inclined to indulge in conspicuous consumption. This will become still more apparent if we agree to include in consumption, taken in its broadest meaning, such investment as used for the construction of luxury dwellings.

When foreign aid is "tied", its availability may induce the planners to change their investment allocation. Some foreign loans, not speaking of direct foreign investment, are likely to be invested in sector K_L at the expense of the remaining two. Again, it is difficult in such an eventuality to consider as "aid" an inflow of foreign capital, which adds to the lopsidedness of the economy and is likely to promote "perverse growth".

The above considerations prompt the following remarks on foreign aid:

(a) The use of it arises on the grounds of insufficient capacity to import.

(b) Giving the country concerned an opportunity for additional exports, either from existing stocks or from unutilized (or improperly utilized) existing capacities, is the best form of "aid".

[35] The absolute low level of national income per head makes the volume of investment per head low, but the share of investment in the national income may be, as a rule, considerably raised without inroads into popular consumption, as long as the share appropriated by the rich and devoted to conspicuous consumption remains high.

(c) Inflows of capital in the form of credits[36] may be helpful, if such credits are properly utilized. Under no condition, however, should an inflow of long-term capital be automatically equated with "aid".

(d) The evaluation of foreign aid and its allocation requires a deep insight into the working and structure of the economy, and proper handling of it is only possible if comprehensive planning has been adopted.

(e) The simple cases discussed above serve to indicate the types of problem the planner is likely to face with respect to foreign aid.

---

[36] The longer and the softer, the better they are, as the servicing of the foreign debt will place less burden on the balance of payments.

CHAPTER 6

Forms of Foreign Aid—An Economic Analysis (1966)*

Introduction

Few topics are the object of a more voluminous literature than foreign aid. And yet the very concept of "foreign aid" needs clarification.[1] This will be the main purpose of this chapter, which, at the same time, will review the principal forms of economic aid and evaluate them.

The chapter is in three parts. The second reviews the different modalities of economic aid. The third discusses the problem of aid through trade.

Use has been made of contributions and reviews of literature prepared by the following authors, to whom go our thanks: I. Blaszczyszyn, J. Kotowicz, T. Kozak, M. Paszynski, C. Prawdzic, and W. Rydygier.

Foreign aid and economic development

DEFINITION OF ECONOMIC AID

From the point of view of the recipient country foreign economic aid occurs when:

(a) The country receives additional resources in foreign currency (or its equivalent in goods) over the capacity to import generated by exports or financed from accumulated reserves, without the need of

* Paper written with Michal Kalecki.
[1] To quote the so-called Jeanneney report, "L'aide est une notion ambigueë et sa mesure chiffrée malaisée" (*La Politique de Coopération avec les Pays en Voie de Développment*, Paris, 1963, p. 51).

immediate repayment and at a cost lower than the prevailing rates of commercial loans.

(b) These additional resources are used in order to improve the recipient country's economic performance above the level otherwise attainable, i.e. either the country achieves a higher rate of growth without reducing the anticipated consumption of working people or it implements the anticipated rate of growth, managing to increase the volume of popular consumption over the anticipated level. (A combination of the two situations described above is, of course, possible.) We assume that this higher rate of growth implies changes in the structure of the economy, although in the short view structural rigidities or imbalances which give rise to scarcities in supplies of determined commodities and services can only be relieved by additional imports.[2]

The country's economic performance is not improved, however, when additional resources are used to increase the consumption of "luxuries", i.e. permit the implementation of the anticipated rate of growth with an unchanged level of popular consumption and a lower volume of internal savings.

This is why we cannot equate all the inflows of foreign capital with foreign aid.[3] Whether it should be considered as "aid" or not depends, on the one hand, on the comparative cost of such captial and, on the other, on the use made of it by the recipient country, which may not always have a free hand to act without taking into consideration the suggestions of the donor. Thus, a certain measure of arbitrariness cannot be entirely dissociated from evaluations of the foreign aid received.

We should discard as fallacious all ideas of assisting a country by putting at its disposal an amount of accumulated local currency, as long as it remains unconvertible. Two situations may occur: either the country concerned has no free productive capacities, and in this

---

[2] For a good analysis of problems and policies of developing countries arising from pivotal scarcities and the role of foreign aid in relieving structural bottlenecks, see *United Nations, Work Economic Survey 1964*, part I, New York, 1965.

[3] The necessity of making a distinction between the inflow of foreign capital and that of "aid" is today more or less accepted. See for example, F. Benham *Economic Aid to Underdeveloped Countries*, London, 1961, and P. N. Rosenstein-Rodan, "International aid for underdeveloped countries", *Rev. of Econ. and Statist.*, May 1961, pp. 107–138. For an all-inclusive treatment of aid see H. J. P. Arnold, *Aid to Developing Countries, A Comparative Study*, London, 1962.

case the additional demand generated by releasing accumulated local funds will lead to inflationary pressures, or free capacities do exist and then the financing of additional production by having recourse to deficit financing has the same effect as that of financing it by foreign loans in local currency.

Turning now to the definition of aid from the point of view of the donor country, we should make a clear distinction between two positions:

(a) The donor country has no free productive capacities (as, for example, usually happens in socialist countries).

(b) The donor country does not fully use its productive capacities, because of lack of effective demand (a frequent situation in developed capitalist countries).

In the former case giving foreign aid, embodied in an export surplus, means a sacrifice because the aggregate internal expenditure (i.e. national income less exports plus imports) will be less than the income generated, which cannot be stepped up above the maximum level warranted by the productive capacities. Would there have been no export surplus the aggregate internal expenditure would be equal to the income generated at the maximum level.

In the latter case, the picture changes entirely: the export surplus, similarly to investment, has a "multiplier" effect, so that the aggregate domestic expenditure after deduction of the export surplus from the income thus generated is higher than the income which would be generated without the export surplus. We may say, therefore, that by giving economic aid to other countries a developed country with free productive capacities assists its own economy in obtaining a higher level of economic activity. Foreign aid, far from being a burden for it, can perform a very useful role in achieving full employment while it serves a better purpose than encouraging the armaments race, provided it does not compete with public expenditures other than armaments, which are of considerable importance for the country in question.[4]

[4] When foreign aid is granted by a country with free productive capacities, such aid does not necessarily lead to the reduction of the gap in the rates of growth between the donor and the recipient countries, because it contributes to the simultaneous increase of these rates in both countries. The concern of the developing countries with overtaking

CRITERIA OF EVALUATION OF FOREIGN AID

From the definition established above, it follows that:

(a) Foreign aid means essentially an improvement of external conditions of growth.

(b) Its evaluation depends essentially on the full knowledge of the general problems of economic development of the recipient country.

We can measure with some precision the extent to which a given volume of foreign aid, provided on certain conditions, increases the recipient country's capacity to import in the short run and how it will adversely affect the future position of the balance of payments through the servicing of the debt and the repayment of the principal.

From the quantitative point of view foreign aid can be compared to a positive shift in terms of trade to the extent to which both increase the capacity to import of the country without any effort on its part. But foreign credits must be repaid. Moreover, a positive shift in terms of trade has a continuous effect, comparable, strictly speaking, to a continuous flow of foreign assistance. It will be easily seen, therefore, that an adverse shift in terms of trade cancels the effects of the inflow of foreign aid and, what is more, must be compensated by a continuous inflow of that aid as long as the worsened terms of trade do not improve. In such circumstances a perfectly legitimate procedure consists in subtracting from the net inflow of capital[5] the "losses" suffered on account of adverse terms of trade, even though such an operation involves a somewhat arbitrary choice of the initial level of export and import prices, considered for the purpose of the calculation as fair. Data collected by different United Nation agencies point to the rather disturbing fact that the "real" inflow of long-term capital to the developing countries in the last decade was to a great extent offset by the growing burden of servicing foreign debts and the losses motivated by the adverse shifts in the terms of trade. Without going into the details of the matter,

---

the developed countries is thus misplaced: we should aim at a situation where massive flows of aid from developed countries will help the developing countries in achieving higher rates of growth and in reaching thus higher absolute levels of income per capita, while contributing at the same time to a higher rate of growth in the developed countries and retarding, therefore, to mutual profit, the moment when the two groups of countries will find themselves on the same level of income per capita.

[5] By net inflow we mean the inflow of capital less its servicing.

which will be dealt with below, we should like to emphasize even at this stage of the argument that a positive shift in the terms of trade of developing countries or a reduction in the volume of the transfer of profits arising from direct foreign investment would improve the external conditions of their growth in just the same way as a flow of foreign aid of the same volume, with the difference, however, that no increase in foreign indebtedness would occur.[6]

Turning now to the second aspect of the problem, mentioned at the beginning of this section, we shall examine at some length the role of foreign trade in the process of economic development of an underdeveloped country.

All the tensions and bottlenecks of such an economy can be translated into an additional demand for imports. This demand arises with regard to the products of the "supply-determined" industries which cannot push their volume of production beyond a certain level[7] and must be paid for by export surpluses produced by "demand-determined industries. The higher the postulated rate of growth, the greater will be the necessary volume of imports. To pay for them it will be necessary to resort to less and less "effective" exports[8] and to introduce more and more capital-intensive export[9] up to the point where the advantages arising from a higher volume of foreign trade will be offset by the disadvantages resulting from the increase of the capital–output ratio.

From these considerations we see that an inflow of foreign aid may be instrumental in stepping up the rate of growth of an economy faced by the barrier of foreign trade. But such a result by no means follows automatically from the inflow of foreign aid, which may be dissipated in additional consumption of "luxuries".

[6] The indebtedness of the developing countries is increasing at an alarming rate. Developing nations are paying their debts at the rate of 5 billion dollars a year, as against less than 1 billion dollars a year ten years ago. Some countries have to devote 50 per cent of the value of their exports to the amortizations of their foreign debt. The total foreign debt of the underdeveloped countries rose to 10 billion dollars in 1955, and at the present rate it will be 90 billion by 1975. (*Commercio Exterior de Mexico*, May 1965, p. 11).

[7] We may consider non-existing branches of industry as supply-determined at the level of production equal to zero.

[8] The lower the cost in local currency of a unit of foreign currency earned the more effective is an export.

[9] Of course, after having exhausted all the possibilities of less-capital-intensive export-oriented investments.

We may look at the matter from still another angle. Given an initial economic structure we may construct on the basis of an assumed income distribution and of a postulated rate of growth, a plan anticipating the trend of demands for necessities, luxuries, capital goods, and intermediate goods, the inputs of which are necessary for the production of final goods. These demands will be met partly by domestic production and the rest will have to be imported. In principle the necessary imports can always be covered by production for export. But the feasible structure of this production may not fit the conditions prevailing in the foreign markets. The country is thus faced with a deficit in foreign trade and the non-utilization, to the same extent, of its productive capacity. In such a situation of sectoral imbalances between supply and demand, after having taken full advantage of all the possibilities of foreign trade, the possibility of taking foreign aid to the tune of the potential import surplus might be considered.

But such an inflow of foreign assistance automatically adds to the financial resources of the country which permits increasing investment without reducing consumption, or vice versa, without risking inflationary pressures. In evaluating foreign aid we should, thus, clearly see its double function.

Two questions, therefore should be asked here:

(a) To what extent has the inflow of foreign aid improved the country's balance of payment position; and has this improvement been used to remove the bottlenecks in the supply of capital goods, necessities, luxuries, or intermediate goods?

(b) Were the additional financial resources instrumental in raising the rate of growth by increasing investment over the level of domestic savings or releasing local savings for consumption; and, if so did they finance an increase in the consumption of necessities or of luxuries, or materialize in a higher volume of social services?

Aid may be considered appropriately utilized if:

(a) It adds, *ceteris paribus*, to investment other than those increasing the output of luxuries.

(b) It adds, *ceteris paribus*, to the consumption of essentials and/or the output of social services.

But it defeats its own purpose when it releases local savings for an additional consumption of luxuries by foregoing the taxation of higher income groups and/or non-essentials, or it fosters investment leading to an increased output of luxuries.[10] Such investment merely adds to the lopsidedness of the economy, and leads to "perverse growth": in the short run it promotes growth but in the long run it adversely affects the growth prospects of the economy. For it ties up capital goods, intermediate goods, and essentials, which otherwise would have been used to expand productive capacity and employment in the sectors of the economy which turn out essentials, capital goods, and intermediate goods.

Thus, the role played by foreign aid can be evaluated only in the context of a comprehensive analysis of the development problems of the recipient country seen as a whole. Such an analysis requires the framing of a plan and, therefore, comprehensive planning should be considered as a prerequisite of any action aimed at a rational utilization of available foreign aid.[11]

Before going into a more detailed examination of some aspects of the impact of foreign aid on the economy of the recipient country, we should like to stress that, of the two functions of foreign aid, the one pertaining to the realm of foreign trade is by far the more important, contrary to some entrenched prejudices.

For quite a time many economists believed that foreign trade would never become a bottleneck, while in a poor country the barrier of

[10] In his report on the Conference on Development Aid, held in Dar-es-Salaam in September 1964, D.A. Lury refers to the point, raised there, that some of the aid given to African countries is in fact working against development. "It was alleged that aid to some countries was being used to build up a small urbanized élite which was losing contact with its fellow-countrymen. It is difficult to assess the true benefits flowing from the development of aid but at the least it seems clear that it would be wise for recipients to follow the rule given by Dr. Kiano, Kenya Minister for Commerce and Industry, in his speech at the beginning of the Conference: 'Look gift horses in the mouth'", *East Afr. J.*, December 1964, p. 30.

[11] This point, rather obvious to economists from countries with experience in comprehensive planning, is being increasingly accepted today even by authors who represent a school of thought which for a long time denied the need to plan. See, for example, J. K. Galbraith, "A positive approach to economic aid", *Foreign Affairs, New York*, April 1961. At the United Nations Conference on Trade and Development the developing countries were pressing to get foreign assistance on a long-term basis in the context of development plans, instead of piecemeal annual commitments.

insufficient accumulation would put a low ceiling on the rate of growth. Yet, by means of appropriate taxation and other institutional measures, the relative share of investment in the national income of developing countries can be greatly increased without affecting the consumption of working people. However, the majority of developing countries must struggle against the obstacle of an inadequate and inelastic world demand for their feasible exports.[12]

The foreign currency gap is, therefore, likely to be retained in practice for the evaluation of needs in foreign aid, although from a purely technical point of view the planner should perform two independent calculations of the foreign trade currency gap and savings gap arising at a postulated rate of investment to implement it. Where the savings gap is higher than the foreign currency gap, it should be reduced to the level of the foreign currency gap by measures of taxation purporting the reduction of non-essential consumption. Failing this, it would be necessary to increase the foreign currency gap up to the level of the savings gap.

THE IMPACT OF FOREIGN AID

It is sometimes believed that the evaluation of foreign aid can be inferred from the commodity pattern of the additional imports financed by such aid.

This, however, is absolutely wrong. Additional imports of equipment may prove detrimental if they are earmarked for the expansion of productive capacities in the industries turning out luxuries, while additional imports of necessities, by helping to close the gap between supply and effective demand, may, in fact, permit the stepping up of the level of investment without the danger of inducing inflation. Also, credits tied to the purchase of specified sorts of goods should not be rejected

---

[12] In their "Proposals for the creation of the Latin American Common Market" (Supplement to *Commercio Exterior de Mexico*, **XI**, no. 5, May 1965, p. 3) the four wise men of Latin America—Jose Antonio Mayobre, Felipe Herrera, Felipe Sanz de Santamaria, and Raul Prebisch—speaking of "common denominators" existing today among the developing countries, state in the following words their foreign trade problem: "Markets for the traditional export of our primary commodities are shrinking and closing, without new ones being offered for our manufactures. The trend towards imbalance in foreign trade is placing a serious brake on the economic development of many of our countries. And deterioration of the terms of trade is materially reducing the positive contribution of international financial resources to our development."

by the recipient country, as long as those goods belong to the actual list of preferential imports. Obviously, foreign currency which would have been spent otherwise for the purchase of these goods is being released for other destinations. In such a way shipments of grain on credit—if imports of grain cannot be prevented—may amount to an indirect financing of purchases of equipment.

We may turn now to a more complex instance of dislocation, when the final impact of the foreign aid is by no means apparent. Let us suppose that instead of building a machine industry which is technically feasible a country chooses to spend the same funds on a motorcar factory. It will subsequently use the available foreign aid to import machines of highest priority, which will, in fact, amount to financing the superfluous motor car industry. To make our example still more convincing, we may imagine that our automobile industry can produce trucks or passenger cars, the former having a high social priority and the latter a very low one, Without foreign aid, the factory would have a programme of production of trucks. But foreign aid becomes available and is utilized for imports of trucks, while the local factory specializes in passenger cars Nobody would question the necessity of putting new trucks into service, but under the circumstances, aid coming in the form of trucks is, in reality, used to finance the production of passenger motorcars.

The substance of our argument is, therefore, the following: we should always look at the final impact of foreign aid, following step by step all the successive dislocations caused by the additional imports financed through foreign aid. Aid will be efficient to the extent to which it closes gaps between effective demand and supply in the process of the development of the recipient country.

THE ABSORPTIVE CAPACITY[13]

How much aid can a country take? On a purely theoretical plane, any amount of economic aid can be swallowed, as an inflow of foreign

[13] For a not-too-satisfactory attempt to define different aspects of the "absorptive capacity", see P. N. Rosenstein-Rodan, "International aid for underdeveloped countries", *Rev. of Econ. and Statist.*, no. 2, May 1961, pp. 107–138, and the criticism formulated by D. A. Baldwin and G. Ranis in the May 1962 and November 1962 issues of the same journal.

capital will always increase the volume of aggregate domestic expenditure and, whenever properly used in accordance with a plan, will materialize also in a higher rate of growth of the national income. But the higher this rate, the higher will have to be the relative share of imports in the increment of the national income, because of the lack of free productive capacities, including the skilled labour force which we consider for the moment to be an importable item. In other words, the "effectiveness" of the foreign aid measured by the marginal ratio of the increment of the national income to the additional imports will tend to zero, while the ratio of the increment of the aggregate expenditure to the additional imports will tend to unity.[14]

Before we reach this limit, however, two other factors are likely to set a ceiling on the "absorptive capacity" of the recipient country.

On the one hand, there is the problem of financial capacity to service the debt. The better the terms of credit the lesser will be, of course, the burden of servicing of a given volume of credits. But unless new outlets for exports are created,[15] servicing of the debt is likely to become a problem if the country indulges in taking credits for some years. An increasing share of foreign currency earned through exports will be devoted to this aim and the net capacity to import will in consequence decrease, unless new credits are taken. This will start a snowball process, which only shows that even a sustained foreign assistance will not solve the problems of the developing countries as long as the stalemate in foreign trade persists. We must never lose sight of the fact that credits are but a form of postponing the payment for a delivery of goods, but ultimately this payment will normally have to take the form of an export.

On the other hand, the capacity to absorb foreign aid depends to a great extent on the country's availability of skilled manpower of different grades and types. Obviously our previous assumption, made at the beginning of this section, that skilled labour could always be imported from abroad is unrealistic. At best a developing country can rely for some time on highly qualified foreign technicians, but already

[14] Compare for this point: D. Doser, "National income and domestic income multipliers and their application to foreign aid transfers", *Economica*, February 1963.

[15] From the point of view of the balance of payments the impact of import substitution is, of course, identical to that of additional exports.

the medium grades required in great numbers cannot be brought from abroad both due to difficulties in recruitment and the political complications that are likely to arise. That is why technical assistance and the so-called investment in human resources should be considered as the complement of economic foreign aid in the form of credits for the purchase of goods. The volume and forms of such assistance must be carefully harmonized with the economic development plan. Normally, contracts for the supply of complete industrial plants should contain clauses about technical assistance. But the problem is, of course, broader.[16]

Principal forms of economic aid

Before we pass on to review the different modalities of economic aid—grants, credits, grain loans, direct investments—we should like to comment on two general aspects of all such types of aid, namely:

(a) Their relationship with the public and the private sectors, both in the donor and in the recipient countries

(b) The pros and cons of bilateral and multilateral arrangements

As far as the first issue is concerned, the developing countries have good reasons to prefer aid coming from public funds which are put at the disposal of the recipient country's government. Such aid eliminates, or at least reduces, possible pressures on the part of powerful private corporations of the donor countries, operating in the recipient countries. At the other end, it makes easier the proper utilization of available foreign assistance in harmony with the economic plan objectives. The least we can say is that it is always possible for the authorities of the recipient country to make use of the foreign aid received in such a way as to strengthen the private sector, if it chooses to do so, while the contrary is not true: it is difficult to imagine that a private concern in the recipient country will avail itself of foreign loans put at its disposal for any other purpose than that of expanding its own

[16] To some extent, it implies the choice of a strategy for development. Some writers would advise the underdeveloped countries to concentrate for a certain period of years on investments in "human resources" before starting industrial investments. Such a strategy is open to two criticisms. On the one hand, it retards unnecessarily the beginning of the actual process of development. On the other, all plans for manpower training must rely on long-run economic plans, and not vice versa, the more so since vocational training in industrial crafts could not succeed in the absence of industrial plants.

productive capacities, however low might be the social priority attached to such a project. The individual interests of the firms cannot be taken, of course, as identical with the social priorities established in the plan, unless we believe that the market mechanism allocates investment in the best way. The whole experience of the developing countries belies such a belief; were we to go by market indications alone, we should have a completely lopsided development with an excessive part of the sector turning out luxuries. At any rate, planning would have to be considered as perfectly redundant. Actually, making foreign loans available to specified private firms amounts in some cases to influencing the pattern of investment in the recipient country by the donor institution.

Besides, several developing countries are interested in expanding their public sector, as an objective of their economic and social policies, aimed at strengthening their independence and speeding up the necessary structural transformations.

While asking for an increased stream of aid coming from public funds and going to the public sector, many economists and politicians at the same time advance unexceptionable arguments in favour of multilateral aid, channelled through the United Nations and their specialized agencies, rather than offered through bilateral government-to-government contacts. Such a shift towards a system of multilateral international aid distribution would, in their opinion, reduce to a minimum the political aspects of aid-giving.[17] They might be right, although not quite in touch with the complex realities of the present world political

---

[17] In an essay, *The Political Case for Economic Development Aid* (mimeographed), Professor Max. F. Millikan of MIT (Cambridge, Mass.) recognized that "foreign aid is not a goal of the United States nor even a separable element in our foreign policy but rather a handy multipurpose instrument of that policy which we have been tempted to use in an increasingly wide variety of ways for an increasingly broad range of purpose". Time and again the American press opens the debate on the same subject. The conflicting positions are aptly summarized in the following excerpt from an editorial published by *The New York Times* (international edition) on 12 January 1965: "Some critics, taking the simplest, balance-sheet approach, insist that the quid of United States aid must be held back from any country that does not provide the quo of support for American policies. But such a policy would be self-defeating. To try to make docile puppets out of aid recipients would lead to bribery and blackmail, destroying all that the program has already accomplished and ending in complete futility." The political functions of American foreign aid are clearly stated by H. Feis in his recent study, *Foreign Aid and Foreign Policy*, New York, 1964. For a brutal assessment of the strategic importance of developing countries for NATO and the consequent call to subordinate entirely foreign aid to political and military criteria, see M. W. J. M. Brockmeijer, *Developing Countries and NATO*, Leyden, 1963.

scene.[18] Whatever the opinions expressed on this subject, we must be prepared to work in the immediate future mainly in terms of bilateral economic relations.

I am convinced, furthermore, that bilateral assistance has something to recommend it: it does not require very heavy machinery, it can adjust itself to new and elastic forms, and it can be more easily co-ordinated and harmonized with trade relations, at least between countries adopting some measure of long-term planning. In this context I should like once more to stress the necessity of thinking simultaneously in terms of trade and aid.

GRANTS (GIFTS)

From the strictly economic point of view a free grant is, of course, the best form of foreign aid. Aggregate internal expenditure exceeds the income generated by the total of the grant and no repayment is involved, either at the moment or in the future. But economic aid has been

---

[18] Senator Fulbright is one of the American advocates of multilateral rather than bilateral aid. In a long article written for *The New York Times Magazine* and reproduced in *The New York Times* (international edition) on March 27–28 1965, he makes it clear, however, that he seeks only a "psychological difference", as he advocates channelling American foreign aid through international institutions which are controlled to a large extent by the United States: "It should be understood", writes Senator Fulbright, "that while the World Bank and the I.D.A. are independent international agencies, the influence of the United States on their policies is considerable because decisions on loans are made by votes weighted according to contributions. As the largest single contributor, the United States has the greatest voting power. In channeling its development loans through the I.D.A., therefore, the United States would be renouncing exclusive control, with its attendant disadvantages, while retaining great influence on the disposition of its contributions."

In an article on the World Bank's relations with India a contributor to *The Economic Weekly, Bombay.* 4 April 1964, p. 630, stated: "Dispensation of aid has invariably been accompanied by dispensation of advice; the latter has varied from mild suggestions to outright interference in the policy formulations of the recipient country. We were hitherto at the milder end of the advice-scale. We are moving, one fears, rapidly to the other end."

The distinction between public and private loans proves, moreover, deceptive to the extent to which some public lending agencies such as the World Bank insist on the so-called "bankability" of projects to be financed, extending the market test to projects in the public sector without much concern for the social external economies. this attitude has been criticized at the Geneva Conference on Trade and Development by representatives of developing countries.

too much of an instrument of policy, not to have some strings or second thoughts attached in many actual cases of free grants (with the exception of rather minor contributions, made on a humanitarian basis, to assist countries affected by some natural calamity, feed destitute children, or help victims of war and refugees).

This is why grants cannot be judged just on their face economic value. But no precise measure can be given either of the political price attached to them.

CREDITS

Loans given on terms better than the currently prevailing ones in standard commercial transactions, usually tied to specific investment projects and associated with some form of technical assistance, constitute the bulk of what is termed "foreign economic aid" given to the developing countries. The borderline between the "commercial" loans and "long-term" loans is, of course, rather arbitrary and, rigorously speaking, aid should be computed as the difference between the actual cost of credit borne by the recipient country and the cost-to-be of a standard commercial credit. Such an approach would lead, however, to endless complications of a purely technical nature and make our quantitative estimates of foreign aid still more shaky—the more so because the terms of credits granted to developing countries have recently been changing quite substantially, not to speak of the differences attached to the kind of supplies which are offered on deferred payment basis, so that it would be quite difficult to define for reference the "standard commercial loan". (The recent downward trend in the cost of foreign credits can be, to a great extent, ascribed to the action of the Soviet Union and other socialist countries, which not only broke the Western monopoly for the supply of industrial equipment to the former colonial and dependent countries but also introduced and generalized the practice of loans, repayable in 10 to 12 years and bearing a low rate of interest of no more than 2.5 per cent. Even if the conditions offered by the socialist countries are from time to time overbidden now, we should not forget that before the emergence of the socialist countries on the world market for industrial equipment the developing countries had to content themselves with much less favourable conditions of deferred payment[19]).

Moreover, the whole approach of this chapter is that of not separating foreign aid from trade. We suggest, therefore, that credits should be classified by ranging them from expensive commercial loans to "soft" credits repayable in local currency over such a length of time and that they approach asymptotically the category of grants.

Apart from the distinction, already discussed in general terms, between public and private loans, we can classify the different types of credits available to the developing countries according to the cost of servicing (including the repayment of the principal) and the modalities of such repayment.

The cost of servicing depends on three elements: the grace period, the length of the credit, and the rate of interest. The average yearly burden decreases with the length both of the grace period and of the credit itself and increases with the level of the rate of interest. It is more sensitive to the first two elements than to the third one.

Of course, the lower the cost of servicing the loan the better the loan is, from the point of view of the recipient country, subject to the note of caution already expressed about grants: the more "commercial" a loan the less likely it is to have political strings attached.

In our opinion, in the evaluation of a loan the stipulations about the way of its repayment are just as important as its "cost". Broadly speaking, we can distinguish three modalities:

(a) Repayment in hard (convertible) currency
(b) Repayment in local, unconvertible currency of the recipient country (soft loans)
(c) Repayment in goods

In the first case, the recipient country must increase its income from exports, in order to earn the necessary hard currency to service the debt, or be prepared to reduce its potential imports to the same amount. Otherwise, it will have to seek new loans to consolidate its foreign debt. At the risk of being repetitive, let us stress that a loan does not solve the problems of foreign trade but merely postpones them. Without

[19] For a recent study of aid provided by the Socialist countries see G. M. Prochorov, *Dvie Mirovyie Sistemy i Oswobozdivsijesia, Strany*, Moscow, 1965.

a lasting solution in the sphere of foreign trade, the only economically—but by no means politically—viable alternative is that of a continuous inflow of grants!

In the second case, the recipient country's situation is somewhat better, because the creditor country becomes interested in finding in the recipient country new exportable goods, to be purchased with the local currency received in repayment of the credit. But two dangers always loom: that of financing from these funds part of "normal" imports, which otherwise would have been paid for in hard currency, or of accumulating a huge sum in local currency, which either will have to be finally converted (we fall back on the first case then) or might be used as an instrument of interference in the economic life of the recipient country.

The soundest from the point of view of the recipient country is the third modality, especially if repayment in goods is negotiated in addition to the "normal" volume of trade between the countries concerned or, at least, constitutes part of the foreseen increment in trade relations between the two partners. If equipment for a plant is being furnished on a deferred payment basis and the credit is going to be cancelled out by shipments of part of the output of the new plant, we are in the presence of a truly "self-liquidating" and mutually advantageous credit. Different variations of the pattern described above have been suggested, from the Indonesian "production-sharing" formula to the industrial branch agreements (discussed below in the section on aid through trade), which combine elements of loans and of long-term trade arrangements. These arrangements do not necessarily involve payments in terms of products of a given plant, but may be based on equivalent future exports of other goods. In our opinion relatively cheap loans repayable in goods are the most viable form of aid to developing countries, for they combine, to the mutual interest of the recipient and donor countries, elements of assistance and trade and contribute to a lasting solution of the problem of insufficient export outlets, at present affecting so many developing countries. The current practice in this respect, already existing between some socialist and developing countries, should be considerably expanded and equally extended to the sphere of economic relations between the developing and the capitalist developed countries.

GRAIN LOANS

A substantial part of American aid to the developing countries takes the form of supplies of grain under the provision US PL 480. This is a highly complex form, combining elements of trade, loan, and grant. An attempt to analyse its different aspects follows.[20]

From the point of view of the donor country, i.e. the United States, the whole operation consists of shipping abroad a part of the agricultural surpluses, which are anyhow purchased by the Commodity Credit Corporation as part of the policies of support to agricultural incomes. That is why, strictly speaking, no cost whatever is involved on the side of the donor country.

Public Law 480 established four titles under which grain surpluses are delivered to foreign countries, as well as some general conditions, such as the obligation to transport at least 50 per cent of the grain by ships under the American flag, the necessity of making some additional cash purchases of American agricultural products, the acceptance of the clause forbidding competition with American agricultural goods in third markets, etc. The most important is Title I with which we shall deal below in more detail. As for Titles II and III, they relate to operations of relief, charity, and barter transactions. Title IV relates to long-term loans, repayable in dollars, with an additional clause giving to the United States some control on the way of utilizing the proceeds from the sale of grain in local currency by the government of the recipient country.

Title I (as mentioned above, by far the most important) technically deals with cash sales of grain against local unconvertible currency which are credited to a special account of the donor country, thus creating the so-called "counterpart funds",[21] but at the same time establishes directly or by supplementary bilateral agreements an elaborate

[20] For an analysis of the impact of "grain loans" see, in particular, Said El-Naggar, *Foreign Aid to the United Arab Republic*, Institute of National Planning, Cairo, 1963; Ch. Beringer, *The Use of Agricultural Surplus Commodities for Economic Development in Pakistan*, Institute of Development, Karachi, 1964; K. N. Raj, *Indian Economic Growth—Performance and Prospects*, New Delhi, 1965.

[21] The "counterpart funds" are calculated from the dollar cost of supplies by applying a fixed exchange rate. For this reason and also because of the possible variations of stocks of grain, the counterpart funds do not correspond exactly to the proceeds from actual sales of grain.

mechanism for the utilization of the counterpart funds. Part of these funds serves to finance the expenditure of American agencies in the recipient country. Another share is earmarked for loans granted to American private companies operating in the recipient country or local enterprises affiliated to them (the so-called Cooley loans). The rest of the counterpart funds is usually lent or granted by the United States to the government of the recipient country for projects mutually agreed upon. In other words, to the extent to which the counterpart funds finance American activities, this is tantamount to a transfer of funds, which otherwise would have taken the form of transfers of dollars. Similarly, the Cooley loans take the place of an inflow of foreign capital to a particular section of the private sector.

To the extent of this utilization of counterpart funds, PL 480 amounts to replacing certain dollar flows from the donor to the recipient countries by shipments of grain and, therefore, no foreign aid whatever is involved. Roughly speaking one-third of the value of shipments of grain to the developing countries from 1954 till the end of 1964 should be deducted to allow for these transfers (including the Cooley loans). Let us turn now to the remaining two-thirds.

The grain supplies, which in fact are nothing but grants, have the same double effect as imports of capital in general. On the one hand, they supply the deficient necessities, and thus permit the country concerned to develop at a higher rate without inflationary pressures, or counteract existing inflation. On the other hand, they ease the problem of financing investment, because the proceeds from the sales of grain provide a source of this financing.

As to the release of the counterpart funds for loans and grants for development (excluding the Cooley loans), this has, as do all loans in local currency (see above), an effect fully equivalent to deficit financing government investment and must not affect its total volume determined by the considerations of full utilization of resources without creating inflationary pressures. If, however, the donor country is reluctant to permit the blockage of counterpart funds and insists on playing the game of releasing them for projects mutually agreed upon, and further supplies of grain depending on the "utilization" of the counterpart funds, this creates a channel for the donor country's influence upon public investment in the recipient country. This effect will grow in importance very quickly unless shipments of grain under Title IV become the dominant form of exports of American agricultural surpluses.

The imponderability attached to this situation might be of such a nature as to make it preferable to the developing countries to avail themselves of Title IV rather than of Title I, even though the imponderability will not be entirely eliminated in this way[22] and the necessity of servicing the debt in hard currency will have to be faced.

Of course, a still better solution would consist in convincing the American Government that an accumulation of counterpart funds should not be considered as an obstacle to further supplies of grain under PL 480. Such accumulation could be viewed as a transfer of funds to finance the future activities of American agencies in the recipient country after the deliveries of grain under PL 480 come to an end.

The above is not meant as denying the positive effect of the supplies of grain in question, apart from the handling of the counterpart funds. However, even with regard to the positive impact of grain deliveries, care should be taken to avoid two negative side-effects: a mood of complacency towards the problem of agricultural backwardness on the part of the ruling classes in the recipient country and the temptation to sell the available additional grain supplies at low prices, in order to gain popularity among the urban population, with no regard to the fact that such a policy may discourage local agricultural producers and compel them to reduce the area under food crops. Experiences of several developing countries show that both dangers are real.

FOREIGN DIRECT INVESTMENT

The widespread practice of including the inflow of foreign direct private investment in the category of "aid" can be explained, though not justified, on two grounds: it results from the application of a purely technical criterion, by which all inflows of long-term capital are considered as "aid" with no regard to their cost and purpose and/or from

[22] In its issue of July 1965, *New Africa*, Lond., commented on the action taken by the American Congress to withhold supplies of American grain to the United Arab Republic (a decision subsequently reversed): "To withhold bread from the starving has never been considered moral. It is in the light of such considerations that the action of the Congress in using the surplus for political blackmail comes as a shock even to those who have become hardened to the realities of aid with strings" (p. 6).

the doctrinal position, that investment of foreign private capital is by definition sound and necessary to the recipient economy, because it passes through the test of the market, the only reliable guide to orient the allocation of investment.[23]

Enough has been said already in this chapter to discard these two criteria as irrelevant. But a few other misconceptions about direct foreign investment should still be dispelled.

It is sometimes argued that direct foreign investment is cheaper to the recipient country than any credit because it need not be repaid. Even if we assume that foreign capital will not be repatriated at any moment, the argument is based on a sophism: it is true that on the "capital account" the inflow of foreign direct investment will never be offset under such an assumption by an outflow of repatriated capital. But the profits transferred abroad may exceed the cost of servicing a foreign loan,[24] while the reinvested profits add to the book value of foreign investment with no further inflow of foreign capital (at best

---

[23] For an apologetic view of foreign direct investment, though skeptical about its volume, see the important book of F. Benham, *Economic Aid to Underdeveloped Countries*, London, 1961. For an open criticism of aid through public channels and an outright plea to increase the flow of private direct investments, see E. G. Collado, "Economic development through private enterprise", *Foreign Affairs*, New York, July 1963. H. Feis (*Foreign Aid and Foreign Policy*, New York, 1964) insists on the traditional philosophy of American "free enterprise" with respect to the division of roles between public and private investments. The former should concentrate on infrastructure in order to pave the way for the latter.

A 1963 amendment to the foreign aid bill, voted by the United States Congress, requires that 50 per cent of development loans be channelled into private business activities. This measure was criticized even by a top AID administrator (see F. M. Coffin, *Witness for Aid*, Boston, 1964, p. 123).

[24] In his lectures, *India Economic Growth—Performance and Prospects* (New Delhi, 1965), Professor K. N. Raj of the Delhi School of Economics, on the basis of data from a sample study of the Reserve Bank of India on foreign collaboration in the chemical industry, estimates that total foreign exchange outflow per annum in the case of companies with private foreign collaboration covered by the sample works out to nearly 24 per cent of the capital invested by the foreign participants, "which is higher than the servicing burden on even the most onerous of loan capital received so far" (p. 23). Dr. Raj reaches the following conclusion about types of foreign aid suitable to India:

"If our interest is in minimizing the burden on foreign exchange we should really be concentrating on loans which either carry with them a long period of repayment or an understanding that the lending country will take more exports from India and help the whole process of repayment by raising the export earnings of the country. In the case of foreign private investment there is often a bias against export of the

they can be said to diminish the outflow of profits). Profits earned by foreign investors from these reploughed profits will again be transferred, at least partly, abroad. We are thus in the presence of an endless snowballing process, as contrasted with a loan which creates obligations for a definite number of years. It may be easily shown that in the long run the impact of continuous foreign direct investment on the balance of payments of the recipient country must be negative (we do not discuss here the indirect consequences in the form of additional exports or import substitution, which would be the same whatever the form of financing the new plant), unless the inflow of foreign investment grows substantially from year to year.[25]

To illustrate our argument, we may well imagine that a country seeks a net inflow of 100 units of foreign capital per year. This capital yields profits, starting from the end of the year of the inflow, of 15 per cent per annum of which 10 per cent are transferred abroad and 5 per cent reinvested. We want to ascertain what should be the inflow of foreign investment.

Table 6.1 gives the results of the exercise performed for six years. We see that by the sixth year the ratio of gross inflow to net inflow exceeds 2 to 1.

Table 6.2 performs the same exercise on the assumption that two-thirds of the annual profits are reinvested and only one-third are transferred abroad.

The results are somewhat better for the recipient country, but the trend is the same; in the sixth year, the ratio of gross inflow to net

---

products concerned since investment itself comes now mainly from international companies which have similar stakes in other countries.

"It is only in the case of loans from the Soviet Union that aid has been closely tied up with trade, and this has produced good results. Though the annual servicing burden on Soviet loans has been nearly 12 per cent the rapid expansion in exports to the Soviet bloc in the last few years has made it possible to meet this liability without much difficulty. In fact Soviet aid is really in the nature of trade credits tied to more trade, and this is advantageous to both the lending and the receiving countries. The Soviet Union is able to offer an expanding market for Indian products because it has need for them and because it is in its own interests to accept these products in exchange for the machinery and capital goods it exports to India" (pp. 23–24).

[25] Compare the well-known essay by E. D. Domar, "The effect of foreign investment on the balance of payments", originally published in the *American Econ. Rev.*, December 1950, and included in his *Essays in the Theory of Economic Growth*, New York, 1957.

TABLE 6.1

Year	Gross inflow of capital	Foreign investment at beginning of year	Foreign investment at end of year	Profits transferred abroad	Net inflow of capital
	1	2	3	4	5
I	111.1	111.1	116.7	11.1	100
II	124.1	240.8	252.8	24.1	100
III	139.2	392.0	411.6	39.2	100
IV	156.9	568.5	569.9	56.9	100
V	177.4	774.3	813.0	77.4	100
VI	201.4	1014.4	1065.1	101.4	100
	910.1			310.1	600

inflow is already 1.47 to 1. The results of the two operations for the six-year period are compared in Table 6.3.[26]

Even if there were no other arguments, beyond that of the long-term worsening of the balance of payments, the case for private foreign investment would be very weak. There are obviously no prospects to set into motion a continuously growing stream of direct foreign investment in the developing countries, not to speak of the political inconvenience of having a big foreign private sector, likely to act as a powerful pressure group.

Let us not forget that a conservative figure for the average rate of profit has been given. It is in fact not unexpected that from the recipient country's point of view private foreign investment should prove more costly than the majority of commercial loans. After all, by its very

[26] Looking at the matter from a different angle, given a constant yearly gross inflow of capital C, a rate of profits transferred abroad, and a rate q of profits reinvested, the net inflow of capital will become zero after a certain number n of years, which can be calculated from the following formula:

$$n = \frac{\log\{(p+q)\}/p}{\log(1+q)}$$

With the assumption of our first case, that is, $p = 10\%$ and $q = 5\%$, the positive effects of a constant yearly inflow of C units of foreign capital would be entirely offset by the outflow of profits in the ninth year, while in the second case ($p = 5\%$, $q = 10\%$), the same effect would take place in the twelfth year.

TABLE 6.2

Year	Gross inflow of capital	Foreign investment at beginning of year	Foreign investment at end of year	Profits transferred abroad	Net inflow of capital
	1	2	3	4	5
I	105.3	105.3	115.8	5.3	100
II	111.4	227.2	249.9	11.4	100
III	118.4	368.3	405.1	18.4	100
IV	126.6	531.7	584.9	26.6	100
V	136	720.9	793	36	100
VI	146.9	939.9	1033.9	46.9	100
	744.6			144.6	600

TABLE 6.3

	Case A	Case B
1. Book value of foreign investment as percentage of the gross inflow of foreign capital	117.4	138.8
2. Book value of foreign investment as percentage of the net inflow of foreign capital	177.5	172.3
3. Profits transferred abroad as percentage of the gross inflow of foreign capital for the whole period under consideration	34	19.4
4. Profits transferred abroad as percentage of the net inflow of foreign capital for the whole period under consideration	51.7	24.1

nature and avowed purpose it is guided by the profit motive. Normally foreign investors will not put their money in a developing country unless they expect a rate of profit not lower than in their own country, plus a substantial risk premium; the more independent and progressive a country, the higher this premium will be.[27]

[27] Several limitations of the direct foreign investment are recognized in a study, "Balance of payments problems in developing Africa" published in the *Statistical and Economic Review of the United Africa Company Limited*, no. 29, April 1964.

The author reaches the following conclusion: "For developing countries with their current balances already in deficit or tending that way, an unduly large outflow—more particularly in the form of servicing charges, which are of a recurrent nature—is a matter of understandable concern and one apt to prompt them to impose those very curbs on capital and dividend repatriation which can only act to discourage further capital inflows in the future. Yet a point must sooner or later be reached at which the rise in the debt servicing bill has to be halted" (pp. 44–45).

There are, of course, instances of huge foreign direct investment, motivated not so much by the immediate profit expectation as by the desire to control sources of oil, minerals, and other raw materials, although in the case of oil the two motives usually coincide.[28]

The crucial importance of oil royalties for the budgets of several developing countries should not make us oblivious of the fact that a considerable proportion of very high profits is still being transferred abroad in spite of some progress in the redistribution of income from oil production, achieved by a few developing countries in the last years. And there are still the dangers to which a country becomes exposed when it depends to such a degree on a monoexport controlled by powerful foreign firms involved in world-wide operations which may prompt them at any time to take decisions affecting the whole future of the recipient country (e.g. to reduce the output in one place in order to put into operation a new field in another country). At any rate one fails to see how these situations could be brought under the heading of "foreign aid", even in the most remote manner.

One more argument frequently invoked by the partisans of direct foreign investment is that it brings the necessary know-how to the developing country. This fact is beyond dispute, but in most cases this "know-how" could be purchased even at cheaper rates on a commercial basis, not to mention the technical assistance available free or on credit, when complete plant equipment is imported on a deferred payment basis. Substantial tax-fee profits are transferred abroad by foreign-owned corporations under the cover of payments for the "know-how" and the patents.

From what was said above, it follows clearly that in our opinion foreign direct investment should be excluded from the category of foreign aid. At a time when so many developing countries are asked to promulgate "codes of investment" giving privileges and guarantees to foreign private investors, it might be useful to enumerate the minimum conditions which, from the recipient country's point of view, should be respected in order to make the inflow of foreign private capital useful, if not part of aid:

[28] For an assessment of developed countries' vital economic and strategic interest in the natural resources of the developing countries, see M. W. J. M. Broekmeijer, *Developing Countries and NATO*, Leyden, 1963.

(a) Foreign private investment should be licensed from the point of view of branch allocation, localization, and concentration of foreign capital in different sectors of the recipient country's economy.

(b) Foreign-owned enterprises should be submitted to the same taxation as local enterprises and their books audited by the officials of the recipient country's government, especially with the view of ascertaining whether the declared export prices are not too low and the declared import prices for materials and equipment are not too high.

(c) All payments abroad including royalties, transfers of profits, and repatriation of capital should be limited and controlled.

(d) Reinvested profits should be treated as domestic private capital (e.g. the transfer should be prevented both of these profits at any future date and also of the profits derived from their reinvestment).

In all fairness, we doubt whether much new direct foreign investment would be available under these regulations. It should, however, be emphasized that the inflow of foreign private capital to the developing countries does not reach substantial levels even in those cases where economic conditions offered by developing countries are quite attractive. This can be explained by two sets of reasons: on the one hand, prospective investors consider that the political risk involved is very high (possible nationalization or introduction of regulations of the type described above); on the other there is no scarcity of good investment opportunities in the developed countries.

Aid through trade

In the first part of this chapter we have come across several interconnexions between trade and aid. In particular, the following points were stressed:

(a) Of the two functions of foreign aid—that of adding to the import capacity and of increasing the financial resources of the recipient country—the former is the most important.

(b) In the long run the capacity to service the foreign debt depends anyhow on the progress achieved by the recipient country in export promotion (and import substitution, it is true), so that an inflow of foreign aid does not as yet constitute a lasting solution, permitting a sustained and satisfactory rate of economic growth.

(c) A positive shift in the terms of trade is comparable to a continuous inflow of grants with no strings attached.

This leads us to the consideration of "aid through trade", by which we mean either measures aimed at improving the conditions of existing trade (improvement in the terms of trade) or the creation of additional markets above the "normal" volume of trade.[29] The opening of such additional export opportunities would increase the capacity to import of the developing countries and, thus, permit a higher rate of growth.

To the extent to which these additional exports would consist in sales of accumulated stocks, they would mean releasing reserves previously accumulated but "frozen", as they could not be either traded or consumed. This would bring about either an increase in the personal available income without a corresponding decrease in the level of investment or an increase in investment with an unchanged level of consumption.

In the case of exports from idle capacities, the national income would increase over the level previously assumed without any additional investment. The aggregate capital–output ratio would be correspondingly reduced and either the country concerned could achieve a higher overall rate of growth with an unchanged relative share of investment in the national income or it could implement the assumed rate of growth with a higher relative share of consumption. These effects would be comparable to those arising from the provision of foreign aid, with two differences however: namely that, on the one hand, the aggregate expenditure would not exceed the national income, because no inflow of capital occurs, and, on the other, the country would not become indebted.

[29] "Despite—indeed because of—the greater resistances that must be encountered by aid in the form of market, as against aid in its other forms, the case for its provision appears to be inescapable if the developing countries, certainly of Africa, are to succeed in developing their economies beyond the constraints of current domestic capacity and ahead of slowly moving economic forces. And, what is more, short of a sufficient enlargement of their export markets, however this comes about, it will become increasingly difficult to continue to put other forms of aid to profitable use: to continue, that is to use them to *promote growth* instead of to subsidize resistances to it" ("Balance of payments problems in developing Africa", *Statistical and Economic Review of the United Africa Company Limited*, no. 29, April 1964, p. 54).

Even the opening of markets for new lines of exports which do require investment but have a relatively favourable "investment efficiency ratio" (cost of investment per unit of earned foreign currency) might be considered as "aid", as it helps the assisted country to overcome the barrier of foreign trade with a lesser volume of investment, i.e. improves its economic performance by lowering the aggregate capital–output ratio. This applies in particular to enabling the developing countries to export certain types of finished goods or semi-manufactures.

"Aid through trade" could include both multilateral and bilateral measures. While wishing all success to the search for world-wide schemes, evolved with a view to stabilizing commodity prices and regulating international trade, we should like to offer below two suggestions to be explored in bilateral relations. Although they are less spectacular than these schemes, they offer some advantages: they can be easily put into practice, at least between countries having some measure of long-term planning; moreover, they seem to offer a good and realistic point of departure for the process of integrating the economics of developing countries, step by step, on a regional or on a wider basis. We have in mind long-term export contracts with stable prices and the so-called branch industrial agreements.

LONG-TERM EXPORT CONTRACTS

These contracts should cover, first of all, the traditional exports of the developing countries, such as tropical foodstuffs, other cash crops, minerals, oil, metals, and also semi-processed and finished goods, the production of which may be easily expanded. The contracts should provide for growing volumes of sales at stable or partly stabilized prices by means of clauses, either stipulating the maximum amplitude of the price fluctuation admissible in a year or establishing a procedure about the sharing between the buyer and the seller of the difference between the price agreed upon in the contract as "basic" and the price actually quoted on the commodity exchange or considered by the two parties as representative for the "world price".

Quite obviously such contracts would give the planners in the developing countries a fair degree of certitude with respect both to future incomes from feasible exports and the volumes involved, so that they could take decisions about investment in advance. This knowledge of the trend of future trade is particularly important for perennial crops, when decisions about planting new trees antecede the first crop by several years and at the same time set the level of production for quite a long period. Generally speaking, fluctuations of income from exports due both to price and volume variations have been affecting the economies of the developing countries so adversely[30] that even where a chance of future higher prices exists a premium on stability is worth paying.

Those partners of the developing countries who have a planned or even a directed economy should normally also be interested in knowing in advance what supply of specified goods they may obtain from given sources and what would be the cost involved. Stability is always welcome to the planner and worth being paid for by the renunciation of uncertain gains from shifts of terms of trade, which he is not likely to take into account in the process of planning anyhow. At any rate, for a country normally employing most of its productive capacities, it should be much easier to assist the developing countries by accepting stable prices than by extending credits, which have to be offset by a lower volume of internal investment or consumption.

So many schemes of price stabilization have failed to materialize that the plea to introduce stable prices in bilateral exchanges may seem very daring. But the least we can say is that in contrast to international compensation schemes, our proposal can be easily tested and introduced progressively. We are, moreover, convinced that the mere fact of signing a certain number of long-term contracts with stable prices would bring about an attenuation of price fluctuations in the commodity markets concerned, thus paving the way for more ambitious and general solutions.

INDUSTRIAL BRANCH AGREEMENTS

The long-term contracts discussed above apply in the first instance to the already existing exports. But in the process of economic growth

[30] During the last fifty years, the eighteen basic tropical products, accounting for 90 per cent of their total, registered average annual fluctuations of 14 per cent with respect to unit prices, 19 per cent with respect to the volume, and 23 per cent with respect to the incomes from exports. Moreover, taking into consideration the costs of marketing, a 10 per cent variation of the final price means a 20 to 25 per cent difference in the income of the producer (*La Politique de Coopération avec les Pays en Voie de Développement*, Paris, 1963, p. 95.)

the developing countries should obviously establish new lines of exports and this requires a thorough restructuring of the international division of labour prevailing at present. It was suggested at the United Nations Conference on Trade and Development (see Doc. E/conf.48/c.2/REC/2) that a practical measure with this end in view could take the form of "industrial branch agreements" based on partial division of labour between the countries concerned. On the basis of bilateral consultations between representatives of a given branch of industry a long-term agreement would be drawn up, establishing over a given period of time a changing pattern of mutual supplies, not necessarily balanced, including raw materials, intermediate goods, final products, and equipment, with a final aim of implanting in the developing countries new industries partly or wholly export-oriented and creating, at the same time, complementarity of economies based on specialization and partial division of labour.

The resolution adopted by the Second Committee of the United Nations Conference on Trade and Development, referred to above, mentioned specifically the developing countries and the countries with centrally planned economies, and linked the whole matter with supplies of equipment by the socialist countries on a deferred payment basis, so that industrial branch agreements appear as a generalization and a complement of the "self-liquidating credits", discussed in the second section of this chapter. But a parallel can be drawn between this specific measure, devised for the expansion of trade between the developing countries and the socialist ones, and the so-called "complementary agreements" which were foreseen by the Montevideo Treaty as a means to promote regional economic co-operation in Latin America, which have seldom been put into practice.[31] Mutual guaranteeing of stable and growing markets for new exports and the adjustment of long-term

[31] Compare the following assessment, made in the "Proposals for the creation of the Latin American Common Market", by Jose Antonio Mayobre, Felipe Herrera, Carlos Sanz de Santamaria, and Raul Prebisch:

"As is well-known, the import substitution process is entering a new stage. Easy substitutions are wholly or nearly exhausted in the more advanced Latin American countries and technically complex industries are beginning to be set up requiring large investments and a sizable market. None of our countries, no matter how large or vigorous, could begin or continue this stage of industrialisation on its own economically viable conditions.

It is therefore necessary to plan the development of these industries on a regional scale. This planning refers principally to iron and steel, some non-ferrous metals, some

plans to these decisions seems to be the only viable way of approaching the problem of the diversification of the pattern of exports of developing countries both in the context of regional integration and of a modified division of labour in the world economy.

Conclusion

At the end of this effort to clarify some issues related to foreign economic aid, we should like to stress the following points:

(a) Foreign aid essentially means an improvement of external conditions of growth, even though it adds automatically to the financial resources of the recipient country whenever it involves grants or credits.

(b) The impact of foreign aid on the recipient country cannot be properly assessed out of the context of a development plan.

(c) To evaluate the effort of a donor country two different yardsticks must be used, depending on whether the country concerned has free capacities at its disposal or not.

(d) Long-term credits repayable in goods are the most attractive form of foreign aid from the point of view of the recipient countries.

(e) Another advisable form of aid can be achieved without import of capital through multilateral schemes of trade promotion, bilateral

---

groups of heavy chemical and petro-chemical industries, including the production of fertilizers, and the manufacture of motor vehicles, ships and heavy industrial equipment. This involves a limited number of industries which, in addition to being import-substitution industries, cover fields of vital importance for strengthening the economic structure and accelerating the pace of our countries' development. It is precisely in such fields that economies of scale, the advantages of suitable siting, the utilization of productive capacity and better operational efficiency will be most strikingly achieved. One of the paradoxical situations existing side by side with the Treaty of Montevideo has been that some of these industries have been established or expanded in various countries without regard to the objectives of an integration policy.

It would be appropriate for the Governments to decide now to conclude these sectoral agreements in such industries so that a start can be made without delay on the studies needed for carrying out the relevant negotiations.

One result of the investment policy in all these industries might be the conclusion of a series of sectoral agreements within the next few years. Although these agreements are provided for in the Treaty of Montevideo, very few of them have so far been concluded, and those that exist do not relate to the industries that are of basic importance" (Supplement to *Commercio Exterior de Mexico*, **XI**, May 1965, pp. 8–9.)

long-term export contracts on the basis of fully or partly stable prices, as well as the so-called branch industrial agreements. "Aid through trade" is thus a complement—though not an alternative— to "pure" aid.[32]

[32] This last conclusion broadly coincides with the prevailing opinion among the delegates of the developing countries to the United Nations Conference on Trade and Development, who quite understandably insisted on having the best of the two worlds: a substantial improvement in trade and an increase in the net inflow of capital.

CHAPTER 7

Problems of Implementation of Industrialization Plans (1970)

Preliminary remarks

If we consider planning to be a continuous process and a permanent dialogue between planners and industrial executives rather than a procedure to draw at fixed time intervals pluriannual plans, the usual distinction between plan-building and plan-implementation loses much of its sharpness. As a matter of fact, realistic planning, as distinct from industrial programmes consisting of a mere set of goals, involves detailed inquiries about the feasibility of the proposed targets, i.e. an anticipation of the problems of implementation likely to arise and their confrontation with the disposable means. Thus problems of implementation of industrialization plans must be already dealt with at the planning stage, while other shortcomings are likely to appear at the implementation stage proper. For the sake of clarity, I shall discuss them separately, although I am aware of the arbitrary character of such a distinction.

I find it useful to examine first the case of developing countries involved in comprehensive planning, i.e. having a system of planning which embraces the whole economy and which, for the implementation and more specially for investment, relies heavily on the public sector. This case is in many respects simpler than that of mixed economies, a condition very widespread for the time being, where the private sector plays an important role in industrialization side by side with the public sector. I shall then approach the case of mixed economies by indicating the additional problems of implementation which arise there as compared to the former case.

While discussing problems of implementation of industrialization plans in developing countries, we shall keep in mind the following general guidelines for the development strategy:

(a) Rapid industrialization is an important objective as it brings an increase in labour productivity, the much needed diversification of the commodity pattern of the economy, and, at least in the long run, generates a substantial increase in employment.

(b) The pace of industrialization cannot be fixed arbitrarily. The following limiting factors are likely to restrain it:

(i) Availability of food—the main counterpart of wages in a poor developing country—and the consequent need to harmonize rates of industrialization with rates of supply of necessities, at the risk of generating inflation and thus upsetting the social goals of the development process and, in the long run, the rate of growth of the economy.

(ii) Shortage of foreign currency to finance the import content of investment[1].

(iii) Shortage of skills and know-how, which cannot be entirely obviated by turning to foreign experts, not speaking of the cost involved[2].

In each country these barriers will act with different intensities and the ceiling to the rate of growth will be imposed by the most intense one.

(c) Industrialization is not an aim in itself but a means to ensure a continuous increase in the well-being of the people. But its impact on the standards of living of the working people will depend very much on its pattern: the "growth potential" of an economy and its capacity to generate a continuous process of improvement in standards of living of the broad masses of population depends on a balanced increase in supply of both goods of popular consumption and producer goods (produced in the country or obtained through trade), while a premature and excessive emphasis on the supply of luxury consumer goods is likely to benefit only a minority and to endanger the long-term prospects

---

[1] Theoretically it is possible to overcome the barrier of foreign trade through investments in export-oriented or import-substituting industries. But if such investments are highly capital intensive the advantages of an additional gain in foreign currency are offset by the increase of the overall marginal capital–output ratio and the whole operation becomes self-defeating.

[2] That is why I speak of the limited "absorptive capacity" of some countries for foreign aid. Even if foreign currency were made available, it would have been impossible to finance productive industrial investment with it.

of growth and social improvement in the country considered. It is so because, in an economy with a limited capacity to step up the pace of industrialization, an excessive growth of industrial sectors turning out luxuries (or the misappropriation of scarce foreign currency for imports of luxuries) will reduce the rates of expansion of the remaining industries turning out essentials and producer goods. Thus the pattern of industrialization which gives a place of pride to luxuries is likely to prove deceptive after some time, even if in the short run it creates a state of euphoria on account of high rates of growth of the national income. Experience accumulated by several developing countries over the last few decades would strongly support the view that such a pattern of "perverse growth" is likely to happen in a mixed economy whenever the allocation of industrial investment is operated through the unhampered market mechanism. A major function of the industrialization plans should consist precisely in preventing the developing countries from following that deceptive pattern of perverse growth and trying to set for each country and period of time not only a realistic rate of growth of industrial output but also a reasonable commodity structure and a time sequence for the implantation of new industries.

Implementation of industrialization programmes under comprehensive planning

SOME PROBLEMS ARISING AT THE PLANNING STAGE

I shall discuss in this section the following topics:

(a) The capacity for industrial planning.

(b) Instruments used to ensure that concrete project and implementation conforms to macroeconomic preferences.

(c) The impact of implementation problems on the long-term plan.

(a) Chronologically the first difficulty of the implementation of industrialization programmes stems from an insufficient capacity for designing and industrial planning. The passage from a tentative choice of general options to detailed planning requires working on the basis of preliminary projects, at least for the major establishments, in order to get a more

accurate picture of capital–output ratios, import content, and requirements in terms of the supply of energy, water, raw materials, transport
facilities, and manpower—both qualified and unqualified. The more
industrialized a country the less necessary the preliminary project
becomes for the planner, as, on the one hand, he can work out tentative
estimates on the basis of knowledge accumulated from the already existing plants and, on the other, the impact of the new project on the
industrial structure of the country and its infrastructural facilities is
likely to be less. In a country, however, which is about to embark
on industrialization, lack of preliminary projects often proves a major
hindrance to effective planning, increasing thus the likelihood of bigger
difficulties at the implementation stage proper. It is, of course, possible
to rely to some extent on the experience of other countries, but cross-
country comparisons must be handled very cautiously because of the
different economic and environmental conditions prevailing in each
country. Moreover, detailed and unbiased information on projects going
in other countries is not easily available. Much can be done to improve
this situation through international action, and in this connexion one
should think that the elaboration of catalogues of basic technical and
economic indicators for industrial plants of different types and two
or three standard capacities should enjoy a high priority in the programme of activities of the UNIDO.

The preceding considerations also show the importance of creating,
as soon as possible, local services in the developing countries, equipped
if not to take care of industrial design at least to evaluate in an independent way the projects submitted by foreign engineering consultants.
Such a screening of submitted projects would put a brake on the undiscriminating transfer of foreign technology and designs, not necessarily
suited to the needs of the country concerned, and, at the same time,
would help the planners to gain the necessary experience in the evaluation of concrete projects.

It would be, in general, advisable that the machinery for planning
and implementing industrial development should include a special
agency for project evaluation, working in close collaboration but enjoying some autonomy with respect to the planning commission. Such
an agency would prepare a few variants of each preliminary project
submitted by the industrial designing units, both national and foreign,

in order to find out whether it conforms to the macroeconomic preferences and constitutes the right solution under given circumstances.
Needless to say, such a careful screening would normally lead to a
greater efficiency of the investment process and would also help to
anticipate the possible difficulties of implementation better; by taking
proper measures in advance. Such difficulties could be avoided or
minimized.

(b) The preceding remarks should not be understood as a plea for
complete centralization of all the investment decisions. While the authorities should screen, in my opinion, all the important projects, there
still remains considerable room for decentralized decision and decentralized implementation. It is, therefore, extremely important to find ways
of ensuring that concrete solutions worked out both at the control and
the decentralized levels conform to macroeconomic preferences.

The decision problem can be approached by attempting to fix appropriate evaluation criteria for individual decision-taking, based on a
system of shadow prices. A good practical approximation to this solution
consists in using only very few shadow prices in order to avoid complications which a general solution would entail. Thus, for example, Polish
planners use two shadow prices in their formula to evaluate the
"efficiency of investment"[3] namely the "recoupment period" and the
"exchange rate" for imports. It has been shown that solutions chosen
by means of application of this formula are optimal to the first degree
of approximation from the macroeconomic point of view.

The formula of the efficiency of investment applies to the choice
of the best project from a set of alternatives, linked by the common
denominator of the same output in physical terms. If we shift, now,
to the case of export-promoting or import-saving projects, it becomes
possible to compare projects located in different branches of industry,
as the criterion consists in minimizing the net domestic cost per unit
of foreign currency earned through exports or saved through import
substitution.

As for influencing the decentralized implementation of industrialization programmes it should depend on an imaginative system of incentives

[3] The efficiency is measured essentially by the ratio of investment to the so-called
recoupment period plus current cost per unit of product. The formula used is slightly
more sophisticated because of a few refinements which need not be discussed here.

and disincentives, conceived on such a way as to:

   (i) Avoid unnecessary investment, where productivity could be increased by proper organizational measures.

   (ii) Avoid costly new projects, where it is possible to get approximately the same results by modernization and expansion of the existing plants or simply by increasing the number of shifts.

   (iii) Avoid unnecessarily heavy investment in construction whenever it is possible to leave the industrial installations in the open air or under light shelter.

   (iv) Reduce the gestation period of the investment so as to minimize the period of immobilization of capital, which is tantamount to an increase in the overall capital–output ratio.

   (v) Minimize the import content and give preference to imports payable in soft currency.

Proper handling of notional (or actual, whatever the case) rates of interest for capital, differentiated for each type and duration of the loan, coupled with bonuses depending on the maximization of notional profit of the enterprise (or actual profit if we operate in a non-socialist economy), as well as using, at least for accounting purposes, a multiple exchange-rate system, should in principle cause to some extent the undesirable features listed above to be avoided. But experience has shown that it is extremely difficult to conceive such a system of incentives and to put it into practice.

Now, the shortcomings enumerated above do not apply exclusively to projects implemented at the decentralized level. Many instances of these features could be found in important projects carried out under the direct responsibility of the central government in many countries.

One is tempted to offer a sociological rather than economic explanation of the propensity to excessive investment in new projects. A new project, and still more a big new project, is more appealing on political grounds than less spectacular efforts to get the same results at a lower cost from the existing plants. Also, it is easier to carry out a new investment than to improve the performance of already existing installations. At the enterprise end there are also reasons to prefer new investment: as long as it goes on, it is always easier to get finances for other purposes and to justify possible shortcomings in the operation of the plant.

There are no general ways of eliminating the shortcomings listed above from the implementation of industrialization plans. The only possible suggestion is to have these shortcomings always foremost in mind and to scrutinize all the projects already at the planning stage from that angle.

(c) A useful distinction from the point of view of the construction of a long-term plan is that between demand-determined and supply-determined industries. Among the latter we should consider separately those which are affected by a lack of appropriate natural resources and those where the rate of growth cannot exceed a certain ceiling on account of technical and organizational difficulties.

In other words, this last subcategory consists of industries where problems of implementation appear as a major constraint. This may be due to an absolute lack of skills, which cannot be accounted for in the delays considered as the time factor cannot be easily manipulated in educational programmes; whatever the amount of resources we decide to put into it, there will always be a time lag of several years between the beginning of such programmes and the first additions to the availabilities of skilled manpower.[4] Moreover, even in conditions of a relatively good supply of skilled manpower (a situation rarely found in developing countries) it is extremely difficult to assimilate many new workers at the same time to many new techniques and to organize industrial cooperation if the rates of growth become too high.

This underlies the importance of choosing a proper time path for starting new industries and the importance of specialization in selected lines of production.[5] By successive concentration of efforts and realistic assessment of limits to industrial expansion, set on account of implementation difficulties, it becomes possible to avoid wasteful immobilization of capital in too many projects started at the same time and to master one by one the new techniques, while working in too many directions at the same time brings the danger that none of the new products will easily meet the quality and cost standards. Of course, this argument should not be carried too far. We know by experience that industrial output can increase for long periods at fairly satisfactory rates, much

[4] That is why implementation of industrialization plans is closely linked to that of educational programmes. In particular, vocational and in-job training should be closely correlated with industrial investment.

[5] Such a specialization could be made easier by long-term trade agreements.

higher than those presently achieved in the majority of developing countries. Still, some sense of proportion and awareness of the existence of organizational and technical ceilings are necessary.

Finally, I should like to point out the importance of manpower planning in the context of taking long-term measures aimed at decreasing the implementation bottleneck. Three difficulties arise in this connexion:

  (i) The time horizon envisaged in manpower and education planning exceeds the usual five- or ten-year span of industrialization plans.

 (ii) Manpower requirements are closely linked to the industrial structure of future output and its volume, but demand for qualified manpower should be assessed independently for such categories as research, designing and training, planning and management, and current production, of which only the last can be derived directly from estimates of future industrial output.

(iii) Developing countries must resort to training specialists abroad, but it is very difficult to estimate what proportions of the drain on their skilled personnel is caused by the chance of getting attractive jobs in America and Europe.

PROBLEMS ARISING AT THE IMPLEMENTATION STAGE PROPER

As I have already pointed out, the better the planning the lesser the likelihood of unpleasant surprises at the implementation stage proper. But it would be wholly unrealistic to assume that such unexpected difficulties do not appear.

The following are the most likely, as experience shows:

(a) Increase in the cost of the project, as compared to the initial estimate, due either to incorrect calculations or changes in prices. The calculation might have been biased on purpose in order to get the investment started; at the implementation stage, it becomes impossible to retract and additional funds must be provided. "Local patriotism" of executives responsible for different branches of industry or even single factories makes them compete for investment funds in this way. The only practical way to cut down such practices has been already indicated: more careful screening of the investment projects by a special agency.

(b) Delays in the implementation due to organizational shortcomings, delays in the supply of materials and equipment, etc. The higher the share of investment in the national income, the annual rates of increase of investment, and the number of similar projects started at the same time which are competing for the same skills and supplies, the more likely such delays will occur. If the economy is submitted to a big strain and the rates of growth are put at excessively high levels, any exogenous and random interference (such as, for example, unusual weather conditions affecting transport) may make a severe impact and generate a cumulative process of disorganization of the investment activities, ending up in delays with the consequent immobilization of capital and an increase in the overall capital–output ratio.

The impact of exogenous disturbing factors can be cushioned by providing special reserves, i.e. by keeping certain capacities free and by increasing the working capital to finance stocks. This is again tantamount to increasing the overall capital–output ratio and, therefore, a delicate balance must be sought for an empirical way between the desire to protect oneself against uncertainties and the inconvenience of increasing the capital–output ratio, i.e. reducing the rate of growth for a given volume and share of investment in the national income or increasing the volume and share of investment for a given rate of growth. To my knowledge, a satisfactory theory of reserves in planning has not yet been worked out.

(c) Lack of foreign exchange to finance the import content of the investment programme, arising from unforeseen worsening of the balance-of-payments position due to such contingencies as emergency imports of food, adverse shifts in the terms of trade, failure to attract foreign capital according to expectations too hastily incorporated in the plan, delays in effective utilization of credits pledged by foreign governments and international institutions, etc. The bigger the share of foreign trade of a country conducted under long-term agreements and pluriannual contracts, the lesser the danger of these fluctuations. But the better the discipline of foreign trade (which means exclusion from imports of all non essential items) the greater the chance that the reduction in the import capacity will affect the imports of investment goods. Slowing down and, if the worst comes, interrupting or even abandoning some investment projects are lesser evils than cutting down absolutely necessary imports of essential consumer goods and of materials and intermediate goods for the already existing factories turning out essentials and producer goods enjoying a high social priority.

Once more, the only way to protect the economy against the negative effects of uncontrollable fluctuations in import capacity consists in accumulating some reserves, subject to the same qualifications which have already been expressed when we discussed investment reserves.

At the same time, great emphasis should be put on minimizing the import content of investment programmes, but not to the extent of seeking self-sufficiency with no regard for cost and quality. In particular, substantial savings of foreign currency could be achieved if local consulting, designing, and engineering services were organized, if building were entirely based on local materials, and if full use were made, whenever possible, of labour-intensive and import-saving techniques in such activities as road building, construction, etc. I am not taking sides in the controversy on capital-intensive versus labour-intensive techniques, as I do not believe that it should be discussed for practical purposes as an antinomy, any more than export promotion versus import substitution or industrialization versus development of agriculture should. In all three cases, what really matters is to find appropriate weights for each term and to work out a mixed strategy. In many industrial projects, the range of available technical solutions, as far as capital–output and capital–labour ratios are concerned, is extremely narrow and the import content is very high, because nearly all of the equipment must be purchased abroad. Therefore it becomes very important to compensate for these capital-intensive and import-intensive items by reducing the capital intensity and the import content of other projects.

The most significant area for such compensatory operations lies, let us stress once more, in the field of construction activities, and in particular of residential and administrative building. Quite frequently developing countries try to emulate industrialized Western countries in modern architecture. The result, on the whole, is disappointing, whatever the formal and aesthetic value of the designs. Beautifully designed structures prove ill-adapted to the local climate and tremendously expensive; imported steel, glass, aluminium, and cement displace local materials and in addition it becomes necessary to import air-conditioning equipment and lifts. All these items could frequently be avoided if closer consideration were given to the traditional local architecture as a source of inspiration, both with respect to designs better suited to the climate and the use of local building materials. To this I should add that construction activities conducted along traditional lines (with some modifications, of course) might be an important source of employment, while designs and techniques borrowed or imitated from industrial countries frequently induce the use of costly foreign-made building machinery, which displaces local labour and even calls for contracting, from time to time, foreign technicians.

Implementation of industrialization plans in a mixed economy

Practically all the problems reviewed in the last section are relevant also in the case of a mixed economy, although their form might change. It is sometimes argued that reliance on the market mechanism and on competition of profit-oriented enterprises, both private and public,[6] would prevent the appearance of many undesirable features, discussed above, and, in particular, of the high propensity to invest. Such a view can be challenged, however, both on theoretical and empirical grounds.

Apart from the likely distortion of the investment pattern brought about by the allocation of investment through the market mechanism (see above), it would be wrong to expect that a developing mixed economy could actually conform to the pattern of an ideal competitive market. Protection rightly granted to new industries and measures taken to prevent further worsening of the balance-of-payments position in the form of duties, tax exemptions, subsidies, preferential credit arrangements, etc., are precisely meant to correct the market mechanism. To this I shall add that many firms enjoy a monopolistic or oligopolistic position in the market, and the size of the market as well as the necessity to channel scarce investment resources to other areas with high social

[6] Public enterprises do not differ in this case from the private ones, except for the fact that the owner is the State.

priority do not leave room for the formation of additional competitive firms; to the extent to which such a competition in some areas would mean temporary creation of excessive capacities at the expense of investment in other vital fields, the whole operation should be considered wasteful. Finally, we should keep in mind that the price policy of the public sector enterprises is an integral part of the financial policies of the State; it is a matter of expediency whether public enterprises should yield high profits, permitting thus a reduction in the level of taxation, or whether they should sell below cost, so as to subsidize the rest of the economy submitted to a higher incidence of taxes. The adopted solutions vary for different types of public enterprise and also depend on conditions prevailing in each country. However, there is no direct link between the costs and the price policy of the enterprises in the public sector.

Thus, both private and public industries in a developing mixed economy are inclined to rely heavily on investment without much regard for costs. This is the combined effect of the following factors: the availability of cheap credit,[7] the lack of problems on account of insufficient effective demand, and the propensity to imitate technical solutions from advanced countries, where it pays to substitute capital for labour.

To the problem discussed in the last section I must add that of financing industrial expansion in the case of mixed economies. Under comprehensive planning this problem does not arise except in the case of foreign currency. Decisions embodied in the plan[8] about the share of investment and consumption in the national income in successive years and the commodity pattern of production constitute the basis for price and wage policies framed in such a way as to implement the planned distribution of national income. Obviously, it is possible to devise a large number of alternative solutions conforming to the same set of goals but differing in terms of relative prices and relative wages, and one should stress here the political importance of the choice of a reasonable variant. But there are no other autonomous financial

[7] I do not have in mind absolute rates of interest, but the possibility of easy repayment of credit on the part of the entrepreneurs under conditions prevailing on the market and the existing mechanism of price formation of the products turned out by new industries.

[8] Of course, we assume that the plan is balanced and, in particular, that supplies of food match the demand so that no inflationary pressures arise.

decisions to take, just technical operations to perform.[9] In a mixed economy we are confronted, however, with two problems:

(a) Financing public investment (including transfers to the private sector) without creating inflationary pressures (i.e. without upsetting the balance of supply and demand of essentials, mostly food; see the first section).

(b) Channelling private savings into investments of high social priority (i.e. on the one hand, ensuring that private capital takes up projects foreseen in the plan and not meant for the public sector and, on the other, preventing it from investing in plants which do not fit at all in the plan and would lead to perverse growth as defined in the first section).

Implementation of industrialization plans is thus closely related to the fiscal policies pursued by the government. By proper taxation it should be possible to transfer funds to the public sector, while at the same time slowing down the rate of growth of consumption of luxuries. In particular, indirect taxes levied on luxuries together with direct taxes imposed on owners of sumptuary dwellings and motorcars would have a two-pronged effect: they would increase the revenue of the State and, at the same time, they would discourage consumption of luxuries and, by implication, excessive investment in the sector turning out luxuries.

It is impossible to discuss within the limits of this paper the whole issue of fiscal policies in a developing country engaged in industrialization. I should, therefore, like simply to emphasize, once more, the great relevance of fiscal policies to our main topic and to indicate my personal preference for a flexible system of taxes. In such a system there should be room for incentives granted to those who invest their savings in projects enjoying high social priorities; at the same time, taxes should not burden the poor. As personal income taxes tend to be inoperative in most developing countries, except for the share paid by the lower middle classes (office and public administration employees), I believe

---

[9] In practice the role of banking and financial institutions is broader; they are well placed to control and influence the actual implementation of investment at the enterprise level; moreover, continuous analysis of the investment expenditure is an important part of the planning process.

that, without abandoning at all the idea of getting the rich to pay income taxes, more imagination should be used to devise a variety of personal taxes on real estate and personal property which are easy to evaluate. In countries where sizable tracts of land belonging to big landowners are not properly put into use, a progressive land tax could be applied as a means of increasing revenue (and thus contributing to industrialization) and at the same time either inducing them to operate their land more intensively[10] (the increased supply of food thus obtained would again assist the industrialization drive) or forcing them to sell the land to the State (this in turn would help to carry out the land reforms, which in my view constitute the prerequisite of rapid growth of agricultural output—the necessary counterpart of industrialization).

Fiscal measures alone are not sufficient, in my opinion, to ensure that the private sector implements the industrialization plans established by the government. The government must resort to direct controls with respect to licensing of medium and large projects, foreign trade, and operations of foreign capital:

(a) Licensing is necessary to guide both the branch distribution of investment and its geographical location. Contrary to an entrenched prejudice, the administrative effort involved should not be too great, taking into consideration that in practically all the developing countries a construction licence is required and special services exist to this end. We consider that the scope of such services could be easily expanded.

(b) The impact of foreign trade on the process of economic growth is such as to make us believe that effective planning requires some measure of control over foreign trade, even in countries which do not experience any balance-of-payments difficulties. This is more evident in import-sensitive developing countries, where small fluctuations of the capacity to import may upset the whole investment programme. Such control should aim at banning all the non-essential imports, as long as there are difficulties in the balance of payments. Now, by essential imports we do not mean investment imports as opposed to maintenance

---

[10] An underlying assumption of the argument on progressive land taxes is that the behaviour of the traditional landlord does not consist in maximizing the profit derived from the land he owns, unless he is compelled to act in such a way.

imports. Such an interpretation, followed for years in several developing countries, led to distressing results: industries already existing and turning out goods with high social priority were forced to cut down their output due to a lack of materials and spare parts, while all facilities were given to imports of new machinery for industries whose implantation could have been postponed for a number of years.

(c) Several developing countries pin their hopes, as far as industrialization is concerned, on direct investments of foreign capital. Such investments must be submitted, however, to the same controls as local investors for the reasons already explained, and, in addition, it is necessary to investigate the likely effect of the inflow of capital on the balance-of-payments position and to regulate the remittances abroad of projects. Contrary to loans, which create a liability limited in time, direct investments generate a continuous outflow of profits, dividends, and royalties. We should also remember that profits ploughed back will in their turn generate further profits, dividends, and royalties subject to transfer abroad, unless reinvested capital is given, by laws of the recipient country, the treatment reserved for domestic capital.[11]

The apparent advantage of getting machinery from abroad without having to pay for it has been frequently misinterpreted in two directions: that of granting excessive concessions to foreign private capital, to the point of excluding even the competition of local private investors,[12] and that of accepting foreign investment without laying down any restrictions as to the choice of the field of activity and of localization. Such a policy is, in my opinion, shortsighted. A project belonging to the category of investments which the plan tries to restrict is bound to have negative effects even if its import content is wholly financed by an inflow of foreign capital. It will probably affect the balance of supplies of several scarce goods, add to the inflationary pressures, and in the long run adversely affect the balance of payments. We should dismiss, therefore, the justification so commonly heard in such

[11] Some developing countries attempted to pass regulations in this respect, but without much practical success up to now.

[12] Foreign investment is frequently carried out by powerful international firms well prepared to compete with weaker firms local to the enterprises with a view to eliminating them from the market, to the detriment of national and economic interests of the developing country.

instances that, whatever the project chosen,[13] it is better to have some inflow of foreign capital than none at all.

A note of caution should also be expressed about the justification of an extremely liberal policy towards foreign capital in terms of the need to get "know-how" from abroad. I do not dispute such a need and the implementation of industrialization plans would be impaired without the transfer of knowledge from more developed countries. But there are many instances when this knowledge can simply be purchased, not speaking of the assistance given on behalf of international organizations; from the macroeconomic point of view the purchase of patents, licences, and hiring of foreign technicians often proves much less expensive than getting the "know-how" in a package deal of which a direct investment of foreign private capital is an integral part.

The above observations should not be understood as an outright condemnation of foreign private investment, but rather as a warning against the widespread belief that it automatically helps to implement industrialization plans and as a plea for a policy of selective imports of capital, with strong preference for long-term loans.

Fiscal and other incentives may be used to persuade the private sector to take up projects in line with the plan. Controls of the type discussed above are helpful in order to prevent undesirable kinds of investment and to influence the implementation of the approved projects. But none of these measures can guarantee that a project considered essential will really be taken and implemented in the due course of time. Only direct participation of the public sector can do this. I shall discuss in the following paragraph a few issues related to this topic.

(a) State participation can take the form of supplementing private investment whenever it fails to materialize or of creating in certain fields of production public enterprises meant to remain in the public sector. An intermediary form is that of promoting new investment

---

[13] The argument that a foreign investor would automatically be prevented from taking up a "bad" project, because it would not offer a sufficient profit margin, does not hold true, as long as he is able to sell at monopoly prices or to substitute imports of goods which used to be sold at prices inflated by excessive transport costs and a handsome margin of profit. This was, for example, the case of beer in some African countries, where in spite of excess capacities already existing foreign investors were seeking permission to build new breweries.

through industrial and financial corporations and of selling new plants to private interests as soon as they become economically viable (according to market economy criteria). We have thus a situation diametrically opposed to that visualized by Schumpeter: the State and not the private investor is the real innovator. The argument frequently used to justify the handing of successful enterprises promoted by the State to private investors on the assumption that they will better succeed in managing them does not convince me. Why should people who failed to show entrepreneurship be good managers, while those who succeeded in promoting the enterprise mismanage it, just because they are State employees? If vigorous efforts were made to prepare managerial cadres for the public sector there would be no more mismanagement, on the average, in the public than in the private sector.

Furthermore, what is the guarantee that the private entrepreneurs will not show their skill in carrying out monopolistic practices, which maximize their profit but keep part of the productive capacity idle with clear-cut loss for the national economy? But it is not my intention here to pass value judgements, as the choice of the pattern of the public sector is a political one and belongs to the realm of a long-run strategy of economic development. I shall simply say that this choice is directly relevant for the implementation of the plan. The more the plan relies for its implementation on the public sector, the smaller the probability of discrepancies between the intention of the planners and the actual implementation.[14]

(b) Besides taking up projects earmarked in the plan, the public sector can play an important promotional role in organizing, financing, and assisting technically small-scale private and co-operative industries. Here the case for private or co-operative rather than public ownership becomes much stronger, as a means of attracting the savings of private traders and craftsmen to industrial investment and of using managerial talents which are suited to small enterprise frequently run as a family business. Promotion of small-scale industries may prove of great relevance in the context of regional planning and whenever transport facilities are lacking and transport costs are high—a good way to satisfy local demand at competitive prices, even if production costs are consider-

---

[14] Assuming, of course, that the plan was designed realistically.

ably higher than in large-scale plants. Encouragement of small-scale industries with low capital coefficients is also a way of compensating for the high capital–output ratios in modern large-scale industrial projects.

How big a share should be allotted to small-scale enterprises, both traditional and modern, in the implementation of industrialization plans is a matter for empirical consideration. In any case, for small-scale industries to be viable they must be supported by public sector special institutions. As for the argument that their capacity of contributing to capital formation is less than that of bigger units, I believe that this matter can be dealt with by appropriate taxation of the rich and the well-to-do.

(c) Implementing industrialization plans requires, as a rule, considerable activities in the field of construction. In almost all the developing countries those activities are carried out by private firms, including the construction of projects belonging to the public sector. Experience shows that this is a source of very important transfers of funds to the private sector and of profits, not always legal, which could be tapped for investment if they were earned by public enterprises.

To sum up, the public sector has a very significant role to play in the implementation of industrialization plans in a mixed economy. Its *differentia specifica*, as compared to the private sector, is that it can be geared to this task, while private enterprises act on a profit motive.

CHAPTER 8

Transfer of Technology and Strategy of Industrialization (1970)

"From where do inventions come?", the late Michal Kalecki used to ask his astonished students. Very few would reply by stressing the role of the human brain. For Kalecki, this experience, often repeated in university tests, was proof that teaching of theories of growth and of economics at large had become so sophisticated as to kill common sense in the students. Technology, i.e. knowledge organized for production, has always played its role in economic activity—whether embodied in manpower (skills), in equipment (hardware), or disembodied (software). The only marked difference today lies in the fact that software and know-how are becoming more and more a commodity and, therefore, have become a subject for political economy. It is, indeed, not necessary to accept all the simplifying assumptions of the Cobb–Douglas, or other similar production functions for ascertaining that technical progress has its impact on output. Yet, the economics of research and development—and for that matter also education—are wasting a lot of intellectual effort, time, and money in unconvincing attempts to measure the impact of scientific, technological, and educational progress on output, instead of concentrating on more relevant issues.

At the same time, discussions on the so-called transfer of technology suffer from sweeping, and often contradicting, generalizations. On the one hand, there are those who claim many advantages for the latecomers who, supposedly, should be able to use at their will all the accumulated wealth of world science and technology in order to grow quickly and smoothly. And, on the other, one finds the pessimists who consider that the technological gap between the leading industrial powers and the rest of the world is bound to widen even larger, and to handicap ever more, the developing countries. Paradoxically, both these schools of thought advocate heavy reliance on transfers of technology: the former because they consider it a bargain, the latter because they do not see any escape from a position of permanent technological dependence. Quite obviously, the indiscriminate transfer of technology has also its foes who rightly emphasize the need for a big domestic effort in science and technology, but from time to time go so far as to claim that the ultimate solution consists in a scientific and technological autarky—a proposition hardly acceptable even to very big countries, not to speak of the smaller and of the very small ones which number high among the developing countries.

It is not my purpose in this chapter to go into this kind of discussion: I should rather like to analyze the very concept of "transfer of technology"[1] which lacks precision and then to discuss its possible place in the formulation of a strategy of industrialization.

As already mentioned, the concept of technology comprises the concept of software (denoted hereafter as S) and overlaps with those of skills (M) and hardware (H).[2] Even if we were to narrow down the concept of technology to S, the question of complementarity between S, H, and M would always arise at the operational level; it is particularly meaningless to speak of transfer of technology without inquiring into the existence of H and M necessary to use a given S for production. If we agree now to denote domestic S, H, M with subscripts d, and foreign S, H, M with subscripts i, the matrix of the possible situations is the following one:

---

[1] Even this term commonly used could be questioned on semantic grounds: nobody speaks of the transfer of raw materials when imported raw materials are used as inputs for production; on the other hand, there are no reasons to believe, as I shall show later on, that whenever foreign technology is made use of, a real transfer of knowledge and spill-over effects take place. I am thus using the term just questioned for mere convenience, because putting new terms into circulation makes little sense.

[2] To the extent to which a technology may depend on the use of specific intermediate goods imported from the firm which provides the technology, such inputs are also part of the technological "package deal" and, incidentally, represent a substantial part of returns on the transfer of proprietary technology supplied by foreign private firms (e.g. pharmaceuticals, cosmetics, and chemicals at large). This is one of the reasons why it is impossible to evaluate the cost of technology from figures related to nominal fees paid for patents, licences, and know-how.

(a) $M_i \, S_i \, H_i$: foreign specialists apply a foreign-invented technology[3] and operate equipment from abroad.

(b) $M_i \, S_i \, H_d$: foreign specialists apply a foreign-invented technology but were able (or compelled) to find suitable locally made equipment (an unusual though not impossible case).

(c) $M_i \, S_d \, H_i$: foreign specialists have been called to operate locally made equipment, but S was provided by local research and development (once more an unusual but not impossible case).

(d) $M_i \, S_d \, H_d$: foreign specialists have been called to operate locally made equipment and use domestic software (to make this case at all realistic we might assume that H_d is but a copy of H_i).

(e) $M_d \, S_i \, H_i$: local manpower works with foreign technology and on imported equipment (contrary to the previous three cases, it is a quite frequent one, together with cases f and g dealt with below).

(f) $M_d \, S_i \, H_d$: local manpower produces on locally made equipment a product using foreign patents and/or know-how.

(g) $M_d \, S_d \, H_i$: equipment has been imported for domestic-designed and domestic-manned production.

(h) $M_d \, S_d \, H_d$: all the three factors are local.

Case (a) is obviously one of *total technological dependence*; case (h), on the contrary, is one of *total technological independence*. The remaining six denote varying degrees and forms of reliance on foreign technology.

The above matrix thus provides a suitable frame for analysing the technological dependence of a country at a given moment. But it can also be dynamized, (a) being the point of departure, (h) the final goal, and the remaining six cases the intermediary stages of a dynamic process (see Table 8.1).

The above scheme does not imply that reaching of $M_d \, S_d \, H_d$, in all types of production, should necessarily be the goal of development strategy. The strategist has considerable freedom of choice and, in many lines of production, he might opt for $M_i \, S_i \, H_i$ as a long-term solution. But in others, he might opt for $M_d \, S_d \, H_d$, and then it should be useful for him to consider cases in columns 2 and 3 as intermediary stages

---

[3] My classification is based on the origin of M, S, and H, but it has nothing to do with the ownership of the plant; $M_i \, S_i \, H_i$ may occur in a domestic-owned or even public-owned factory, though there is more likelihood they would be found in a foreign-owned subsidiary.

TABLE 8.1

1	2	3	4
(a) $M_i S_i H_i$	(b) $M_i S_i H_d$	(d) $M_i S_d H_d$	(h) $M_d S_d H_d$
	(c) $M_i S_d H_i$	(f) $M_d S_i H_d$	
	(e) $M_d S_i H_i$	(g) $M_d S_d H_i$	

t_0 —————————————————————————→ t_n

between 1 and 4, though direct passage from 1 to 4 could be envisaged also, and all sorts of short-cuts and skipping over 2 and 3 are possible. A strategy of technological development should spell out precisely the priorities involved, the paths to be followed, and the time-scheduling of the operations—taking into consideration the overall industrial strategy and the capacity of the three systems involved: the educational (for M), the industrial (for H), and the scientific (for S). Ultimately, it becomes an exercise in the ways to expand and connect these three systems and in the ways to decide what should be made at home and what should be imported.

At this stage, in order to inquire into the conditions of such a dynamic policy and to evaluate the efficiency of transfers of technology, I may complicate the argument by observing that an imported S may serve as an input both for production and for research, although these two functions are by no means automatically performed at the same time. This observation holds true *mutatis mutandis* for "imported" specialists. Having in mind the double function of technology, transfers of technology can take one of the four following forms:

(a) *Adaptive transfer*: foreign technology T supplied in the year

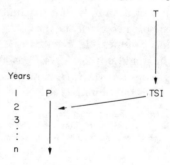

1^4 is adapted by domestic technological-scientific infrastructure TSI before going into production P in the year 2.

(b) *Full transfer*: technology T is being supplied in the year 1 and simultaneously used in production and made the subject of domestic research. In the year n, when technology has to be renovated, domestic TSI will be able to perform the task.

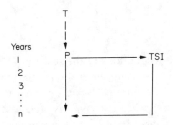

(c) *Full adaptive transfer*: it is a combination of cases (a) and (b).

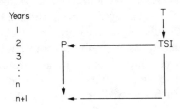

(d) *Pseudo-transfer*: in this case foreign technology T functions only as an input into production with no repercussions whatsoever on TSI. Strictly speaking, such a form of using encapsulated foreign technology does not constitute a transfer at all. Its spill-over effects are kept at a minimum; domestic skilled manpower performs a passive role.[5] Still, such pseudo-transfers constitute the bulk of what comes today under the broad denomination of transfers of technology. It is certainly the case of most "transfers" being big private companies and their subsidiaries abroad. Under this type of arrangement, a kind of "principle

---

[4] The concept of "year" is here purely notional to signify time lags.

[5] One more reason to look for more stimulating jobs abroad.

of echo" operates with respect to imports of T: every n years in order to renovate the technology it is necessary to purchase it abroad.

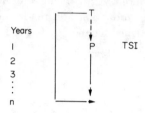

We can thus take a second look at the strategy of technological development. It consists in deciding what should be the respective proportions and areas for autonomous domestic creative effort and for the four types of transfers defined above, as well as the time-scheduling of all this. The latter consideration is of tremendous importance because types of solution applied to definite areas may change over time while new subjects will be added every year. At this moment I might reintroduce the matrix discussed above and, once more, emphasize the links between S, H, and M.[6] While it is easy to construct a scale of preferences (autonomous effort > full adaptative transfer > full transfer > adaptative transfer > pseudo-transfer), quite obviously all the five solutions will have to be employed, including the pseudo-transfer, as no developing country is able overnight to start research in all fields. But choices should be made with full knowledge of the differences between the alternative solutions and their advantages and weak spots.[7]

It also follows that the implantation of TSI is of crucial importance for an adequate transfer machinery. The latter question should be particularly stressed at a moment when the United Nations and the World Bank come forward with the idea that developed countries should spend 5 per cent of their research and development budget on research which

[6] It should be noted, furthermore, that research may be engaged both on S initially imported and H which serves to produce by means of S.

[7] Thus, pseudo-transfers are in the short run the easiest to work out and they create the comfortable feeling of getting access to the most up-to-date technology, whenever considerations of economies of scale permit the transplantation of technologies applied abroad. But they ignore the specific conditions of the importing country; furthermore, they perpetuate a situation of complete technological dependence, not to mention burdening the balance of payments.

is of interest to developing countries. I consider this a paternalistic, and therefore politically unacceptable, solution (if at all realistic in terms of the willingness of developed countries); instead of consolidating a situation of dependence on transfer of ready-made products of science and technology with all the ensuing negative aspects, including the high cost of transfer, of proprietary knowledge, a much bolder effort than hitherto should be made to create the TSI in the developing countries. Such a TSI should comprise:

(a) A strong and active industrial information component, able to provide domestic investors (including the public sector) with independent knowledge on sources of S, H, and even M abroad and thus strengthen their bargaining power.

(b) Engineering, designing, and consulting offices, as technology cannot be really mastered so long as local competence is not entrusted with responsibility for development projects (even though foreign consultants may be associated on an *ad hoc* basis).

(c) Fundamental and applied research institutes, performing a treble function—educating scientific manpower, doing some research (which usually requires some concentration thresholds to be attained with respect to personnel and resources), and assisting science policy-makers.

(d) A science policy-making and implementing agency, which should on the one hand frame the suitable strategy and on the other control the actual transfers of technology and go as far as screening big investment projects with respect to the choice of technology and of their sources.

In other words, TSI should be viewed as an integrated system established in order to promote the necessary change in the supply of technologies as part of the overall process of development, which may be viewed as a passage to an accumulative model of economy.[8] Thus, to be mean-

---

[8] I assume that practically all economies produce some surplus but that the use of the surplus for investment purposes and the consequent technological transformation do not occur automatically. Surplus may be dissipated in a "primitive economy" through non-productive uses such as conspicuous consumption of the élite, the drain abroad, or the socially accepted collective ceremonial consumption. Similar phenomena reappear in the affluent capitalistic economies. Thus economic history unfolds in a dialectical succession of three models: the dissipating model, the accumulative model, and the affluent accumulating–dissipating model.

ingful, any discussion of the strategy in the field of science and technology must replace the problem we are dealing with in the context of socio-economic conditions of the country concerned. In particular, there is no point in discussing the transfer of technology and its ill-effects in many countries without going into a thorough analysis of the workings of the imperfect market there; one might argue that market conditions and relative prices between agriculture and industry are such as to make science and technology an unprofitable proposal to the great mass of farmers, while price formation in the industrial field favours wasteful expenditure on costly technology, ill-adapted to factor proportions, at least in the private sector.[9]

The argument that the implantation of the TSI in developing countries would be costly and its functioning inefficient boils down to the fallacy of the static comparative advantage. The principle of protection to infant industry within reasonable limits is today a commonplace of development economics. Why should there not be protection to infant science and technology in order to compensate for the unavoidable cost of apprenticeship in this crucial field of modern life?

Imaginative work is needed to define such a principle in operational categories without falling into excesses of scientific autarky and paying too high for the lesson. Most probably, one of the answers lies in a much more effective co-operation among the developing countries. The United Nations should concentrate on the creation of a "south–south" communication network bringing together scientists from Asia, Latin America, and Africa, instead of duplicating the existing "north–south" bilateral channels.

At the same time, a comprehensive analysis of the world movements of technology is called for, transcending the statistical description and cutting deep into the institutional aspects of the existing transfer machinery and of the market of technology and skills and the distribution of gains. It should be recognized that international movements of technology come within a comprehensive definition of international economic relations, side by side with movements of goods, services, capitals,

---

[9] In particular, it is vain to expect that transfer of "advanced technology" from enterprise to enterprise will render the recipient enterprise competitive to the extent to which the sources of its uncompetitiveness are external to the enterprise and arise out of the general inefficiency of the "environment".

and labour, both skilled (as in the case of the brain drain) and unskilled (as in the case of mass migration of workers to Western Europe); at the same time a *political economy of knowledge*, as distinct from the economics of research and development and of education, should be developed in order to assist the planners.

CHAPTER 9

Selection of Techniques: Problems and Policies for Latin America (1970)

Introductory remarks

If we agree, as a first approximation, to define a technique by the amount of fixed capital necessary to produce a unit of output (or, in other words, the capital–output ratio c) and the labour input per unit of output (i.e. the reverse of labour productivity p), the problem of the selection of a technique will arise whenever it is possible to produce the same output by alternative methods, which are efficient, i.e. compensate for higher fixed capital investment by lower labour inputs, or vice versa. The problem is illustrated in Figure 9.1. Let T_1 be a reference technique characterized by labour input OA and capital investment OB. All techniques inside the angle AT_1B will be better than T_1, as requiring at the same time less capital and less labour. The problem of selection does not arise: they should be preferred to T_1. All techniques situated inside BT_1A' are worse than T_1 because they require at the same time more capital and more labour; such techniques are therefore inefficient and should be disregarded. But all the techniques inside AT_1B' and BT_1A' are efficient: those inside AT_1B' require less capital but more labour than T_1, while those inside BT_1A' require more capital and less labour inputs than T_1.

To choose the best technique out of the set of all efficient ones according to the factor proportions prevailing in a given economy, we must know the marginal rate of substitution between capital and labour, i.e. how many units of additional fixed capital we are ready to sacrifice in order to save one unit of labour input on current costs of production. In other words, we must know the length of the prevailing or postulated

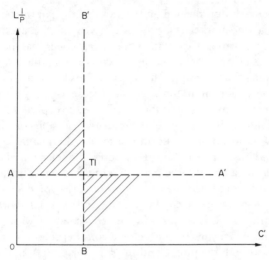

Fɪɢ. 9.1   Selection of techniques

recoupment period of the invested capital, which is just a convenient way of expressing the cost of capital. If the recoupment period is n years, it will pay to substitute up to n units of capital for one unit of yearly labour costs.[1]

Let us imagine two techniques with the following features:

	Technique A	Technique B
Fixed investment per unit of output	100	200
Labour input per unit of output per year	100	80

Technique B is more capital intensive, as it requires 100 units of additional investment and allows in compensation for saving 20 units of labour per year. Technique B will be preferred whenever the recoupment period n is longer than five years. For $n < 5$ (i.e. in situations where capital is very expensive), the more labour-intensive technique A will be preferred.

[1] Needless to say, the recoupment period is not tantamount to the actual life span of the equipment. All the complications we have been dealing with in this paragraph arise from the fact that we are in the presence of a stock (capital) and a flow (labour).

The choice will thus depend on the value of the parameter *n*.

Now, in a free-market economy *n* is given by the prevailing rate of interest on borrowed capital. The entrepreneur has no problems in reducing fixed investment and current costs to a common denominator and of choosing the technique which, given a price and a capital market structure, allows for minimum production costs, so long as we do not take into account any possible difficulty of access to capital. In a centrally planned economy it should be theoretically possible to choose *n* in such a way as to optimize the utilization of the available factors of production. Thus, for all practical purposes, the selection of techniques is automatic in an ideal free-market economy, while in a centrally planned one it could become an important area for decision-making and optimization, were it not for certain institutional shortcomings.[2]

Let us turn now to the case of a mixed economy with a dynamic though not necessarily big public sector, a considerable amount of public investment (in both the public and the private sectors), and some controls built into the economy.

The agencies entrusted with public investment and lending of public funds to private investors should be able to apply methods of project evaluation similar to those of the centrally planned economies. Such methods consist of using in one way or another criteria of macroeconomic and macrosocial benefit instead of microeconomic entrepreneurial ones based on profit expectation within the prevailing market and price structure.[3] Of course, we assume here implicitly that collective long-term interests do not necessarily coincide with those of individual profit-motivated enterprises, or, in other words, we recognize the need for State intervention into the realm of economic affairs, with both an economic and a social purpose.

Is, however, intervention with respect to the selection of techniques at all possible within the private sector of the economy?

Without ignoring the difficulties involved and the narrow limits of

[2] Experience shows that project evaluation and comparison of alternative techniques should be separated from investment decision-making and project implementation. If all three functions are concentrated in one agency (e.g. the planning commission), project evaluation may suffer biases and often becomes a justification *ex post hoc* of a choice made on some other grounds.

[3] We are not concerned at this point with the different proposed techniques of social cost-benefit analysis. This aspect will be dealt with later on.

manœuvre, this chapter endeavours to reply in the affirmative to this question. On the one hand, it should be possible to influence private investors' choices (whenever alternatives exist, which is not always the case) out of the available stock of techniques through adequate price, credit, trade, and fiscal measures. On the other, the supply of alternative techniques should be increased by means of vigorous and purposeful science and research policies. Finally, some results could be obtained by influencing the output-mix of the economy by means of action of the demand pattern, mainly through income policies and a judicious catalytic use of public investment.

Policies with respect to the selection of techniques should thus become an integral part of development policies in spite of all their limitations, or rather because of those limitations. The lesser the scope for choosing techniques according to their capital–labour ratio, the more important it becomes not to miss the opportunities of lowering that ratio in selected areas of activity where they really exist, as, for example, in agriculture, building, certain public works, ancillary activities in industry, etc. At any rate, the process of industrialization is bound to include many projects with high capital–labour ratios, so that at best all we can hope for is to mitigate the unfavourable relationship between increases in industrial output and employment creation. We assume the selection of techniques to follow, in principle, the choice of the output-mix, based on considerations of market, resource availabilities, and the requirements of the adopted strategy of growth. But feedbacks are possible, i.e. the pressure of employment goals may motivate biasing the proposed output-mix in favour of activities where labour-intensive techniques exist, to the extent to which some substitutions in the demand pattern may be feasible.

The same observation applies to foreign trade: exports of goods produced by labour-intensive techniques should be actively promoted, and even subsidized to a reasonable extent, not because developing countries have necessarily a comparative advantage in such types of production, as is often argued,[4] but because it is for them a more rational way of using the existing resources to overcome the foreign exchange bottleneck.

---

[4] We should recall here Leontieff's paradox on the comparative advantage of the United States in labour-intensive products.

Finally, it should be possible in certain countries to step up the rate of overall growth above the level forecast or planned, by launching an additional popular housing programme, based on locally produced building materials, labour-intensive methods of construction, and even some self-help schemes.

I should like to end these introductory remarks on a note of cautious optimism. Though the incorporation of the selection of techniques into the realm of development policies broadens the area for strategic decision-making, there is bound to be very little elbow-room for manœuvring in the short and medium run, chiefly because of the inexistence of modern techniques devised for the factor proportions prevailing in developing countries. Some improvements can be sought, however, by making the access to existing alternative techniques easier and by reducing the scope for wrong decisions prompted by inadequate policies of support for industrialization which boils down to an excessive lowering of the opportunity cost of equipment for the entrepreneur.

In the long run I see more reasons for optimism than for pessimism, provided it is realized that the key to a less-disturbing future lies in a real breakthrough in the realm of science, technology, and education. Autonomous scientific and technological development, which is by no means tantamount to a trend towards technical autarky, should be given utmost priority by Latin American countries, and ways of organizing purposive and concrete co-operation among developing countries should be sought. Many developing countries which managed in the last few years to establish important industries suffer today from a painful technological dependence. Modernization has too often been associated in these countries with a passive reception of patterns and techniques evolved in other contexts, and a certain mood of euphoria with respect to the possibility of producing up-to-date industrial goods goes hand in hand with an inferiority complex with respect to their scientific and technological potential. The field of science does not comprise only nuclear energy and space; many vital areas of fundamental and applied research could and should be developed in Latin America with a view to solving the specific problems of the continent. Nor do I accept the argument that poor countries cannot afford to spend more on science. They should do it precisely because they are poor and are looking for short-cuts.

My argument should not be taken as an unqualified profession of faith in the so-called scientific revolution, understood as a panacea and a substitute for social reforms. I believe that the "development potential" of a country rests on a reasonable industrial structure (varying from country to country and changing over time), an institutional set-up which allows for using a fair measure of "operational controls" (in Myrdal's sense of the term)[5] and taking autonomous decisions, as well as on an intellectual structure capable of continuously feeding the socio-economic system with new ideas and technologies. Thus, the scientific and technological breakthrough must come as part of an overall strategy of attack on underdevelopment, all the more so since, in order to develop, science and technology need a climate of freedom of research and speech incompatible with acute social tensions.

A peep at some theoretical controversies

Before beginning the analysis of the Latin American experience I shall very briefly refer, without any pretension of being exhaustive, to some of the discussions which have been raging for quite a time and seem relevant to our subject.

A MACROECONOMIC CONFLICT: INCOME VERSUS SURPLUS MAXIMIZATION?

Given a limited stock of capital and a postulated level of real wages, should we strive to maximize output by spreading capital over a large number of working posts or, on the contrary, should we make use of more capital-intensive techniques which maximize investment surplus?[6] Figure 9.2 illustrates the controversy.

Income is maximum when we reach D, but surplus is maximum at the point A where the marginal productivity of labour equals the wage. The first alternative is advantageous in the short run, as consump-

[5] See Gunnar Myrdal, *Asian Drama*, vol. III, New York, 1968.
[6] A. K. Sen, *Choice of Techniques: An Aspect of the Theory of Planned Economic Development*, 2nd ed., Oxford, 1962, remains the standard reference on the subject. For an interesting critical analysis see Z. Dobrska, *Wybor Technik Produkcji w Krajach Gospodarczo Zacofanych*, Warsaw, 1963 (in Polish).

tion *EF* is higher than *BC* and employment *OF* exceeds *OC*. But the future rate of growth depends on investment and surplus *AB* is higher than *DE*. Thus, choosing the income maximization in the short run means compromising the pace of income increases over time. The longer the time horizon considered, the more advantageous the second alternative looks. We thus reach the conclusion that even underdeveloped countries with scarce capital and plentiful labour resources should resort to capital-intensive techniques of production.

Sen's argument is unquestionable so long as we accept the assumptions of his model: there are no exogenous inflows of capital apart from the initial stock; no technical progress takes place; and income distribution is perfectly even.

Now, one may argue that such assumptions are not very realistic. Accumulation takes place not only in the modern sector, just started from scratch, but also in the traditional sector, so there is bound to be each year some inflow of exogenous capital, even if we disregard foreign loans. In these circumstances the opposition between the two maxima becomes less. The introduction of technical progress into the model would have the same effect. As for the income policies, either of two things may happen. On the one hand, we may really operate a perfectly egalitarian economy and then the case for manipulating with a rate of increase of real wages in the context of a dynamic economy[7] becomes quite strong: it might be conceivable to lower the postulated rate of increase of real wages and to keep at the same time the employment roll large enough as to enable total consumption *FE'* to exceed *BC*, while surplus *DE'* becomes equal to *AB*. On the other hand, the social distribution of income may be skewed, and then the whole problem becomes immaterial to the extent to which it would be possible to reconcile, by adequate income and fiscal policies, high levels of investment with reasonable levels of popular consumption: the stepping up of investment should take place on the basis of high marginal savings ratios imposed on higher income classes.[8]

[7] In his important paper on "Determination of the rate of growth of a socialist economy under conditions of unlimited supply of labour" in vol. III of *Essays on Planning and Economic Development*, Warsaw, 1968, M. Kalecki advocates using labour-intensive methods in order to draw on the reserves of labour, subject to the condition, however, that at no moment of the growth process should real unit wages fall.

[8] See also *supra* chapter 3.

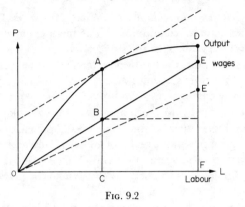

FIG. 9.2

At this stage we should observe that Sen's findings are often misinter-preted by private industrialists in developing countries, who are eager to find social arguments in favour of profit-maximizing techniques at the level of individual enterprise. Needless to say, their argument is invalidated by their failure to take the implications of the prevailing income distribution into consideration.

In a sense, Sen's model gives a useful insight into one more aspect of the fundamental problem of planning—the need to choose between present and future advantages and the lack of objective criteria for optimization of such choices. But he does not provide the planner with a clear-cut rule of conduct because of the complications already men-tioned and, above all, of the limitations which arise when, from the macroeconomic and general level of argument, we get down to earth and try to work out actual technological choices.

INTERMEDIATE TECHNOLOGY: A PANACEA?

The opposite case, stressing the scope for primitive labour-intensive techniques meant to become a major component of the development strategy, is not entirely convincing either.

How far should we go in diluting the capital? Does it make sense to employ people at levels of productivity where value-added is not enough to cover the minimum acceptable wage? How big is the real scope for labour-intensive investment activities of the "pick-and-shovel" variety, i.e. virtually unmechanized? What can we expect from the so-called "intermediate techniques"?[9] The mere enumeration of these questions shows the vastness of the subject. We can at best try to sketch in some replies. We must start, however, by summarizing the arguments in favour of labour-intensive solutions.

The reserves of idle or semi-idle labour, far from being a liability, should be transformed into the major asset of a developing country. By drawing on this resource, it should be possible to carry out extensive investment programmes in the realm of infrastructure and social services and to expand output in agriculture and cottage industries by making use of "£1-technology instead of £1,000-technology", to borrow a symbolical expression from E. F. Schumacher.[10]

Such was the underlying assumption of the Chinese "big leap forward" and, to some extent, of the community development programmes and related schemes sponsored by various governments in Asia and Africa and United Nations agencies, though the latter were never meant to constitute the main engine of growth of a wholesale strategy.[11]

In reality neither in China, which had at least the advantage of strong social discipline, nor in the non-socialist developing countries did this kind of programme yield the expected results. The reasons are manifold:

(a) The scope for employing techniques which in spite of low capital intensity are efficient and meet the minimum productivity criterion is, at present, quite narrow, *inter alia*, because of a lack of substantial research on such techniques.

(b) Even in public works straightforward substitution of capital by labour is often difficult, if not quite impossible, because of organizational problems involved and of the extension of the gestation period of the projects under construction.

[9] These techniques are being advocated by the Intermediate Technology Development Group Ltd., in London, and the Volunteers for International Assistance in Schenectady, New York.

[10] E. F. Schumacher, *Social and Economic Problems Calling for the Development of Intermediate Technology*, July 1965 (mimeographed).

[11] Among University economists who in the West worked on the problem, Ragnar Nurske and Arthur Lewis should be mentioned above all. Among the French-speaking economists, Gabriel Ardant is the most active propagandist for the *investissement humain*.

(c) Resorting to voluntary labour is only possible when the population has a strong feeling of participation, usually arising out of radical land reforms, even though one should not expect that this capital of goodwill is inexhaustible.

(d) Whether paid or not, people in order to work must be adequately fed, and there is little hope of mobilizing for this purpose the parcel of food which they would have eaten were they to remain semi-idle in their local village, to say nothing of the fact that their diet must be improved to sustain a reasonable labour productivity. Food availability thus sets the upper limit to growth of employment,[12] even if we were to suppose that efficient labour-intensive techniques are available in areas of the economy that are worth developing.

But rejection of labour-intensive investment as a wholesale strategy is not tantamount to ignoring the untapped opportunities of a fuller use of labour reserves in developing countries and, even less, to closing the eye to wasteful uses of capital.

In the same way, I believe, that the partisans of intermediate techniques have a strong point, provided it is reduced to its real proportions and stripped of the missionary zeal often present in discussions on the subject.[13] I agree with E. F. Schumacher when he stresses the impossibility of the traditional sector being absorbed in the short and medium run by the modern one and the consequent need to help people of the traditional sector (see footnote 13). Such a view does not imply giving up the expansion of the modern sector but merely re-establishing the proportions hitherto biased almost exclusively in favour of the modern sector. I also agree with Barbara Ward's contention that for 50 years and more practically all research has been concentrated on

---

[12] See P. C. Sah, "The choice of investment techniques in under-developed economies", in vol. III of *Essays on Planning and Economic Development*, Warsaw, 1968, and by the same author an unpublished Ph.D. thesis, defended in 1968. Dr. Sah shows that the limit of food availability can be exceeded if labour-intensive techniques are employed to earn additional foreign exchange (or to save it through important substitution) in quantities higher than the import requirements of food for the workers employed in these foreign-trade-oriented industries.

[13] Schumacher, *op. cit.* See also the interesting article by C. Bobrowski, "Algerian traditional agriculture", in *Essays on Planning and Economic Development*, vol. III, Warsaw, 1968, where the methodological consequences of the need to include the traditional sector in the plan are explored.

large-scale, labour-saving technologies, the least suitable for the developing world, and the following conclusion drawn by her: "This is a disproportion which the developed world never knew since it invented and pioneered and adapted its technology to its own needs as the process of development went on. But now the technology exists in its own right and can be purchased and introduced into societies in which in fact it is quite inappropriate. One can see the consequences of this maladjustment very clearly in some parts of Africa today. Inexperienced governments, trying out their hand in economic decision-making, find it terribly tempting to buy the most up-to-date machinery which persuasive gentlemen from the North Atlantic area come to sell them."[14] Finally, I sympathize with D. R. Gadgil's plea for creating large-scale employment out of agriculture in rural areas.[15] Under such circumstances it is very useful indeed to catalogue, diffuse, and demonstrate labour-intensive techniques, suitable for small-scale applications, whether these techniques are in use today, adapted from past practices or developed anew for some particular task. More emphasis on studying such techniques is certainly called for, and developing countries should develop, side by side with modern research, a kind of "do-it-yourself research guerrilla";[16] the example of war economy in North Viet-Nam is there to show the potentialities of such an approach. But the condition of minimum productivity should never be neglected and, thus, the scope for the application of "intermediate technology" remains narrow, even though it should displace more obsolete and altogether inefficient techniques still existing in the traditional sector. Moreover, the adjective "intermediate" leads to some confusion; I am speaking in reality of efficient labour-intensive techniques which in a reasonable development strategy should find some useful application side by side with most capital-intensive techniques in other areas of the economy. Emphasis on "intermediate technologies" implies, therefore, the acceptance of technological dualism, rather than overcoming it; trying to avoid wide

---

[14] Barbara Ward, "The decade of development. A study in frustration?", in *Reshaping the World Economy—Rich and Poor Countries*, ed. by J. A. Pincus, Prentice-Hall, Englewood Cliffs, N.J., 1968, pp. 27–28.

[15] See D. R. Gadgil, "Notes on rural industrialization", *Artha Vijnana*, **VI,** no. 1, March 1964, pp. 9–15.

[16] Michel Leiris, *Cinq Etudes d'Ethnologie*, Paris, 1969, p. 142.

disparities in capital intensity per worker between one sector of the economy and another as a matter of policy sounds quite unrealistic.[17]

MAKING VIRTUE OF NECESSITY: TECHNOLOGICAL DUALISM

I shall now sum up the position. There are many arguments for and against capital-intensive technology. An ILO study[18] lists the following points:

In favour of capital-intensive technology

(a) The building up of an industrial sector employing the most modern and advanced technology is the hallmark of an economically developed country.

(b) It is necessary to invest with the future in mind.

(c) Advanced technology enables managements and workers to acquire the technical skill and knowledge that are indispensable to a modern economy.

(d) The industries with the greatest growth potential are those employing advanced technology.

(e) A high degree of capital intensity permits large profits to be made and a large proportion of these profits to be ploughed back to promote faster growth.

Against capital-intensive technology

(a) Advanced industrial technology has developed, in response to the needs of industrially advanced countries with large markets, a relative abundance of capital and entrepreneurial and managerial skills, and a shortage of labour.

(b) Transplanting industrial technology to countries where it will

---

[17] This is our only but fundamental quarrel with the stimulating paper, *Progressive Technologies for Developing Countries*, by Keith Marsden from the Small Industries Unit, ILO, 1967 (mimeographed).

[18] See ILO, *Human Resources for Industrial Development*, Geneva, 1967, chap. 7, pp. 201–217, condensed in *Development Digest*.

operate under conditions for which it was not designed can be an expensive mistake.

(c) Countries should not seek to make a sudden break with their past; instead they should develop and adapt their traditional skills, knowledge, and techniques.

(d) Where capital is scarce, capital-intensive technology means concentrating it in a few large plants while keeping the rest of the economy starved of capital, and this accentuates the contrast in living standards between the modern and the traditional sectors while limiting at the same time the number of people that can be gainfully absorbed into the modern sector.

(e) If capital-intensive technology does enable a few large modern plants to make big profits, this does not mean that the total profits, both public and private, for the economy as a whole are necessarily greater. Nor is it necessarily the case that more resources will be invested than if capital had been spread widely.

The obvious conclusion is that a comprehensive development strategy should try to make use of both capital-intensive and labour-intensive technologies or, in other words, that it should be two-pronged.

From the operational point of view, this means under present circumstances that special attention should be given to reducing the present bias towards capital-intensive technological sectors. I shall briefly discuss both these points.

Reducing the bias in favour of capital-intensive technology

As a matter of fact, efficient intermediate technology either does not exist or is hardly known, and the least one can say about experiments with a labour-intensive investment is that they have not hitherto been encouraging.[19] On the other hand, various reasons combine to expose developing countries to an excessive absorption of capital-intensive techniques. Here are the main ones:

---

[19] We should not forget, however, that the process of rapid industrialization undergone by the Soviet Union and such Eastern European countries as Poland was for quite a time based on "extensive" methods, i.e. large increases in employment and moderate gains in productivity.

(a) Capital and foreign exchange are made available to investors at excessively low rates, while costs of labour are inflated by unsuitable fiscal policies.[20]

(b) The imperfections of the markets are often strengthened by the irrational working of operational controls over foreign trade and finance, so that profits run very high,[21] enhancing the propensity of the entrepreneurs to use profit-maximizing techniques.

(c) Lack of appropriate research infrastructure, of equipment-producing industries, and of local engineering and designing firms in most cases puts foreign consultant firms and suppliers of equipment and know-how in a position of monopoly.

(d) This dependence on imitative transfers of capital-intensive technology is enhanced by the mechanisms of foreign direct investment and foreign aid, which, furthermore, frequently distort the investment pattern and give it an unnecessarily high import content.[22]

(f) A false concept of modernity,[23] too often assimilated with foreign-made gadgets and symbols of scientific achievement that are not in harmony with the basic needs of the population,[24] on the one hand, gives tremendous prestige to foreign trade-marks of companies from developed industrial countries and, on the other, generates a mood of pessimism and an inferiority complex with respect to all products of local science and industry. Paradoxically enough, unnecessary imports of sophisticated technology and its use by insufficiently trained workers add to the inefficiency of the industrial system.

[20] The same view is expressed, *inter alia*, in the ILO study already quoted (see footnote 18).

[21] Compare Gunnar Myrdal, *Asian Drama*, vol. III, New York pp. 2077–2108 ("A note on positive operational controls").

[22] I. M. D. Little calls "an economic horror" an import bias of this kind, so frequently associated with projects financed from abroad, whether from private or from public funds. He goes on to say that the shortage of project-designing capacity accounts for neglecting small projects in favour of big ones (I. M. D. Little, "Aid: project programme and procurement tying", in *Towards a Strategy of Development Co-operation with Special Reference to Asia*, Rotterdam, 1967, pp. 54–56).

[23] For an excellent analysis of the irreducible opposition between "autonomous" and "imitative" (*refleja*) modernization, see Darcy Ribeiro, "Política de desarrollo autónomo de la Universidad Latino-americana", *Gaceta de la Universidad*, Montevideo, April 1968, pp. 27–39.

[24] Exploration of outer space and the armaments race are two instances of scientific rationality put at the service of irrationality, so emphatically exposed by Herbert Marcuse (see, for example, his *One-Dimensional Man*).

The ways of remedying this situation are by no means easy. I shall deal with this matter in the last section of this chapter. Here I shall limit myself to indicating the broad approach:

(a) A revision of policies of support to industrialization is called for with a view to increasing the opportunity cost of capital and decreasing the opportunity cost of labour, which is by no means tantamount to decreasing wages.

(b) Imports of technology should be continuously scrutinized and made selective on the basis of a long-range research and industrial policy.

(c) At the same time financial and fiscal advantages (tax rebates, subsidies, government contracts) should be given to industrialists who develop and apply domestically designed technologies and purchase locally produced equipment, subject of course to some broad criterion of efficiency of such technologies and equipment.[25] It is to be hoped that such technologies and equipment would be better adapted to the specific conditions and factor proportions of the country concerned (the latter will be better reflected by the price system thanks to fiscal and financial measures mentioned above).

(d) Such advantages would be meaningless without an elaborate policy of research oriented towards the basic problems of the country and carried out with active support from the State with a view to increasing and diversifying the supply of viable domestically designed techniques.

(e) Although the emphasis in the above policy guidelines has been put on indirect controls, some direct controls, such as scrutinizing and licensing of major industrial projects, seem advisable. The opportunity of entrusting a single government agency with all imports of technology should also be examined;[26] such imports should be dissociated whenever possible from imports of capital.

---

[25] The UNESCO conference on Application of Science and Technology to Asian Development, which met in New Delhi in August 1968, adopted a resolution to this effect (see UNESCO, *Conférence sur l'Application de la Science et de la Technique au Développement de l'Asie, Partie I: Conclusions et Recommandations*, Paris, 1969, pp. 20–21).

[26] Such a suggestion is contained in a paper by Y. Nayudamma, Director of the Central Leather Research Institute in Madras, published in *Science and the Human Condition in India and Pakistan*, ed. by W. Morehouse, Rockefeller University Press, New York, 1965.

(f) Finally, through concerted political, economic and cultural action it is necessary to create a climate of greater self-reliance, which should not be mistaken, however, for autarky, xenophobia, and ethnocentric exaltation of real and imaginary national achievements.

Coexistence of asynchronic technologies

It has often been said that India is passing directly from the cow-dung to the nuclear energy age. This is true, but so long as the transition lasts, Indians will continue to live in both ages; for quite a time it will still be possible to find Indians who work in the most up-to-date industrial plants but use cow-dung as fuel for their cooking at home.

So long as such asynchronism opposes industrial economy to household practices, the conflict is not dangerous, at least economically. But the problem becomes quite different when an artisan-type workshop must face the competition of a modern plant. Free access of British manufactured goods to the Indian market in the past ruined local crafts that had been flourishing. It is true that history passed the same verdict on European crafts and cottage industries in the nineteenth century, but if the destructive process was no less intense, the opportunities of getting jobs in the new industries were probably bigger, as production processes were still quite labour-intensive and the numbers of competing workers were not so frightfully big in relation to the plants which were being built; even so, Europe paid an excessively high price, in social terms, for industrialization and was unable to solve the employment problems until the middle of the twentieth century. At any rate, with the present galloping population growth in the developing countries and the prevailing capital intensity in production processes, a repetition of the European path becomes altogether impossible. In these circumstances, protection must be offered to crafts and cottage industries, on social if not on economic grounds, as it would be unwise to add to the already existing pressure of overt and disguised unemployment that displaced cottage industries workers.

The best protection, of course, consists in keeping certain lines of production of consumer goods free from modern industrial competition by operating a selective system of investment and import controls. But such a policy is untenable in the long run, because of concerted pressures from consumers and industrialists. The former do not want to be deprived of the advantages—some real, others imaginary but nevertheless strongly believed in—of being catered for with modern industrial goods, mostly when they are cheaper than traditional goods (but this is not always the case). The latter use—and often misuse—the argument of competitiveness to claim access to a market which offers the easiest opportunities (in terms of the amount of capital required and degree of complexity of technology) of setting up modern industries; profits in such industries may run quite high if costs of production are considerably cheaper than in cottage industries, but prices are still governed by the costs of the latter.

As to government intervention, while it could be reasonably effective with respect to import controls (although we are not too optimistic about their ability to prevent contraband altogether), applying controls to all private industrial investment, including small and medium plants, would require the setting-up of heavy and probably inefficient administrative machinery. At any rate, what we are discussing here is a somewhat theoretical case, as in practically all the developing countries the introduction of modern industries has started in lines of production that were directly competitive with the existing cottage industries.

The next best solution would be to operate a system of subsidies for the cottage industries financed out of special additional taxes imposed on competitive products manufactured by modern industries. This is actually the Indian practice as far as certain cotton textiles are concerned. This solution has three weaknesses, however. First, it has a negative effect on the consumers, who pay an additional indirect duty imposed on an item of mass consumption which should, on the contrary, be exempt from duties.[27] Second, paying subsidies to altogether inefficient industries makes little sense; the minimum productivity criterion (value-added equal at least to a minimum wage) evoked in the

---

[27] The textbook preference for direct taxes and horror of indirect taxes should be opposed, as it is based on two wrong assumptions:

(a) Direct taxes are not equitable so long as the richer taxpayers can evade them while the poorer ones cannot.

(b) Indirect taxes may be equitable if they are not imposed on mass-consumption goods but, instead, made strongly progressive when we get into the range of "non-essentials" and "luxuries".

context of intermediate technologies comes once more to the fore. Third, it is to be feared that owners of workshops and cottage industries will try to compensate for the economic inefficiency of their establishments by exploiting their workers to the utmost limit; no amount of sound legislation is likely to be effective in conditions of acute competition for jobs.

Thus subsidizing of cottage industries should be made selective and, at the same time, efforts should be made to rationalize them along intermediate technology lines. Data assembled for different Indian cottage industries point to an extraordinary diversity of economic performance, ranging from industries that are utterly uneconomic and undefendable, even on social grounds, to a few quite reasonable and prosperous ones (see Table 9.1).

An altogether different solution would consist in integrating cottage industries into the industrial structure of the country through an elaborate pattern of collaboration with modern industries. The case of Japan and its articulated dualism is often quoted, though discussions on the subject lack some clarity, as cottage and small-scale modern industries[28] are altogether different things, especially when small-scale modern industries become so narrowly specialized that they can practically enjoy all the advantages of economies of scale while remaining a family business from the managerial point of view, as well as that of the capital necessary to start them. It might be useful to examine, at this stage, whether the Japanese experience really offers useful lessons for present-day developing countries.

Japan: a model for developing countries?

I should start by pointing to four differences which sharply differentiate Japanese growth from that of the great majority of developing countries.

First, for the last hundred years Japanese development has been oriented by effective government action, even though appearances may

---

[28] See, for example, the important study of Dhar and Lydall, *The Role of Small Enterprises in Indian Economic Development*, Bombay, 1961. See also Staley and Morse, *Modern Small Industry for Developing Countries*, New York, 1965, and Shigeru Ishikawa, *Economic Development in Asian Perspective*, Kinokuniya Bookstore, Tokyo, 1967.

TABLE 9.1

Selected indexes by techniques affecting the choice of techniques in cottage industries : India's case

	Number of persons employed per unit of production	Number of working days per person employed	Amount of fixed capital required per unit of production (rupees)	Annual earnings of unit of production (rupees)	Self-employment (SE) or wage employment (WE)	Cottage ratio (percentage)
Rice milling						
The *pestle-and-mortar* method	2	150	10	131.4	SE	80
The ordinary *Dhenki* method	2.5	150	40	183	SE	
The improved *Assam Dhenki* method	2	150	40	335.7	SE	
The *Chakki-Dhenki* method	5	150	355	432	WE	
Factory sector	53	195	57,552	16,802	WE	
Vegetable oil						
The ordinary *Ghani* method	1.5	300	500	302	SE	80
The improved *Ghani* method	1.5	300	650	764	SE	
Factory sector (ordinary)	55	195	138,020	56,530	WE	
Factory sector (hydrogenerated)	312	303	2,040,667	1,554,599	WE	
Sugar						
The cottage *Gur* industry	4	100	513	120	WE	70
The cottage *Khandsari* industry	4	100	2,125	9,902	WE	
Factory sector	804	138	3,024,923	1,350,925	WE	
Cotton yarn spinning (twenties)						
The ordinary *Charka* method	1	300	10	35.8	SE	30
The *Ambar Charka* method	1	300	100	312.9	SE	
Factory sector	854	300	17,450,000	2,050,000	WE	

Cotton cloth weaving					
The *throw-shuttle* hand-loom method	1.25	300	5	381.5	SE
The *fly-shuttle* hand-loom method	1.25	300	40	576	SE
The *Banaras* semi-automatic hand-loom method	1.5	300	200	1,920	SE
The *Madanpura* semi-automatic pedal hand-loom method	1.5	300	250	2,880	SE
Non-automatic power-loom in cottage sector	1.16	300	4,000	2,250	WE
Non-automatic power-loom in a cottage mill	945	300	2,524,000	1,080,000	WE
Tanning					
As shown by *Aligarh* Survey	2	295	675	240	SE
A village tanning centre	7	300	20,500	1,050	WE
A centre proposed by the *Khadi* Board	20	300	20,000	45,540	WE
Factory sector	99	315	111,350	68,650	WE
Leather footwear					
A cottage establishment	2.5	300	1,035	2,370	WE
Factory sector (1960)	237	295	66,809	24,117	WE
Paper					
A cottage unit operated by bullock power reported by the *Khadi* Board	4	160	3,500	−660	SE
A cottage unit operated by a 3-h.p. motor engine reported by the *Khadi* Board	4	160	4,100	−628	SE
Factory sector	689	299	5,707,680	2,044,790	WE

Continued on page 208

TABLE 9.1 (*Contd.*)

	Number of persons employed per unit of production	Number of working days per person employed	Amount of fixed capital required per unit of production (rupees)	Annual earnings of unit of production (rupees)	Self-employment (SE) or wage employment (WE)	Cottage ratio (percentage)
Matches						
A *Karkhana* establishment as proposed by the *Khadi* Board	7.5	300	2,000	1,500	WE	65
Factory sector	424	278	652,222	815,778	WE	
Soap						
Prasad's personal inquiry	2	300	320	581	SE	75
A *Karkhana* establishment as proposed by the *Khadi* Board	4	300	8,000	1,068.8	WE	
Factory sector	237	296	1,422,754	2,603,419	WE	

Sources: For the figures other than the factory sector, see Kodamath Prasad, *Technological Choice under Development Planning. A Case Study in the Small Scale Industries of India*, Popular Prakashan, Bombay, 1963, pp. 45, 88–147; for the factory sector, Government of India, *Census of Indian Manufactures, Fifth–Thirteenth (1958)*, *Indian Textile Industry, Annual Statistical Digest, 1960*, K. Prasad, *op. cit.*, and Government of India, *Annual Survey of Industries, 1960*, vol. I–XV.

Notes: The annual earnings of a unit of production was calculated in the case of cottage establishments without counting the cost of family labour. In calculating the cost, it is assumed that the fixed and working capital is borrowed at an interest of 16 per cent per annum, which is higher than the rate prevailing in the factory sector. In the case of the factory sector, annual earnings are arrived at residually by subtracting wages and salaries from the gross value added; hence it corresponds to gross profit.

(Reproduced from Shigeru Ishikawa, *Economic Development in Asian Perspective*, Kinokuniya Bookstore, Tokyo, 1967, pp. 432–433.)

suggest an economy with relatively few controls. As early as 1884, a bulky official study of economic conditions in Japan, *Kogyo Iken* (industrial proposal), set out targets for a ten-year time span, matching them with substantial policy recommendations. *Kogyo Iken* should be considered as the world's first development plan.[29]

Second, it was largely autonomous in the sense that it depended only to a very small extent on inflows of foreign capital, while imports of know-how were made selective by means of a long-term policy; one could almost say that policies with respect to science and technology were the backbone of government development strategy. Although Japan's performance in foreign trade has always attracted a lot of attention, we should not forget that Japanese industrialization was strongly import-substituting, partly because of military convenience and partly because of an acute shortage of foreign exchange.[30]

[29] See Ichiro Inukai and A. R. Tussing, "*Kogyo Iken*: Japan's Ten Year Plan, 1884", *Economic Development and Cultural Change*, **16,** no. 1, October 1967. The authors of the article quoted summarize the highlights of this document in the following way: "A few of *Kogyo Iken*'s points of special interest might be mentioned here. First, it reveals in remarkable clarity the impact of the first steps toward industrialization and westernization on the backward Japanese economy. The conflict between modernization and the traditional cultural-economic legacy is a universal aspect of economic development; in the *Kogyo Iken* we get detailed insights into the manner in which these conflicts arose and into their social costs. Second, it was the *Kogyo Iken* which first defined the central role of the indigenous components of the national economy in modern economic growth in Japan and projected the growth of agricultural productivity within a traditional framework of small-scale farming. The *Kogyo Iken* explicitly raised the now fashionable controversy over 'balanced or unbalanced' growth; after considering the outcome of previous industrialization policies, it called for a shift in the emphasis of development efforts in favour of agriculture and rural industries. Third, the development programme outlined was one of self-help. The fact that Japan could not rely on foreign aid in the modern sense directed her to the maximum utilization of her comparative advantages, especially in the setting of export targets which would utilize the supply of the low-cost labour. Last, the role of the government in economic development was closely examined. In the present under-developed countries, there is a tremendous gap between the 'policy-maker's world of economy' and the 'people's world of economy'. Calculations which are rational to the economic planners are not necessarily rational to the people whose participation is crucial to the achievement of the plan. The over-all approach of the *Kogyo Iken* was one of consciously attempting to bridge this gap, an issue often neglected in present-day growth plans."

[30] Compare the following remark by a leading Japanese economist: "In fact, it could even be said paradoxically that if foreign exchange had been more abundantly available in those early Meiji years Japan might have depended longer upon foreign supplies for many of the capital goods required in the development stage. As it was, the very fact of limitation in foreign exchange earnings, combined with the inflow of cheap con-

Third, already at the beginning of the Meiji era Japan had developed an infrastructure and an educational system far more advanced than those existing at present in many developing countries. A modern public educational system was inaugurated in 1872 with an enrolment of 25 per cent of children of school age. The enrolment ratio increased to 95 per cent as early as 1905, and in 1907 six-year school attendance was made compulsory.[31] I believe Shigero Ishikawa, author of an important study, *Economic Development in Asian Perspective*,[32] is right when he insists on the contribution of this infrastructure to the success of Japanese agricultural policies and, at the same time, warns against the hopes of easy transplantation of Japanese labour-intensive methods of cultivation to other countries where such infrastructure (mostly in irrigation) and educational facilities may be lacking. We may add to this an efficient administrative machine—a rare phenomenon indeed—of invaluable importance to the development process.[33]

Fourth, the war—and still more the post-war—performance of the Japanese economy is characterized by a very low standard of popular consumption as compared to the national per capita income. Not only do savings run very high[34] but the social distribution of income is uneven. Before the war Japanese peasants had been subjected to heavy exactions by the fiscal system, although the amount of public investment in agriculture should not be underestimated when describing the pattern of capital accumulation in that country.[35]

---

sumer goods which could not be prevented under the circumstances, helped strengthen the psychological attitude of what is sometimes called reactive nationalism and could be said to have hastened the development of capital goods industries at home" (Shigeto Tsuru, "An aspect of Japan's economic development. The rise of capitalism and the role of agriculture", in *The Structure and Development in Asian Economies*, The Japan Economic Research Centre, December 1968, p. 22).

[31] M. Hiratsouka, "L'enseignement au Japon", *Le Courrier de l'UNESCO*, September to October 1968, pp. 19–24.

[32] This book, issued under the auspices of the Institute of Economic Research, Hitotsubashi University, was published in Tokyo in 1967.

[33] See Kato Shuichi, "Le Japon: pays de contrastes", *Les Temps Modernes*, February 1969, pp. 1348–1349, for some interesting remarks on "occidentalization" based on public institutions and the bureaucratically minded Japanese élite.

[34] Gross savings in 1964 reached 37.4 per cent of the gross national product.

[35] See Ishikawa, *op. cit.*, chap. 4, pp. 290–356.

The Japanese economy now combines modern and efficient production with a consumption which is still low and traditional.[36]

To my knowledge no other society would accept such a pattern of growth, while, with imposed authoritarian solutions, there is a risk of getting the worst of both worlds: the evils of dictatorship and a lack of dynamic development. We should not forget that the bulk of the Japanese population is now having substantial increases in its standards of living thanks to a combination of two factors: a very low point of departure and an extraordinarily high rate of economic growth.

With these general remarks as a background, we may turn now to the more specific problem of industrial dualism. Its existence till a very recent date is attested by the data reproduced in Table 9.2 pertaining to 1957.

According to Okita, about half of Japanese exports still come from small and medium-size enterprises, mostly specializing in labour-intensive products. Several small-scale industries work as subcontractors for large industries. From the managerial and technical point of view collaboration between small- and large-scale industries in Japan provides an example of unequalled efficiency. But we should not forget the important negative features of the system: the big gap in working conditions and wages between workers in the two industrial sectors and the total dependence and subordination of many small-scale specialized industries to big companies which enjoy a monopoly position for their products. Moreover, commendable as it may seem at first sight, the Japanese pattern of industrial division of labour between large- and small-scale industries may prove ill-suited to the needs of developing countries precisely because of its heavy dependence on a highly developed infrastructure and managerial skills.[37]

---

[36] For a general description of the Japanese economy see Saburo Okita, "La croissance rapide du Japon d'après-guerres", *Analyse et Prévision*, no. V, 1968, pp. 1–28.

[37] Compare the following observations of W. Paul Strassman, *Technological Change and Economic Development*, Cornell University Press, Ithaca, New York, 1965, p. 168: "As important as the choice of technique, however, is the modern setting in which small-scale Japanese industry moves. Electric power is cheap; the transportation network is good; and access to auxiliary services, such as sizing, dyeing, mercerizing, electroplating, and case hardening, is convenient. Efficient, above all, are the dependable interrelations among contracting, subcontracting, and sub-subcontracting firms and the meeting of

TABLE 9.2
Capital intensity and wage level in Japanese industry, 1957

Size of enterprise (number of workers)	Ratio of gross output to fixed capitals	Fixed capital per worker	Labour productivity (2 × 3) (thousands of yen)	Ratio of gross profit to fixed capital	Gross profit per worker (3 × 5)	Wage per worker (4 − 6) (thousands of yen)
1	2	3	4	5	6	7
1– 3	0.139	93	13	0.043	4	9
4– 9	0.186	97	18	0.082	8	10
10– 19	0.256	90	23	0.133	12	11
20– 29	0.269	97	26	0.144	14	12
30– 49	0.284	102	29	0.167	17	12
50– 99	0.258	136	35	0.162	22	13
100–199	0.221	186	41	0.145	27	14
200–299	0.202	233	47	0.133	31	16
300–499	0.168	345	58	0.119	41	17
500–999	0.146	447	65	0.103	46	19
1,000+	0.100	769	77	0.068	52	25
Total	0.133	324	43	0.083	27	16

I should not like to end this digression on Japan's experience without insisting once more on the fundamental role which was ascribed in its strategy of growth to a deliberate government policy of acquiring foreign science and technology in such a way as to avoid costly and unnecessary duplication of technological imports, to channel the flow of foreign technology to a few critical areas of the economy, and to combine selective imports with domestic research aimed at assimilating, developing, and frequently improving the imported know-how.[38] This

quality standards and of delivery schedules. Perhaps this disciplined coordination is a unique survival of a pre-industrial hierarchical social pattern, the *oyabunkibun*, or 'boss-henchman' system with its deeply conditioned feelings of mutual obligation. It is worth nothing, too, that modern subcontracting and the great rise of Japanese small enterprises (in contrast with dwarfs employing five or less) came *after* the mid-1920s. Perhaps that crucial dependability was in part a product of industrialization, of what Veblen called the cultural incidence of the machine process.

"Premature copying of labour-intensive, small-scale subcontracting may therefore not be as efficient around the Caribbean Sea and the Indian Ocean as in Japan. Backward economies lack managerial skill and reliability more than capital."

[38] See Okita, *op. cit.*, and also the study on the transfer of technologies by C. H. G. Oldham, C. Freeman, and E. Turkcan (UNCTAD, document TD/28/Suppl. 1, 1 November 1967).

experience of Japan has been recently contrasted by Indian scientists with that of India. Criticism is being levelled at unnecessary foreign collaboration agreements which do not really add new elements to the know-how already existing in the country but are bound to aggravate the balance-of-payments problems; such collaboration agreements would seem to be motivated either by the desire of Indian industrialists to produce under the cover of some attractive foreign trade-mark or by the pressures of exporters of equipment and know-how made possible by means of the mechanism of doubly tied foreign assistance. On the other hand, the existing research and equipment-making capacities in such important fields as the fertilizer and machinery and equipment industries are at present severely underutilized, partly because of the pressure of foreign vested interests.[39]

THREE NOTES ON THE TOOL-BOX

I do not intend to proceed in this section to a review of the various techniques recommended for the selection of techniques. This has become a subject for textbooks and, besides, UNIDO has issued a number of useful papers on the subject.[40] I shall confine myself to a brief comment on the common substratum of such techniques, their applicability, and their limitations. The other two notes contain suggestions for further work, which might perhaps prove useful.

Social cost-benefit analysis: advantages and limitations

Social cost-benefit analysis is a tool by means of which project-makers are expected to harmonize their individual projects with the national objectives set forth in the national development plan, which in turn

[39] See M. M. Suri, *Impact of Foreign Collaboration on Indian Research and Development* (address delivered by the then director of Central Mechanical Engineering Research Institute in Durgapur before the Association of Scientific Workers of India on 13 April 1968) and also the interview granted to the *Hindustan Times Weekly* on 16 February 1969. See also K. R. Chakravorty, *Scientists and National Development* (lecture by the Manager, Planning and Development Division, The Fertilizer Corporation of India Ltd.).

[40] We refer in particular to papers by A. K. Sen, S. Marglin, F. Weisskopf, and K. Laski.

may be modified as a result of knowledge acquired in the process of project-making.

Thus social cost-benefit analysis differs from the traditional commercial profitability analysis in its aims and criteria of evaluation, as it takes into account the different goals of the plan and some external effects of the investment, including those operating outside the market, while commercial analysis is centred on profitability alone.

A practical way of incorporating the macroeconomic preferences into evaluation criteria used in social cost-benefit analysis consists in using shadow or accounting prices instead of market prices for capital, foreign exchange, and occasionally labour,[41] and social rates of discount of future costs and benefits. The different objectives incorporated in the national plans may be, furthermore, given different weights, as suggested by an influential school of thought led by Jan Tinbergen.[42]

But the choice of shadow prices, discount rates, and relative weights assigned to the different goals embodied in the plan involves the exercise of discretion and reflects necessarily political value judgements. Are policy-makers really capable of making their choices in a rather abstract manner consisting in setting values for the parameters mentioned above, or should they be given an opportunity for a more explicit discussion of the alternatives, in particular of the fundamental choice between "more jam today and more jam tomorrow", to use Joan Robinson's words?[43] I am not convinced by the argument that an imperfect quantified hypothesis is better than none at all, unless one postulates the use of sophisticated simulation techniques with different alternative sets of prices.

Is it at all possible to build a homogeneous goal function by means of attributing weights to different and frequently conflicting goals, or would it be a better, though less ambitious, alternative to choose maximization of consumption in a given time horizon, subject to constraints with respect to the relative share of investment in, and social distribution

---

[41] As the planner is primarily interested in changing the substitution rate between capital and labour it is not necessary to manipulate both the prices at the same time to get the desired proportion.

[42] See also A. K. Sen, *The Role of Policy-makers in Project Formulation and Evaluation*, UNIDO, 1968, which gives an excellent idea of the logic of social cost-benefit analysis.

[43] Joan Robinson, *Economic Philosophy*, London, 1962.

of, income? In the latter approach, employment objectives could be taken care of by means of the adequate selection of techniques at the project level and other possible goals kept in mind during the long process of successive adjustment of the plan.

As for the determination of shadow prices, it is often assumed that they should be "equilibrium prices". But, even if we disregard the difficulty of computing such prices,[44] do equilibrium prices really have normative significance? Myrdal's criticism of Tinbergen on this point seems very well taken[45] and the following conclusion of his argument, though written in the context of South Asia, has a wider application: "It cannot be denied that speculation in terms of accounting prices or shadow prices relates to real and important problems raised by the attempts to plan for development in the underdeveloped countries in South Asia. Most certainly there is, for instance, a vast underutilization of the labor force in agriculture and elsewhere in the economies of the region; similarly, in the organized sector there is a greater scarcity of capital, and particularly foreign exchange, than is indicated by their prices. . . . These facts and policy inferences should be taken into account when deciding on institutional reforms and prices policies and other operational controls. Planning should reflect the political choices of the planners and, behind them, the governments and it should be founded on as much factual knowledge as is attainable, including that pertaining to the responses of people to prices and price changes. The abstract and metaphysical concept of accounting prices cannot help to solve the theoretical and practical problems facing South Asian planners. It stands out as a typical example of the pseudo-knowledge, given a learned and occasionally mathematical form, that unfortunately has formed a major part of the contribution of Western economics to the important tasks of ascertaining the facts in underdeveloped countries and creating a framework for policies designed to engender and direct development" (p. 2039).

The doubts and criticisms raised above should not invalidate the social cost-benefit analysis but rather point to its limitations and indicate that it should not serve as the only basis for decision about the advisability

---

[44] Every change in the economic situation or in the plan goals requires a new round on the computer.

[45] See Gunnar Myrdal, *Asian Drama*, vol. III, New York, 1968, app. 5, pp. 2031–2039.

of making an investment.[46] Such a decision should be taken on other grounds in the course of the planning process. The social cost-benefit analysis steps in as a tool for "variant thinking" and comparing alternative designs and technologies with a view to choosing at the project level solutions that are, in a first approximation, optional from the macroeconomic point of view. Reduced to this dimension, it does not differ, except for some technicalities, from the methods of analysis of the "effectiveness of investment" used in centrally planned economies.

Even though I have played down the role of social cost-benefit analysis and its applicability does not extend beyond public investment and, to some extent, private projects subject to screening and licensing by the State, I consider that its systematic application could bring about substantial improvements in the realm of the actual selection of techniques.

Complicating the selection of techniques

At this stage it might be useful to introduce two complications.

One is relatively easy to handle once it is realized. In fact, a project often implies several independent choices of technologies and it may be opportune to have asynchronic technologies and equipment of different vintages and capital intensity inside the same factory (e.g. the selection of an up-to-date highly automated technology for the basic process does not, in itself, preclude the retention of traditional techniques for packing and internal transport, as well as for management and trading).

The other is a more fundamental one. I have hitherto assumed for the sake of simplicity, that a technology is a two-dimensional vector characterized by outlays of capital and labour. But neither of these two factors is homogeneous, and it might be tempting, therefore, to describe technologies as n-dimensional vectors, introducing explicitly such factors as foreign exchange, skills, scarce raw materials and, with respect to agriculture, land.

The set of efficient technologies described in this way will consist

---

[46] Except perhaps for foreign-trade-oriented projects, which are all directly comparable as yielding or saving foreign exchange.

of all technologies which differ from a standard one at least by one lower and one higher input.[47]

How can a selection be made under these conditions? Two approaches are possible.

One leads us back to the use of accounting prices. Subject to their adequacy, optimal solutions can be found.

The other is more pedestrian and does not lead to optimal solutions, but it has the advantage of retaining for further analysis projects which are for some reason outstanding. It consists in successively ranking all the technologies according to each criterion and picking up for further consideration those which either rank very high with respect to one criterion or rank high with respect to several criteria. Such a procedure might eventually lead to redesigning of a syncretic solution. Of course, such an approach makes sense only if several alternatives are possible. But in compensation its applicability extends beyond the selection of techniques proper. When developed, it might become a subsidiary tool for investment decision-making, i.e. the area which escapes the social cost-benefit analysis.

A suggestion for the classification of agricultural technologies

A three-factor analysis on the lines suggested above is attempted below with respect to agricultural techniques in order to overcome the lack of precision attached to expressions like "intensive" and "extensive" agriculture.

Let there be a standard technique T with average inputs of land, capital, and labour per unit of output. I shall distinguish six types of techniques, all of them efficient, differing from T by factor proportions[48] (see Table 9.3).

Instances of each of the six techniques and of their applicability are summarized in Table 9.4.

No doubt actual choices become much more complicated, as agricul-

---

[47] If they only differ by higher inputs, they are inefficient. If they only differ by lower inputs, this means that the standard technique is not efficient and should be discarded.

[48] The exercise could be usefully complicated by introducing the distinction between investment capital and working capital.

TABLE 9.3
Types of agricultural techniques

Denomination	Land	Capital	Labour
1. Land extensive	>	—	—
2. Labour saving	>	>	—
3. Capital saving	>	—	>
4. Labour intensive	—	—	>
5. Land saving	—	>	>
6. Capital intensive	—	>	—

TABLE 9.4
Agricultural techniques and their applicability

Denomination	Examples	Applicability
1. Land extensive	Cattle breeding on natural pasture lands	Very favourable land–man ratio
2. Labour saving	Mechanized agriculture with relatively low yields per hectare (maximization of output per man)	Favourable land–man ratio; shortage and/or expensiveness of labour
3. Capital saving	Settlement of virgin land with little equipment	Favourable land–man ratio; strong demographic pressure; shortage of capital
4. Labour intensive	Intensive agriculture with small inputs (maximization of active agricultural population per hectare)	Unfavourable land–man ratio; strong demographic pressure; shortage of capital
5. Land saving	Intensive agriculture with more inputs (maximization of yield per hectare)	Same natural and demographic conditions as in 4; more availability of capital (higher stage of development than 4)
6. Capital intensive	Industrialized agriculture (maximization of both yield per hectare and productivity per man)	Unfavourable land–man ratio; shortage and/or expensiveness of labour

tural production functions require certain combinations of inputs and accurate time-scheduling of operations. In these circumstances combinations of different techniques may be required. Thus, for instance, capital-intensive irrigation[49] and labour-displacing mechanization of certain

[49] Assuming that it cannot be entirely done by labour-intensive methods.

operations may be a precondition for passing from one low-yield to two high-yield labour-absorbing crops per year. Moreover, as can be seen from Table 9.2, certain types of technology are only possible for given outputs, so that the real choice is between different output-mixes subject to the principle of substitutability.[50]

To the best of my knowledge, little systematic work on these subjects has up to now been made available to planners in spite of their practical relevance to the developing countries. According to the particular case, expansion of agricultural output by means of land-extensive, capital-saving, or land-saving methods should provide a substantial number of additional jobs, while at the same time generating more demand for industrial inputs and consumer goods and, therefore, more employment in the industrial sector. This presupposes, however, that research work on capital-saving and labour-absorbing technologies and crops in agriculture should be given a high priority, a priority which, unfortunately, it has not been given, at least in Latin America.

The Latin American scene

Urbanization, industrialization, and employment

The magnitude of the employment problem faced by Latin America is summarized in the following estimate: in 1960 the equivalent of 25.7 per cent of the active population, i.e. about 70 million persons, were unemployed or underemployed.[51] The demographic explosion is responsible for aggravating the employment situation but deep reasons should be sought in the socioeconomic structure and in the specific features of the recent industrialization processes.

The former account for the severe underutilization of land and natural resources and the consequent migratory push of the rural population towards urban areas. The latter explain that there has been surprisingly little change in the employment structure as a result of the rapid growth of industries. A few data will illustrate these points.

[50] The range of substitutions becomes, of course, very broad when we introduce foreign trade into the picture.
[51] ILPES, *Elementos para la Elaboración de una Política de Desarrollo con Integración para América Latina*, Santiago, 1968 (mimeographed), p. II.1.

According to data produced by Z. Slawinski (Table 9.5), the relative share of manufacturing employment decreased from 13.7 to 13.4 per cent of the active population between 1925 and 1960. These figures conceal, it is true, a sharp decrease of employment in cottage industries and artisan-type workshops—from 10.2 to 6.8 per cent—and a strong increase in the share of organized modern industries from 3.5 to 7.5 per cent. We should note, however, that the additional jobs in modern industries were not being generated quickly enough to offset the decrease of employment in cottage industries.[52]

Moreover, in spite of the spectacular progress in industrial output which accounts by now for about one-quarter of the continent's gross national product, only twenty-five out of every thousand Latin Americans were employed in industry in 1960. Hence the pessimistic but reasonable assumption made by Z. Slawinski that, from 1965 to 1975, industry could not absorb more than 14 per cent of additional labour, as compared with about 13 per cent for construction.

More recent data covering the period up to 1965 confirm the continuation of the trend so exhaustively analysed by Slawinski. Thus Felipe Herrera, president of Inter-American Development Bank, quoted the following figures in a speech: from 1950 to 1965 the urban share[53] of the active population rose from 44.8 to 53.3 per cent but at the same time the share of those employed in manufacturing industries decreased from 14.2 to 13.8 per cent. At the same time, employment in construction and utilities increased from 7.8 to 9.1 per cent, while the most considerable increase in employment took place in "other services", public administration, and non-specified activities (from 22.8 to 30.3 per cent).[54] Some people argue that such an increase in tertiary employment is a positive feature characteristic of modern industrial development and a kind of "employment multiplier effect" generated

[52] We are speaking of relative shares and not of absolute figures. The total number of employed people did increase substantially during the thirty-five years under discussion. But the increase in employment was slower than the population growth rate and the active population decreased from 35 to 33.1 per cent of the total population.

[53] Population is increasing in Latin America by about 3 per cent per year, but urban population is growing at 4 per cent per year and in many towns at even 6 per cent per year.

[54] Speech delivered at the Tenth Assembly of Bank Governors, Guatemala City, 22 April 1969.

TABLE 9.5

Latin America: Distribution of active population by economic sectors and as percentage of total population, 1925 to 1960

	Distribution of active population				Active population as a percentage of total population			
	1925	1950	1955	1960	1925	1950	1955	1960
Agricultural sector	61.3	53.1	50.0	47.3	21.5	18.1	16.8	15.7
Non-agricultural sector	38.7	46.9	50.0	52.7	13.5	15.9	16.8	17.4
1. Production of goods and basic services	19.5	23.4	24.6	25.4	6.8	8.0	8.3	8.4
(a) Mining	1.0	1.1	1.1	1.0	0.3	0.4	0.4	0.3
(b) Manufacturing	13.7	14.4	14.3	13.4	4.8	4.9	4.8	4.8
(i) Industrial sector	3.5	6.9	7.1	7.5	1.2	2.3	2.4	2.5
(ii) Cottage industries sector	10.2	7.5	7.2	6.8	3.6	2.6	2.4	2.3
(c) Construction	1.6	3.7	4.5	4.9	0.6	1.3	1.5	1.6
(d) Basic services	3.2	4.2	4.7	5.2	1.1	1.4	1.6	1.7
2. Services	19.2	29.5	25.4	27.3	6.7	7.9	8.5	9.0
(a) Trade and finance	6.7	7.9	8.6	9.2	2.3	2.7	2.9	3.0
(b) Public administration	2.2	3.3	3.5	3.7	0.8	1.1	1.2	1.2
(c) Miscellaneous	7.9	9.9	11.0	12.1	2.8	3.3	3.7	4.0
(d) Not specified	2.4	2.4	2.3	2.3	0.8	0.8	0.8	0.8
Total	100.0	100.0	100.0	100.0	35.0	34.0	33.6	33.1

Source: OCDE, *La Structure de la Main-d'œuvre en Amérique Latine, son Évolution au Cours des Dernières Décennies et ses Perspectives à Long Terme, Problèmes de Planification des Ressources Humaines en Amérique Latine et dans le Projet Régional Méditerranéen, Paris, 1967. Travaux du Séminaire Tenu à Lima en Mars 1965 et Documents Complémentaires*, p. 182.

by industrialization. This seems to be, unfortunately, a much too optimistic interpretation as far as Latin America is concerned. Herrera formulates the right diagnosis when he insists on the fact that the increase of employment in services has contributed to the gross national products, but only insignificantly, and links the migratory movements from countryside to town with the unsatisfactory social situation of the rural population.

Hence the problem of marginal population besets Latin American urban development and reflects the incapacity of the industrial sector to react more dynamically to the growing pressure for jobs.

We might, at this point, observe that the appalling poverty of an important section of the rural population affects the situation in two ways. On the one hand, it sets people on the road to the towns; on the other, it reduces the outlets for industrial production. The ILPES study already quoted gives 40 per cent of Latin America's population, i.e. roughly 100 million people, as living below their vital minimum calculated at 90 dollars per year and spending about 89 dollars per family per year. These people practically do not purchase any industrial goods. The extreme inequality of social income distribution in Latin America is shown in Table 9.6. In a sense, this problem of the maldistribution of national income is so preeminent as to make some Latin American economists (e.g. Celso Furtado) believe that it becomes immaterial to discuss such matters as selection of technologies, which are of minor importance as compared with the possible effects on employment of reasonable income policies. While agreeing that income policies should be given priority in all discussions on development strategy for Latin America, I consider, however, that the urgency of the employment problem, as illustrated above, makes it necessary to explore all the possible avenues including that of improving the selection of techniques.

In saying this, I do not want to give the impression that much can be achieved, particularly with respect to industrial employment. The experience of other underdeveloped countries is not very encouraging.

A study on West Bengal shows that substantial industrial development in terms of capital outlay and additions to productive capacity may conceivably continue for several decades with little or no additional labour engaged in manufacture. Colin Clark's criterion—conceiving development statistically as a shift of the percentage distribution in the labour force from agriculture towards industry and services—is not a good indicator therefore for the developing countries.[55] Data assembled by C. Hsieh[56] point to the same phenomenon of employment growth rates lagging behind those of output, particularly in manufacturing industries. The situation seems much better in construction. As to agriculture, the range of expectations is extremely wide because some plans attach a great importance to labour-intensive methods of agricultural development while others, for good or bad reasons, insist on mechanization (see Table 9.7).

Finally I might point to the big intersectorial disparities in labour productivity, which so dramatically emphasize the dualistic industrial structure of Latin America. According to data produced by ECLA, in 1962, gross output per worker in Latin America (excluding Cuba) averaged 1,092 dollars. But this average conceals sectoral differences ranging from 353 dollars in artisan-type production and 511 dollars in agriculture to 3,001 dollars in modern industry, and as much as 5,443 in extractive industries.[57] We should, furthermore, note that the range of productivity inside each sector is also very wide. The general

[55] "In point of fact, India's current development is taking place in a manner quite different from that which characterized the industrial growth of Western Europe and North America, and in a quite different setting, India as a latecomer to the process of industrialization can take advantage of the scientific and technological progress of Europe. Productivity per worker in recently installed manufacturing units in India is, accordingly, very much greater than was possible one hundred and fifty years ago in the early stages of the industrial revolution. There are also important differences of scale. For example, the population of India today exceeds by more than forty times that of England and Wales in 1800.

"What we must realize is that the economic trends of the nineteenth century in Western Europe and North America are no longer adequate guides to the path lying before India in the 1970's, 80's and 90's. Technological developments in production seem to render obsolete our standards for evaluating the significance of changes of working force distribution. We shall have to work out new criteria valid for the age of automation.

"As the development in West Bengal has demonstrated, India is well started along the road to becoming a strong industrial power, and shows many signs of continuing in this direction. But from 1961 onward, India's progress toward modernization is unlikely to be reflected in a sizeable increase in the percentage of workers engaged in manufacture."

Alice and Daniel Thorner, "The twentieth century trend in employment in manufacture in India—as illustrated by the case of West Bengal", in *Essays on Econometrics and Planning Presented to Prof. P. C. Mahalanobis*, Oxford, 1964, p. 305.

[56] C. Hsieh, "Les taux d'augmentation d'emploi dans les plans de développement", *Rev. Int. du Trav.*, no. 1, 1968.

[57] The latter figure goes down to 2,610 dollars if Venezuela is excluded.

TABLE 9.6

Latin America: estimated income distribution, 1960

Income bracket (deciles)	Share of total personal income (percentage)	Average of personal income as a percentage of the general average	Annual per capita income (dollars)	Monthly average income per family
1st	2.1	20	80	40
2nd	2.8	28	110	50
3rd	3.6	35	140	60
4th	4.3	43	170	80
5th	5.4	55	220	100
6th	6.5	65	260	120
7th	8.1	80	320	150
8th	10.7	108	430	200
9th	15.4	155	620	280
10th	41.1	410	1,640	750

Source: *Elementos para la Elaboración de una Política de Desarrollo con Integración para América Latina*, Document prepared by ILPES and CELADE, Santiago, Chile, July 1968, chap. III, p. 11.

trend for the productivity gaps is to increase with time. Thus modern capital-intensive industries continue to develop as *enclaves*; the "spill-over" effect of their high productivity is not very substantial. Slawinski summarized the situation by saying that while 11 per cent of the population belongs to the high productivity bracket which is comparable to the average for Western Europe, as much as 40 per cent of the population has not as yet gone much beyond the poorest South Asian standard.[58]

One conclusion which clearly emerges from these data is the need for a concerted attack. While efforts should be made to avoid unnecessarily high capital intensity in the modern industrial sector, the bulk of additional jobs will have to be provided for quite a time by the low-productivity sectors, where minimum productivity standards should, however, be enforced through a process of rationalization.

[58] *Op. cit.*, p. 218.

TABLE 9.7

Planned or projected annual compound rates of growth of output in employment by sectors

Plan	Total			Agriculture			Industries			Construction			Other sectors		
	R_0	R_n	R_n/R_0	R_0	R_n	R_n/R_0	R_0	R_n	R_n/R_0	R_0	R_n	R_n/R_0	R_0	R_n	R_n/R_0
Mal. II (1961–65)	4.1	2.83	0.70	2.83	2.11	0.75	6.34	3.19	0.50	12.35	11.84	0.96	3.40	2.50	0.74
U.A.R. II (1960–65)	7.4	4.90	0.66	4.06	3.17	0.77	8.16	4.44	0.54	8.01	6.81	0.86	8.88	7.85	0.89
Mal. 20/I (1966–70)	4.9	2.80	0.57	4.00	2.30	0.58	4.10	2.90	0.71	8.50	3.70	0.43	4.90	3.60	0.72
Pak. II (1960–65)	3.7	2.11	0.57	2.65	1.92	0.72	7.1	4.40	0.57	—	8.45	—	3.71	1.64	0.44
Ven. (1963–66)	8.0	4.60	0.57	8.00	0.60	0.75	13.50	5.80	0.43	14.80	18.10	1.20	6.60	5.50	0.83
							4.30	3.30	0.77						
Ceyl. (1959–68)	6.0	3.17	0.53	4.72	1.82	0.39	12.10	5.60	0.46	12.15	10.50	0.85	4.54	3.63	0.80
Pak. III (1965–70)	6.5	3.45	0.53	5.06	2.47	0.49	9.99	5.22	0.52	—	—	—	7.11	3.37	0.72
Phil. (1963–67)	5.8	3.00	0.52	3.00	–0.42	0.14	10.01	10.07	1.07	9.35	5.03	0.54	5.24	5.35	1.04
U.A.R. (1960–65)	7.2	3.19	0.46	5.06	3.17	0.63	14.50	6.03	0.41	–0.40	–1.17	–3.00	4.40	2.67	0.60
Ghana (1963–70)	5.5	2.52	0.46	5.15	0.97	0.19	7.60	6.46	0.85	—	—	—	3.70	3.90	1.06
Tur. I (1963–67)	7.0	3.10	0.45	4.20	1.36	0.32	12.60	6.03	0.50	—	10.67	—	7.27	8.88	1.22
Tun. (1962–71)	6.4	2.58	0.40	3.66	1.84	0.50	8.79	4.61	0.52	10.40	0	—	6.79	5.70	0.84
Tur. II (1968–72)	7.0	2.65	0.38	—	0.59	—	—	4.04	—	—	9.03	—	—	7.57	—
Tur. III (1973–77)	7.0	2.65	0.38	—	0.50	—	—	3.71	—	—	7.11	—	—	6.81	—
Gre. I (1960–64)	6.0	1.92	0.32	3.54	0	0	8.01	3.19	0.40	16.20	—	—	6.60	3.54	0.54
Mar. (1960–64)	6.2	1.61	0.26	3.37	—	—	8.74	—	—	—	—	—	5.55	—	—
Inde. II (1956–61)	4.6	1.17	0.26	3.37	0.36	0.11	8.16	2.11	0.26	6.03	6.81	1.13	4.23	2.83	0.66
Inde. III (1961–66)	6.0	1.55	0.26	4.56	0.69	0.15	12.72	2.20	0.17	—	15.43	—	5.71	4.06	0.65
It. (1955–64)	5.0	1.23	0.25	1.84	–1.14	0.62	6.17	2.74	0.44	—	8.20	—	5.70	2.74	0.48
Gre. II (1965–69)	5.5	1.36	0.25	3.89	0	0	7.11	2.47	0.35	—	—	—	5.50	2.29	0.42
Jap. 5 (1958–62)	5.8	1.37	0.24	2.92	–0.80	0.27	6.32	2.10	0.33	—	—	—	6.42	2.36	0.37
Jap. 10 (1961–70)	7.8	1.24	0.16	2.80	–2.04	0.71	9.00	3.50	0.39	—	—	—	8.40	2.90	0.35

R_0 = annual compound projected rates of increase of output.
R_n = annual projected rates of increase in employment.

INADEQUATE SUPPLY OF TECHNOLOGIES

A major reason for the abuse of highly capital-intensive techniques in the modern sector lies in the inadequate supply of alternative technologies.[59] We cannot really blame entrepreneurs for making wrong choices when they have no opportunity for choice at all.

Such a situation is normal for quite a considerable range of modern industries where the only technology available (at least for the basic manufacturing process, if not for all the stages of production and commercialization) is highly capital intensive. But in many other fields it should be possible to choose from a wide spectrum of efficient techniques of different vintages; such techniques must, however, be made accessible, but the present organization of the technological market in Latin America makes this exceedingly difficult. It is a highly imperfect seller's market dominated by dealers in equipment and foreign consultants, and subject to pressures from powerful vested interests which in their advertising and propaganda skilfully play up such arguments as the need to catch up with the most up-to-date solutions abroad and become competitive.

Moreover, a substantial part of the transfer of know-how in manufacturing industries takes the form of direct foreign investment or collaboration agreements between foreign and local private capitalists. Neither such transfers nor the organization and working of the technological market in Latin America have been sufficiently well studied. The scattered information available is, however, enough to reach alarming conclusions.[60]

The duplication and wasteful transfer of technologies that are well

[59] The bias towards capital-intensive techniques resulting from inadequate industrial policies will be examined in the next section.

[60] We are only dealing here with one particular aspect of direct foreign private investment. Its disastrous effects on the Latin American balance of payments are only too well known. It will be sufficient to recall here that the ratio of expatriation of profits to new direct United States investment in Latin America, as computed by the First National Bank and quoted in *Le Monde* on 4 March 1969, are as follows:

	1965	1966	1967	1968
Latin America	4.0	4.3	7.0	5.0
World	1.4	1.4	1.9	2.0

known and have long been mastered is a common practice. Unsuitable technologies are frequently sold at exorbitant prices, as the purchaser has no choice left. Second-hand equipment, which could be profitably absorbed, is being offered at prices which make it a bad bargain while inflating the value of the capital investment of foreign subsidiaries, which get it from their mother companies.[61] The continued pressure of foreign and local vested interests may be very strong indeed, strong enough to prevent even the adequate utilization of the capabilities already existing in the Latin American countries. The recent experience of the Indian fertilizer industry recalls the situation which prevailed in Brazil with respect to the oil industry in the early fifties, when Petrobras was in its early stages.

The lack of a solid research and development infrastructure works in the same direction. A UNESCO study on research and development in twenty-five developing countries shows that Argentina has the highest expenditure per head: 2.8 dollars per year, as compared with an average of 0.45 dollars for the twenty-five countries covered and about 60 dollars for the five most-developed Western industrial powers.[62]

The bulk of funds is allocated to basic research, as is attested by the examples of Mexico[63] and Venezuela, where in 1963 about 74 per cent of research was basic, 21.5 per cent applied, and only 4.4 per cent went to development.[64]

Foreign-owned industries cannot be expected to foster technological research in the Latin American countries, unless they are forced to it by adequate legislation or induced at some future time to shift part

[61] P. Strassman, *op. cit.*, denies that such practices take place on a large scale, but he produces scanty evidence to support his view.

[62] Data communicated to the participants of a UNESCO seminar in December 1968. This figure should be read in conjunction with the following data available for Pakistan: expenditure on foreign consultants exceeds 1 per cent of the national income, while research gets less than 0.2 per cent. Nuclear energy is getting ten times as much money as research on jute and fisheries—two basic industries for the country. M. U. Hag, "Wasted investment in scientific research", in *Science and the Human Condition in India and Pakistan*, New York, 1965, pp. 126–132.

[63] See V. L. Urquidi and A. L. Vargas, *Educación Superior, Ciencia y Tecnología en el Desarrollo Económico de México*, Mexico, 1967.

[64] Data quoted by Marcel Roche at the Second Meeting of Directors of National Councils of Research in Latin America, held under the auspices of UNESCO in Caracas in December 1968.

of their central research laboratories because of the lower cost of research.[65]

The bulk of the effort should be national and probably government sponsored,[66] but fiscal incentives and legal measures should be provided at the same time to compel private industrialists to support and utilize technological research[67] to a much greater extent than hitherto.[68]

Four particularly negative consequences of the present situation with respect to research should be mentioned here.

First, together with political instability, it accounts for the alarming proportions of the brain drain, both external and internal (from science and technology to adminstrative and commercial careers).

Second, it leaves an unnecessarily large area of the economy for which at present no efficient technologies exist at all because the difference in national endowments and ecological and social conditions makes the transfer of technology either impossible or unlikely, as no scientists abroad happen to be working on such problems and the priorities for research in developed countries do not coincide at all with those of developing countries. Here once more we should recall the need of the low-productivity sectors for efficient techniques in the low range of capital intensity.

Third, lack of reasonable research facilities and experience makes a rational, selective policy of imports of know-how practically impossible.

Lastly, imports of technology which are not being absorbed into the stream of local research and followed up by modernization and improvements lead to the creation of "sectoral and spatial enclaves",[69] which, furthermore, after some years of technological standstill lose

---

[65] Though this point may seem at present far-fetched it should not be overlooked. In many fields research is essentially labour intensive and, once skilled personnel becomes available, developing countries should have a comparative advantage over high-living-cost countries.

[66] See, for example, O. J. Maggiolo, "Política de desarrollo científico y tecnológico de América Latina", in *Gaceta de la Universidad*, Mexico, March/April 1968. See also J. Leite Lopes, "La science, le développement économique et le tiers monde", *Le Monde Scient.*, no. 3, 1968.

[67] See Leite Lopes, *op. cit.*

[68] Lack of interest in research on the part of powerful industries that are considered "progressive" is clearly evidenced by the series of lectures published in São Paulo in 1968 in a volume entitled *Pesquisa Tecnológica na Universidade e na Indústria Brasileiras*.

[69] See Manuel Balboa's speech at 1965 CASTALA in Santiago.

all the glamour of their "up-to-dateness". This technological immobilism accounts, perhaps to a still greater extent than the insufficiency of equipment-producing industries, for the Latin American economy's lack of capacity to reproduce itself, pointed out by S. Dell in his analysis of its vulnerability with respect to foreign trade.[70]

A CRITIQUE OF INDUSTRIAL POLICIES

However narrow the range of choices may be, it is not being adequately utilized because of the capital-intensive bias inherent to present industrial policies in Latin America.

In matter of fact, in order to foster an industrialization chiefly hampered, as it was believed, by lack of capital, excessive fiscal, credit, and foreign exchange advantages were granted to entrepreneurs.

Their combined effect is to render the opportunity cost of investment capital extremely low. Examples of situations where it becomes practically nil are easy to quote. Thus, for example, the author of a study on CORFO reached the following conclusion: "Implicitly, but unmistakably, CORFO converted the hard foreign currency loans to enterprises or agencies into domestic loans. This policy was mainly the consequence of two events: the rampant inflation and the fact that CORFO was lending without a dollar or other escalator clauses. As a result, only a fraction of the real value of these loans has ever been repaid by the recipient enterprises."[71] In general, the real rate of interest has often proved negative and conducive to inflation for those firms having access to bank credit in Chile[72] and, I believe, in other Latin American countries. Thus, what really counts is getting access to credit and government favours. For those who manage it—and it is a matter either of public relations or of a solid financial position—capital is neither scarce nor expensive. The trouble is that the bulk of government support thus accrues to entrepreneurs, who really could manage without it,

[70] S. Dell, "The need for economic integration among underdeveloped countries (with special reference to Latin America)", in *Reshaping the World Economy, op. cit.*, pp. 164–176.
[71] M. Mamalakis, "An analysis of the financial and investment activities of the Chilean Development Corporation: 1936–64", *J. of Dev. Stud.*, January 1969, p. 122.
[72] L. J. Johnson, "Problems of import substitution: the Chilean automobile industry", *Econ. Dev. and Cult. Change*, January 1967, p. 213.

while small-scale industries and workshops are really starved for capital. W. P. Strassman is probably right when he says that the "error is in the direction of using capital and labour too little with one another. The sectors with too much of one factor cannot get, or do not seek, enough of the other".[73]

As to fiscal incentives, the Brazilian legislation providing support for projects approved by SUDENE is an excellent case in point: up to 50 per cent of the income tax due from enterprises may be channelled into such investment and finance up to 50 per cent (and in exceptional cases up to 75 per cent) of the new project, while half of the balance is provided as a loan by SUDENE at a 12 per cent—that is to say, strongly negative—interest rate![74] No wonder that in such circumstances the investment cost of a new job works out at about 6,000 dollars and the employment generated is negligible, as compared with the tremendous pressure of unemployed and underemployed in the Nordeste. Hirschman tries to minimize, however, the distorting effects of this legislation, on the grounds, it is true, that new enterprises would anyhow be using the most advanced technology without trying to make it more labour absorptive. The least one can say is that government policies should not be designed in such a way as to reinforce undesirable features in private sector behaviour.[75]

Next, I should mention fiscal incentives to plough back profits, which once more favour overcapitalization so long as similar advantages are not granted for an increase in the pay-roll as for an accumulation

[73] W. P. Strassman, *Technological Change and Economic Development. The Manufacturing Experience of México and Puerto Rico*, Cornell University Press, Ithaca, N.Y., 1968, p. 148.

[74] See for a description of the theme A. O. Hirschman, "Desenvolvimento industrial no Nordeste brasileiro e o mecanismo de credito fiscal do artigo 34/18", *Revta Bras. de Econ.*, no. 4, December 1967, pp. 5–34.

[75] A full assessment of the working of the fiscal credit mechanism based on article 34/18 would require a discussion of alternative public investment foregone because of the reduction in revenue. On the other hand, it should be remembered that red tape makes investment under the scheme a lengthy affair; in the meantime money due as tax is deposited in a public bank and thus, for all practical purposes, it is transformed into a forced loan to the government. Were these funds properly used, red tape should for once be recommended!

of capital.[76] As Celso Furtado points out, subsidies in the form of low rates of exchange for imports and of preferential credits were being granted mainly for the purchase of equipment, less for construction, and practically not at all for working capital. This created artificial conditions for automation and overcapitalization with respect to fixed capital.[77]

Inflation has been exerting a powerful pressure in the same direction, at least among far-sighted entrepreneurs who, distrustful of liquidity, plough back their profits as quickly as they can into fixed investment and stocks of raw materials and also into construction. In fact, the relatively low cost of construction as compared to that of equipment[78] and the belief that the value of buildings at least keeps pace with the general increase in prices make many industrialists indulge in lavish prestige construction, not at all warranted by the needs of production.[79] Thus, we often get a dismaying situation: capital available in the form of subsidized credit and fiscal rebates is wastefully spent on overcapitalized equipment, while the enterprise's own funds go into unnecessarily big investments in buildings. Intensive investment actually goes hand in hand with the acute shortage of working capital.

While capital is made excessively cheap, labour costs exceed the wage bill by a very substantial margin on account of different "social charges" and taxes proportional to the wage bill, which to make things worse are often used inefficiently or altogether diverted to aims which have little to do with their original purpose. Both entrepreneurs and workers complain: the former because labour costs are high when compared with the productivity level, the latter because they are underpaid, as far as wages are concerned, while the fringe benefits financed out of "social charges" are of very poor quality and add little to the worker's level of living. Of the two, the workers have more reason to complain,

---

[76] See W. P. Strassman, *op. cit.*, pp. 127–128.

[77] Celso Furtado, *Um Projeto para o Brasil*, Rio de Janeiro, 1968, p. 43.

[78] According to W. P. Strassman, construction costs in Mexico are about 25 per cent cheaper than in the United States, but, on the other hand, the price of equipment is about double. The ratio is therefore 0.375 if we take that of the United States as 1.

[79] The trend in industrial design today is, on the contrary, to reduce the "shell", leaving equipment in the open air or under a light shelter, whenever possible, in order to save on investment outlays and reduce the capital–output ratio.

as the relative share of wages in value added is very low indeed and moreover keeps decreasing;[80] the adoption of capital-intensive techniques in a highly imperfect market with administered prices explains such a trend, but by no means justifies it. Social unrest becomes in the eyes of many entrepreneurs an additional reason for preferring automatized equipment, so as to reduce labour problems to a minimum, to say nothing of the fact that, paradoxically, it may be easier to staff a highly automatized plant with a few not very skilled hands than a less mechanized factory where hundreds of specialized workers are needed.

The conjunction of the factors described above, all working towards a capital-intensive bias, is so powerful that it would be unreasonable to expect entrepreneurs to behave in a different way from the way they actually do. One might, at most, charge them with bad faith when they invoke the argument of "competitiveness". By working in protected and imperfect internal markets with administered prices they reap all the benefits of technical progress through a higher margin of profits.[81] Why should they want to bring in more competition, at the double risk of reducing the scale of production for individual enterprises and being compelled to share the advantages of increased productivity with the consumers by means of a decrease in prices? As to external markets, at the developing countries' end the problems seem to lie much more with the institutional and organizational factors than with the cost price structure of the new industries[82] (which could always be corrected by means of a subsidy scheme). In any event, the crux of the matter is to be found at the other end: what developing countries need above all to increase their industrial exports is access to the markets of Europe and the United States.

My real quarrel is not with individual profit-seeking capitalists but

[80] In Brazil the relative share of wages in the value added by modern industries decreased from an average of 27 per cent in the decade from 1941 to 1950 to 20 per cent in the decade 1951 to 1960. The corresponding figures for the traditional industries are 22 and 20 per cent (Celso Furtado, *op. cit.*, p. 36).

[81] For this point see Anibal Pinto S. C., "Concentración del progreso técnico y de sus frutos en el desarrollo latinoamericano", *Economía*, **XXII,** fourth trimester 1964, pp. 29–84, and even more particularly pp. 58 and 77.

[82] This is recognized even by A. O. Hirschman in his article, "The political economy of import-substituting industrialization in Latin America", *Q. J. of Econ.*, February 1968.

with the "collective capitalists"—the States—for having confused development goals with maximization of the profits of a handful of entrepreneurs in their industrialization policies. The same instruments—fiscal, credit, foreign exchange policies—could have been used in a different way, along the lines discussed above in the first section, so as to
reduce instead of augment the gap between the growth of output from
newly established plants and an increase in industrial employment.

Some conclusions and suggestions

Throughout this chapter I have been arguing that selection of techniques could meaningfully become an integral part of development
policies even though, in the context of "mixed economies", practical
difficulties may prove considerable.

Designing such policies requires, as a first step, collecting more empirical knowledge about the working of the technological market in its
broadest sense: organizational and institutional aspects of supply of
technologies from local and foreign sources, mechanisms of decision-
making, channels of diffusion in low-productivity sectors, actual proportions between imitative transfers, adaptation and creative innovation,
degree of utilization of the actual opportunities of choice, etc. It is
suggested that such a study should be given high priority.

Effective government intervention in the realm of selection of techniques requires creating or strengthening, as the case may be, of project
evaluation workshops. In order to work efficiently such units should
be staffed with high-level specialists fully aware of the specific conditions
of the country concerned. They should enjoy considerable autonomy
and be independent of the government officials who take investment
decisions in the public sector. It is suggested that evaluation work on
behalf of governments might be done by specially created government-financed institutes for the economics of technology. Such institutes
could be, at the same time, entrusted with advisory functions in policy-
making, research, and post-graduate training of personnel for planning
and policy-making bodies. Emphasis should be on the quality of the
personnel and on the work done rather than on the size of the institute.
Evaluation of selected projects should be done in depth as much as

possible, even at the price of reducing, during the initial period, the number of projects scrutinized.

At the same time the utmost priority should be given to the creation or expansion, as the case may be, of project-designing workshops. It would be advisable to have them, whenever possible, in the public sector or to organize them in the form of co-operatives. Government-owned project-designing workshops should be prepared to accept contracts from the private sector. It is furthermore suggested that the possibility of international specialization and co-operation in the field of project designing be explored on a regional basis. For some Latin American countries project designing in certain fields (e.g. architecture and town planning) might even become an export item to other countries: project designing is a skilled labour-intensive activity; it should give the advantage to countries with a low cost of living with a relative abundance of professionals.

The advisability of creating public agencies for imports of technology should also be examined. Such agencies might be entrusted, in addition, with organizing imports of second-hand equipment on a selective basis. The negative experience accumulated hitherto in this field is mostly due to the fact that such deals, which become a source of easy profits when left in private hands, were being done in a most undiscriminating way.[83]

The scope of action of these institutions need not be limited to the public sector alone. It could be easily extended to those private sector projects which are heavily financed out of public funds through development banks, development corporations, etc. With a certain number of direct controls, such as licensing of big private projects and of foreign collaboration agreements, it might be possible to cover a still bigger part of private industrial investment.

In a mixed economy indirect operational controls play a preeminent role. They are the only way of influencing those private investors who

---

[83] See in this connexion the interesting point made by J. R. Meyer in "Transport technologies for developing countries", *American Econ. Rev.*, May 1966, pp.83–90: it would seem logical to transfer automobiles and trucks from high to low labour cost countries at some point in their life, when the labour required for maintenance becomes relatively substantial.

do not come within the scope of direct controls because of the size of their investment. Furthermore, when properly used, they should very much restrict the need for direct government intervention with respect to big private sector projects. As private entrepreneurs cannot be expected to use shadow prices instead of actual prices in their profitability analysis, policies of support for industrialization should be radically changed. Investment capital should be made more expensive and labour costs lower, without impairing, however, the level of real wages,[84] and working capital should be easier to obtain. Facilities should be extended to those who purchase locally made equipment and technology, while redundant imports of foreign equipment and know-how should be banned. Investment should be discouraged whenever it is possible to increase output by introducing a second or third shift.[85] It should be possible to arrive at these results by using, in a different and more imaginative way, the instruments which are now being misapplied: selective fiscal and credit policies, as well as subsidies.[86]

Up to now I have been dealing with ways of improving actual selection out of the range of available technologies. Long-term policies should concentrate, however, on enriching the spectrum of efficient technologies suited to the specific conditions of each country. Science, education, and research policies should therefore be given in fact, and not only in words, the same status in development strategy as industrial, agricultural, trade, or financial policies.

Research should not only be expanded but made more purposive, which is not tantamount to giving a privileged status applied at the expense of fundamental research. Primary government responsibility in the field of science and research should be recognized, but ways of associating the private with the public sector, at least financially, should be found. The argument that poor countries cannot afford to spend more on science should be opposed; because they are poor, they cannot afford not to take this chance of building a short-cut to develop-

---

[84] Fiscal revenue collected from industries could be increased in such a way as to allow the government to finance all social services for workers out of its budget.

[85] In other words, some kind of fiscal credit or even subsidy should be given to industrialists who fully use their production capacity.

[86] Celso Furtado came out (*op. cit.*, pp. 47–49) with an interesting suggestion of differential taxes on remuneration of capital and the wage bill in consumer goods industries, coupled with subsidies for industries producing equipment.

ment or, to be more precise, of providing one of the essential components to it, the other being social and institutional change.

Nor should "big science" be mistaken for the whole scientific field. Latecomers from developing countries are perfectly capable of doing much more than "reinventing the wheel"; denying them this possibility means either persisting in some kind of ethnocentric prejudice or playing with the ghost of "comparative advantage" understood in the most static way.[87] But scarce resources must be husbanded in a reasonable way, and this means concentration in the triple sense of avoiding wasteful duplication of efforts, guaranteeing scientific institutions the minimum efficient size, and setting out the right priorities for research.

Avoiding duplication implies establishing effective international co-operation. When insisting on the need to foster local research and to ban wasteful import of know-how, we are not taking up a postition against the transfer of knowledge from abroad as such. I think, on the contrary, in terms of a comprehensive policy including adaptable transfers of know-how, followed by local research and development,[88] and strong concentration on creative innovation in areas where the chances of getting an effective technology from abroad are slim.

The import component of technological development will depend on the access to information and know-how. Hence there is an urgent need to radically improve the present highly inadequate technological information network and to find suitable forms of co-operation among countries. It is, in particular, suggested that the United Nations and its specialized agencies should look into the possibility of increasing the flow of information among the developing countries of Latin America, Asia, and Africa and assist them in entering into effective working relations in the field of industrial, technological, and scientific exchanges. The technological and scientific potential of developing countries should be surveyed with a view to making their experience and experts available to other developing countries through the channels of technical assistance. We submit that Latin American experience may prove very useful

[87] For the latter point, see F. Chesnais and C. Cooper *L'Impact des Progrès Scientifiques et Technologiques des pays Avancés sur les Pays Sousdéveloppés*, Paris, March 1968 (mimeographed).

[88] To start from a high point and to go ahead—this is the only strategy which might give an advantage to the latecomer in certain cases. The Japanese example is very instructive in this respect.

to South Asian countries, and vice versa, not only in such fields as tropical medicine and agriculture but also in that of industrial know-how.

Small countries cannot afford to create too many research institutions meeting the requirement of minimum efficient size.[89] But they can either pool their efforts in order to create international insitutes, with or without United Nations support, or work out specialization agreements with other countries of the region, implying the mutual provision of services. The second formula seems less cumbersome, but they are not mutually exclusive.

The priorities of research must be worked out in each country in conjunction with its long-term development strategy, based of course on a thorough assessment of the country's resources and potentialities. I shall limit myself to emphasizing the need to give a great deal more attention than hitherto to low-productivity sectors and the moderate capital-intensity range of efficient techniques.[90] These are areas where there is little likelihood of learning anything very new from developed countries, as they do not happen to be working on such subjects (a great deal could be learned, on the other hand, from exchanges between developing countries on the lines suggested above).

Of course, agriculture, cattle breeding, fishing, forestry, and "biological engineering" are of vital interest for several Latin American countries, the current prejudice among the intellectual élite against this kind of research notwithstanding. The more so that, according to an eminent British specialist in food problems: "We do not at present know what to grow; we may not even know how to farm. More advice, based on temperate zone experience, is of little value because you cannot teach what you do not know. A great deal of research on tropical agriculture has been, and is being done; it is concerned mainly with industrial crops (such as cotton, rubber and sisal) or with foods crops (such as coffee, pineapples, sugar and tea) that can be sold to industrialized countries. Much less attention is even now being given to good

---

[89] The same applies to universities. Their creation for prestige reasons in too many places at the same time leads to a dispersion of scarce talents and resources, which adversely affects their functioning. Unfortunately this happens to be the case in several Latin American countries (see O. Maggiolo, *op. cit.*).

[90] I take into consideration, however, a much wider spectrum of problems and technologies than the partisans of intermediate technologies.

crops for local use".[91] At this point we should recall the need of having a more elaborate typology of agricultural techniques (as suggested in the first section). Another major difficulty is the need to see clearly the pattern of interrelationships between technological and institutional change in agriculture.

Another privileged area should be construction tackled simultaneously at the levels of building materials, methods of construction, and project designing. At all these levels, the present practices bring about a considerable waste of resources and job opportunities. It is believed that construction might play an even more important role on employment creation than hitherto if low-cost housing schemes could be devised[92] and implemented on a large scale. Such programmes would probably bring about an increase of national income and of the share of labour-intensive investment in it while it was being implemented and a lasting shift in the consumption-mix after its completion (if we agree to include the real or imputed value of rent, as the case may be, in the consumption bill of the family which rents or owns the house).

This brings me to my last point, which does not relate, strictly speaking, to the selection of techniques. I mentioned the possibility of improving the overall marginal capital–output ratio and increasing the number of jobs created through new investment by varying the output-mix and loading it with labour-absorbing goods, subject to the limitation that the substitution of such goods for other more capital-absorbing goods and/or for exports of these goods is feasible. At the same time, it was felt that, as a rule, there was little elbow-room for such a manœuvre (which in a planned economy would even be considered as the correction of a planning mistake). Now, in the long run it might be possible to influence more substantially the output-mix and to load it more with labour-absorbing goods, both on account of the altogether new products which are incorporated into the consumption pattern (and eventually production) as a result of scientific progress and because of the changes in the demand induced by income policies. It is even

---

[91] H. W. Pirie, *Food Resources: Conventional and Novel*, London, 1969, p. 111.

[92] Quite obviously, research does not aim only at new processes but also at new products. A new product may, however, have the same impact as a technological innovation in an old line of production when it replaces the goods produced in the old line. This happens frequently in agriculture.

reasonable to expect that the net result brought about in this way could far exceed the combined yield of the measures suggested above to improve the selection of technologies proper. Thus, for example, increasing the relative share of wages in the value added by industries would certainly bring a substantial increase of demand for labour-absorbing consumer goods of both industrial and agricultural origin. The effect of the increase on the incomes of poor peasants could be still more spectacular, so much so as to make the experts of ILPES believe that industries considered at present "vegetative", and which happen to be characterized by moderate capital intensity, might again become dynamic.[93] Such an increase in peasants' incomes could be most effectively achieved were they given the opportunity of, and assisted in, satisfying the growing demand for food on the part of urban workers by efficient labour-absorbing methods of cultivation, animal husbandry and fishing and, at the same time, were their share in the value added also to be substantially increased through appropriate institutional and organizational measures.[94] We know that such a programme of action would meet with formidable obstacles. But we also know that Latin America's economic and social development is at stake.

[93] ILPES, *op. cit.*

[94] The latter should above all rationalize commercialization by guaranteeing minimum prices and, whenever possible, offering advance purchase contracts to producers, while at the same time reducing the margin accruing to intermediaries.

CHAPTER 10

Technological Policies for Latin American Development (1971)

Why technological policies?

Technological policy (hereafter denoted TP) is the latest development policy. The present commitment of Latin American states to lay down comprehensive and consistent policy guidelines with respect both to science and technology[1] reflects the growing awareness of several forces at work, briefly described below.

Technology has played a hoax to humanity at large and to the populations of developing countries in particular. While it has increased tremendously both the range of available products and the productivity of labour, it is having at the same time serious backwash effects. Industrialized countries are primarily alarmed by the deterioration of the quality of life.

The developing countries have reasons to consider the present trends of world science and technology as damaging to their interests. Not only is the bulk of research being conducted on subjects which are irrelevant to the developing countries but part of it is directed against their vital economic activities. It has been estimated that about 1,000 million dollars per year are being spent on research and development (R and D) on synthetic materials in the industrialized countries. This is almost equivalent to the entire expenditure on R and D in developing countries[2] and is bound to reduce still more the demand for some of the natural products exported by them.

[1] This paper is mainly concerned with techniques. However, the borderline between science and technological policies is too artificial to be rigorously respected, and we shall not hesitate to make incursions into the sanctuary of science.

[2] United Nations, *Science and Technology for Development*, Report of the Advisory Committee on Application of Science and Technology to Development, New York, 1970, p. 26.

Most modern technologies are ill-adapted to the conditions of the developing countries because they emphasize production methods suitable for "capital-rich and unskilled-labour-short countries"[3] and insist on economies of scale and product designs adapted to the markets of industrialized countries. To this we should add the difficulties of access to world science and technology and the damaging effects of an external, as well as internal, brain drain.[4]

The control over sources of modern technology gives considerable power with respect to the industries which must rely on transfers of such technology, even if they are owned by local private or public capital. This often leads to *de facto* monopolistic situations and may impose a considerable drain on foreign exchange, not to speak of the reduction of the capacity to take autonomous decisions. The real cost of imported technology thus considerably exceeds the ostensible payments in the form of royalties and fees for technical assistance whenever we are in the presence of a "package deal", by means of which the use of the technology is made conditional on the purchase of overpriced equipment and inputs from sources indicated by the supplier of the technology.[5]

To the extent to which technological processes frequently are the *de facto* locus of political choice,[6] behind the transfer of technologies

[3] *Ibid.* The two quotations are from the document prepared by the Sussex Group and included as Appendix 2 to the report. For more sweeping denunciations of the racist character of Western science see N. Calder, *Technopolis*, London, 1969. See also I. Sachs, *La Découverte du Tiers Monde*, Paris, 1971, also published in the English translation, *The Discovery of the Third World*, MIT Press, Cambridge, Mass., 1976.

[4] Internal drain is meant the alienation of local scientists who follow closely the patterns and fashions of research centres in industrialized countries and do research on subjects irrelevant to their own countries, even in the most remote sense.

[5] Constantin V. Vaitsos has estimated at 155 per cent the overpricing of imported inputs by foreign-owned pharmaceutical industries in Colombia, with the result that reported profits constituted only 3.4 per cent of effective returns to the parent company, royalties 14.0 per cent, and overpricing 82.6 per cent (C. V. Vaitsos, *Strategic Choices in the Commercialization of Technology: The Point of View of Developing Countries*, paper presented at the Dubrovnik Conference of the Development Advisory Service of Harvard University, June 1970). Even if the situation in the pharmaceuticals is particularly bad, Vaitsos' research points to a very important feature of technological dependence. (See also, by the same author, *Transfer of Resources and Preservation of Monopoly Rents*, paper presented to the same Development Advisory Service Conference.)

[6] See J. D. Carroll, "Participatory technology", *Science*, **171**(19), February 1971, p. 649.

it is necessary to see the dependence on imported consumption patterns[7] as a result of the demonstration effect exercised over a large section of the modern sector, i.e. roughly speaking one-fifth to one-fourth of the population which accounts for over half of the global product.[8] What is involved is the entire project of civilization, questioned more or less forcefully by many Latin American writers and social scientists.[9] The implications or technological choices go far beyond the realm of pure instrumentality. More specifically, the excessive reliance on mimetic transfers of technology from abroad reduces still more the already limited freedom of choice of strategies for development, which are adapted to the needs of each Latin American country and make maximum use of the available resources, human and natural. On the other hand, experience shows that without a firmly implanted technological and scientific infrastructure (TSI) a meaningful policy of transfers— not to speak of development of alternative technologies—is practically impossible.

The single most-powerful factor behind the present interest in TPs has been, however, the growing realization that Latin America is at present pursuing a growth path in which the rates of increase in employment lag far behind the rates of growth of the GNP. This applies in the first instance to processing industries. To give an illustration of these trends, amply demonstrated in several ECLA and other studies,[10] the official programme of action of the Brazilian Government for the years 1970 to 1973 anticipates a yearly growth of the GNP of about 9 per cent, while employment will be merely increasing at 3.1 per cent, i.e. at a rate lower than that of the population growth.[11] If the

[7] See also the stimulating paper by Enrique V. Iglesias, "Cambio estructural en America Latina", *Temas del BID*, **12**, April 1971, pp. 5–26.

[8] Estimates contained in Carlo Quintana's report to the ECLA meeting held in May 1971, CEPAL, *Notes Sobre la Economia y el Desarrollo de America Latina*, no. 74, May 1972.

[9] The most outspoken is probably Ivan Illich, *Libérer l'Venir*, Paris, 1971. For a scholarly discussion see UNECLA, *Social Change and Social Development Policy in Latin America*, New York, 1970 pp. 6–8.

[10] *Ibid.*, pt. I (1968) chap. I, 3, and R. Prebisch, *Change and Development, Latin America's Great Task*, IDB, Washington, 1970, and *Economic Survey of Latin America*, 1968: See also Chapter 9 and R. Hofmeister, "Growth with unemployment in Latin America; some implications for Asia", in *Employment and Unemployment Problems of the Near East and South Asia*, vol. II, ed. by R. C. Ridker and H. Lubell, Delhi, 1971, pp. 819–848.

[11] *Metas e Bases para a Ação de Govérno—Sintese*, Brasilia, September, 1970, p. 18.

ratio of 3 to 1 between the rate of growth of the GNP and that of employment were to be retained as representative for Latin America, it would immediately follow that in most countries unemployment will be progressing at alarming rates, as the working force is likely to increase at a rate of 3 per cent per annum and the rate of growth of the GNP for the continent had been 5 per cent per year from 1965 to 1968, reaching 6.5 per cent in 1969 and 6.9 per cent in 1970.[12]

In other words, the integration of the most important social goal—providing jobs for the entire active population—with the objective of growth are postulated. To this I should add that growth with inadequate job creation is likely to prove at the same time regressive in terms of income distribution—another dimension of paramount importance in development strategy.[13]

Hence the idea of looking at the rate of technological change no more as a parameter but as a strategic variable which commands within certain limits the ratio of the growth of employment to that of the GNP. In other words, the proportion between extensive growth obtained through additional employment at prevailing levels of productivity and intensive growth arising out of the increase of labour productivity should not be left entirely to the spontaneous working of market forces. The State should assume a responsibility in this field, so as to reconcile to the maximum possible extent the conflicting goals with respect to output and employment. TPs will imply direct government action in some cases (in particular towards the public sector) and devising of indirect means to influence the private entrepreneurs' decisions (modification of relative prices, fiscal and credit incentives, and disincentives, etc.).[14]

---

[12] UN, ECLA, "Estudio economico de 1970", summarized in *Notas sobre la Economia y el Desarollo de America Latina*, no. 68, April 1971.

[13] R. Prebish (*op. cit.*, p. 178) rightly points with respect to technological progress in agriculture that under prevailing institutional conditions in Latin America it is likely to intensify income concentration and social disparities.

[14] It should be made clear that we are arguing here about the productivity of labour in new projects, i.e. about the desirable capital–labour ratio. Increasing the productivity from the existing plants and thus improving their performance without additional investment is always a commendable goal, subject to restrictions of a social nature (working conditions, etc.). But the mystique of higher productivity has penetrated Latin American entrepeneurs to such an extent that whenever technological choices occur, they choose the capital-intensive alternative, unless somebody proves to them that the other alternative

Looking at the matter from a different angle, we may say that the shaping of TPs is but one aspect of the present concern to redefine development in a more comprehensive way.

Fitting TPs into development strategies

Technology is the dominant component of our present world view to such extent that, without noticing it, we often come to think in technological terms regardless of the nature of the problem under consideration.[15] No wonder, therefore, that some people are under the spell of a true mystique of technology, invested, in their view, with the power to solve the most intractable questions and supposed to pave the way towards painless development. Ingurgitation of modern technology becomes, thus, the major component of, or even a substitute for, more comprehensive development strategies. The rate of technological change will command the modernization process and all aspects will be taken care of by means of more or less automatic adjustments. A particular brand of this technocratic concept of development is the *eficientismo*[16] used as a pretext to push away the difficult and controversial issues of social change. Development boils down to changes in the productive structure and increasingly efficient use of resources.

Fortunately enough, this school of thought has been emphatically rejected by most Latin American social scientists and the originality of their contributions consists precisely in that they go beyond the concept of optimization within fixed structures to explore the institutional change and the conditions for autonomous and steady developmental process.[17]

---

is clearly more convenient to them. A recent study has recommended that the burden of the proof should be, on the contrary, inverted (OIT, *Hacia el Pleno Empleo—Un Programa para Colombia*, Bogota, 1970, p.174).

[15] See H. Ozbekhan, "Toward a general theory of planning", in *Perspectives of Planning*, ed. by E. Jantsch, OCDE, Paris, 1969, p. 64.

[16] See E. Iglesias, *op. cit.*, p. 19: "El reclamo de una maior eficacia en el uso de los recursos que están a su cargo, tanto al Estado como al sector privado, suele confundirse con un falso 'eficientismo' que anularia la metas más nobles del mismo desarrollo, al sacrificarlo a logros materiales puros. parece, sin embargo, ser éste un enfoque por demás superado por los hechos."

[17] See S. J. Gonzalo Arroyo, "Le sous-développement et la dépendance externe au miroir de la littérature latino-américaine", *Cultures et Dev.*, **II**, no. 1, 1970, and *Problèmes Economiques*, no. 1199, 24 December 1970, pp. 19–26.

In this broad perspective, TPs become part of a development package and must be integrated into a coherent set of propositions with respect to income distribution and uses of the economic surplus, transformation of the agrarian structures, uses of foreign exchange, and possibly demographic policies.[18]

The aim of such a package should be to strengthen the development potential of the country, defined in terms of the following three interdependent conditions:

(a) The productive structures ought to be capable of reproducing themselves in physical terms, which implies the implantation of diversified capital goods industries and/or the capacity to pay for growing imports of such goods.

(b) Productive and intellectual structures should be synchronized, as coexistence of modern productive structures with outdated intellectual structures is likely to bring about the most surreptitious form of dependence.

(c) The economic and social systems must be managed by means of operational controls so as to permit efficient implementation of autonomous decisions.[19]

TPs are obviously related with all three. The various ways in which technologies interact with other variables considered in development strategy-making can be deduced from Figure 10.1.[20] In particular, I should stress the following three relationships:

(a) As the range of available technologies is not the same for different kinds of goods and services, the selection of general objectives and their translation into specific goals (and then an output-mix) is likely to heavily influence the technological choices. Hence the importance of relating the current discussion on TPs in Latin America with such major issues as the pros and contra of the horizontal model versus

---

[18] The latter, to be meaningful, should be considered as a complement to the "development package", never as a substitute for development policies aimed at more output and a more equitable distribution of the same.

[19] See I. Sachs, "L'Indépendance du Tiers Monde: structures de production et structures intellectuelles", in *La Liberté de l'Ordre Social*, Recontres Internationales de Genève, Neuchâtel, 1969, p. 116.

[20] See also Chapter 2.

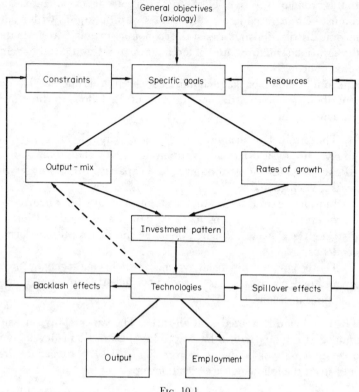

FIG. 10.1

the vertical model[21] and, more generally, the alternative styles of consumption[22] and types of society projected for the future.[23]

(b) Both the spill-over and the backwash effects of technological change need to be carefully investigated. Transfers of encapsulated technology are not likely to have a spill-over effect, not even at the

[21] See in particular a recent ILPES publication with a stimulating restatement of the problem, *Dos Polemicas Sobre el Desarrollo de America Latina*, Santiago, 1970.

[22] See CENDES, *Estilos de Desarrollo*, Caracas, 1969 (also published in *Trimestre Economico*, no. 144, 1969).

[23] This seems to be the orientation of ECLA's research in "integral planning" (*enfoque integral*). See CEPAL, *Notas Sobre la Economia y el Desarrollo de America Latina*, no 74, May 1971.

level of manpower formation. On the other hand, indiscriminate use of capital-intensive technologies will not only lead to growth with unemployment but at the same time compromise the income policies aimed at more equality, unless very strong fiscal measures are applied so as to take a substantial part of the profits from the entrepreneurs (a scenario not very likely to happen, even under a mixed economy with a strong public sector).

(c) We used a dotted line to denote the feedback between the technologies and the output-mix, because of the limited scope for its manipulation with a view to using techniques better adapted to the factors' proportion (and possibly creating more jobs per unit of output). As a matter of fact, output for the internal market is determined by the demand pattern and substitutions have narrow limits. As far as the exports are concerned, the situation so far is not much better, all the advice given to developing countries to concentrate on cheap labour goods notwithstanding. Thus, to load the output-mix with more labour-intensive goods it is necessary to change the composition of the demand by means of income redistribution and, therefore, to act at the level of objectives and goals formulation. The horizontal model and the strategy based on land reforms directed at uplifting the purchasing power of the large masses of poor peasants are called for, as their income elasticity of demand for manufactured consumer goods, as well as for inputs for agricultural production, is fairly high.[24] We are more skeptical about an international economic order coming into existence which will guarantee outlets for cheap labour goods manufactured in developing countries, not to speak of the dangers involved in freezing, at a new level, the international division of labour between the highly industrialized and the developing countries.[25]

[24] This approach has been repeatedly emphasized by ECLA and ILPES. See also W. C. Thiesenhausen, *A Suggested Policy for Industrial Reinvigoration in Latin America*, Madison, September 1970 (cyclostyled). In Thiesenhausen's terms Latin America suffers at present from coercive marginalization, which implies both a minimal participation in the market and a fairly low capital formation.

[25] The idea of re-shaping the world economy in such a way as to promote a division of labour based on the criterion of labour intensity of traded goods has been put forward by Jan Tinbergen and his assistants. As B. Herman summarized it: "Labour-abundant–capital-scarce countries will specialize in labour-intensive industries (low capital intensity), sectors of increasing capital-intensity will become suitable to countries of increasing capital endowments per worker, and the highly capital-intensive industries ending up

Looked at from still another angle, there are at present four views about the place of the technological variable in the development strategy:

(a) The main concern should be the maximization of the rate of growth and, therefore, of the economic surplus. Capital-intensive techniques should be preferred and the volume of investment increased up to a point where the exceedingly rapid rate of growth would take care of the employment problem; this strategy can be called a *fuite en avant*.

(b) The main variable is the output-mix. It should be heavily loaded with labour-intensive goods (i.e. such goods for which efficient labour-intensive technologies exist). These goods should be eventually traded against capital intensive goods.

(c) A more realistic variation on the above theme consists in postulating a change in the demand pattern by means of income policies aimed at broadening the market for industrial consumer goods, which are by nature more labour intensive than the durables, and possibly at curbing the consumption of capital-intensive luxuries.[26] Emphasis on social services and popular housing—so long as they are implemented by labour-intensive methods[27]—belongs to the same category. The same could be still said of measures to improve the human environment, so long as it is understood that environmental concern is by no means a pretext to slow down economic and social development, but, on the contrary, one reason more to insist on it, while broadening the set of pursued objectives.[28] In other words, bigger emphasis on collective consumption and the quality of life could, at the same time, broaden the scope for labour-intensive technologies and in this way contribute to the lessening of unemployment.

---

in capital-abundant–labour-scarce countries. In this way, optimal rates of growth of income and levels of employment would be attained *not only* by the world as a whole *but also* by each of the member nations" (*On the Choice of the Optimal Industry—A Check of a Controversy*, Rotterdam, 1971, p. 19, cyclostyled).

[26] Luxuries may be capital intensive by themselves or indirectly through the required inputs and/or foreign currency.

[27] For a more elaborate discussion of this point, see Chapter 12.

[28] See the Report on *Development and Environment* submitted to the Secretary-General of the United Nations, Conference on the Human Environment by a panel of experts, June 1971.

(d) Those who doubt about the possibility of substantial gains by means of manipulation of the output-mix insist, on the contrary, on the selection of technologies proper, once the output-mix has been defined. The same output can be often obtained by different-process technologies. The efficient alternatives[29] range from labour-intensive to capital-intensive ones. In a market economy, the selection will depend on the relative prices of capital and labour. In a mixed economy, the State should use controls and incentives in order to establish the desired price structure and business environment and thus influence the entrepreneur's decision. Within the public sector shadow prices can be used in cost-benefit analysis of technological alternatives in order to optimize the technological choices.

But the last argument implies that a uniform criterion for optimization does exist, which is by no means true: output maximization by labour-intensive methods does not lead to surplus maximization, if the level of real wages is assumed to be given. And so long as external sources of capital do not exist, the volume of surplus determines the volume of investment and, thereby, the rate of growth.[30]

Moreover, a selection can only be made out of the existing range of technologies. In many cases it is ruled out, because of the limitations on the side of the supply, even though considerable results could be obtained, right now, by making better use of the existing alternatives in such fields as public works, construction, and labour-intensive agriculture, not to speak of the possibility of improving, in the longer run, the supply of technologies by setting out the right priorities for research.[31]

All four points referred to above provide useful guidelines for a pragmatic TP. A high rate of growth is the backbone of development strategy. But this by no means implies that we should not try, at the same time, to make the best uses of this growth by playing with income distribution, output-mix, and choice of techniques.

[29] All the alternatives are efficient which differ by different mixes of capital and labour per unit of product, but compensate a higher intake of one factor by a lower intake of the other.

[30] For a more detailed discussion, see Chapter 9.

[31] See also Chapter 11.

Guidelines for the study of the technological market

Having seen how TPs fit into development strategies, we may now step down to the surrounding realities and inquire about the nature and the doings of the technological market. Unfortunately, available data are extremely scarce. The reasons for this are twofold.

On the one hand, the traditional concepts of international economic relations and of economic circulation still refer to flows of goods and capitals, and only exceptionally to people, but do not include into their purview the circulation of technology, except when dealing with the balance of payments. Even then reference is only made to apparent costs of technology which take the form of royalties, fees for technical assistance, etc. As already mentioned, this is at best the emerging part of the iceberg, most of the costs being indirect. On the one hand, it is extremely difficult to isolate the technological market from dealings in equipment and supply of qualified manpower. Although in a growing number of cases, technology and know-how are dealt with as a separate commodity and special contracts, licensing agreements, etc., are concluded for this purpose, the links with the supply of equipment and of inputs make them an integral part of a package deal. The assessment of the costs and benefits of each transaction requires, thus, going into a painstaking analysis of the whole web of interests involved.

One of the recommendations of this paper is that the utmost priority should be given to the study of the technological market in Latin America. Such a study should explore the following aspects:

(a) Identification of the actors on the stage (Who are the suppliers and the users of the technology? What is the role of the State?).

(b) Identification of the flows, whenever possible in quantitative form.

(c) Institutional analysis of the market forces (What is the bargaining power of the suppliers and that of the users? What are the patterns of relationship between suppliers and users?).

(d) Assessment of the impact of the flows of technology (Is the purchased technology being used merely as an encapsulated input to production or does it also act as an input into research? Is it a pseudo-transfer, an adaptive, or a full transfer in terms of Figure 10.2?).

(e) Evaluation of direct and indirect costs of technology.

(f) Evaluation of the research effort within the enterprise and, eventually, comparison of this with aspect (e)[32].

(g) Assessment of trends on the technological market, subject to the availability of chronological series (Is there a shift from pseudo-transfer to more convenient forms of access to technology? At what rate is domestic research progressing? Is the share of non-proprietory technology increasing or decreasing? What is the changing role of the United Nations and other multilateral agencies as suppliers of proprietory technology on a concessional basis, etc.?).

Due to their importance, three subjects should be singled out for special studies:

(a) Transfers of technology from abroad.

(b) Supply of technology to agriculture, including the individual peasant farmers.

(c) The effective demand for technologies.

I shall briefly discuss them in the next three sections of this Chapter.

Transfer of technology. How efficient and how expensive?[33]

Transfers of technology may take different forms, such as engineering studies on plant construction, choice of machinery and process, technological feasibility studies, turn-key and construction contracts, licensing agreements, and technical assistance. It is important to look at the problem in an all-inclusive way.

The first difficulty often experienced by the Latin American countries is the access to technology. Patents are more often used to protect the market for exports than to transfer proprietory technology. Other

[32] According to preliminary results reached by Jorge Katz, a quite considerable amount of adaptive research is going on in some processing industries located in Argentina.

[33] This section draws heavily on the excellent questionnaire on the transfer of technology, including know-how and patents, addressed by the Secretary-General of UNCTAD (Document TD/B/AC.11/4, 30 April 1971), on studies by C. Vaitsos, already quoted, as well as the "regimen comun de tratamiento a los capitales extranjeros" elaborated by the Comision del Acuerdo de Cartagena.

restrictive business practices, including legislative and political obstacles, may also occur.

Another source of complications arises out of the "technology package": licence agreements often stipulate that the buyer should acquire equipment, intermediate products, and technical assistance at the same source. Such situations seem to affect, in particular, oil, chemical, and pharmaceutical industries. The implications for the cost of transferred technology are obvious and have been already mentioned, the more so because the structure of the market is highly imperfect. The overcharging may take different forms:

(a) High levels of royalties, service fees, and/or dividend payments to a parent company by a subsidiary.

(b) Marked-up prices of intermediate products and/or capital goods imported under the same contract[34].

(c) Higher-than-normal rates of interest on intracompany loans.

(d) Excessive charging of overhead and R and D costs of the foreign supplying enterprise to the purchasing enterprise (often a subsidiary).

(e) Excessive increase in the equity participation by foreign technology suppliers through the conversion of the estimated value of know-how into equity holdings, excessive depreciation provisions, etc.

Other contractual conditions often included in agreements about the transfer of technology result in limitation on competition, whether in the form of excessive protection or exclusively guaranteed by patent. The licensees may, in turn, be prevented from exporting to third markets. Additional fiscal, exchange, and financial guarantees given to the licensor may worsen even more the conditions on which technology is obtained; a quite common feature is the continuation of royalty payments for undetermined periods of time, even though the technology supplied has in the meantime become freely accessible and/or obsolete.

While the licensors usually get a number of guarantees, the licensee has little means of enforcing a fair implementation of the contract, in terms of quality, accounting data, etc. The insistence of many licensors of having the disputes settled outside the jurisdiction of the technology-purchasing country is not made to facilitate matters.

[34] In dealings between a parent and a subsidiary company underpricing of exports may also occur.

The picture which emerges from this cursory review of conditions of transfers of technology is gloomy enough to warrant utmost concern with the problem on the part of Latin American governments and to postulate a concerted international action. Technological dependence considerably reduces the scope for autonomous decisions on the part of Latin American enterprises submitted by the licensor to controls of different kinds, ranging from direct (majority equity participation) to indirect (e.g. control of the supply of key inputs, control over marketing). To this we should add that the transferred technologies frequently prove ill-adapted to the needs of the importing country. This may happen both at the product technology level and that of process technology. Three important objections applying to many imported technologies are excessive capital intensity, inadaptation to the scale of production required, and lack of concern for utilization of local resources. The first characteristic reduces the employment effects of the growth process and, combined with the second, works towards the establishment of monopolies and oligopolies.[35] The last leads to an unnecessarily high import content.

To summarize, the present situation in Latin America has been described in the following way by the Brazilian Minister of Foreign Affairs:

"So long as our countries do not manage to create through their own research technical solutions adapted to their specific needs, they will have to depend for their development on a growing volume of imported technology. It is, therefore, indispensable, side by side with our (research) efforts, to firmly act in international fora in order to prevent our condition of technology importers to bring about, while we further develop, an ever greater gap relative to developed countries than the one caused by our condition of exporters solely of primary commodities. . . As buyers, we participate in an international market of technology of which we have an imperfect knowledge and whose laws have been arbitrarily set by the vendors. Lack of

[35] See on this point M. Merhav, *Technological Dependence, Monopoly and Growth*, Oxford, 1969, and also M. Kaplan, *El Marco Global Histórico en que se Inserta la Problemática del Desarrollo Científico y Téchnico de America Latina*, paper read at Centro de Estudios de Post-Grado, Faculted de Ciencias Economicas y Sociales, Universidad Central de Venezuela, 9 December 1970.

attention to technological alternatives, often compounded by lack
of knowledge about their very existence, makes free competition impossible in the realm of technology causing serious losses to developing
countries. It is not acceptable to see an element of such paramount
importance for our development traded in such unfavourable conditions."[36]

Supply of technology to agriculture

Though our knowledge of the technological market with respect to
industries may be imperfect, the situation is much worse as far as agriculture is concerned. How are technologies diffused? What is the real importance of the extension services and that of other channels, in particular,
dealers in inputs? Is there any chance, in those countries where land
reforms are being implemented, to build a more prosperous agriculture
on the basis of participatory technology, by which we mean active
participation of peasants in research?

The next set of questions refers to the kinds of agricultural technology
which are being supplied. The table on page 218 provides a classification
of agricultural techniques[37] which enhances the need for very careful
planning of technological transfers, the more so because tropical agriculture has hardly been investigated up to now and, for obvious reasons,
in this particular field the scope for pseudo-transfers is very limited
indeed.

Yet, the so-called "green revolution" is being propounded without
much regard to local social and economic conditions. What will be
its impact on environment, natural and human? How will it affect
employment? The last question is all the more important because for
a long time ahead Latin America will have to rely on agriculture to
absorb a substantial part of its labour force.

Opinions about the social and employment effects of the green revolution are polarized, but increasingly students of the problem warn against
the deleterious effects it is likely to have both in terms of social differen-

[36] Statement of the Brazilian Minister of Foreign Affairs, Mario Gibson Barboza, at
the Ninth Session of CECLA (Brasilia, 11 February 1971).
[37] See also Chapter 9.

tiation in the countryside and of employment. Even those capitalist farmers who start by investing in modern inputs will not stop short of mechanization, so that after a temporary increase in labour intake farms involved in the green revolution are likely to enter a second labour-saving stage, unless serious corrective measures are taken well in advance. Once more we are in the presence of a sharp conflict between the entrepreneurial and social rationality and of a complex web of interfering interests on the part of technology suppliers. To end this section I would like to draw attention to a recent, quite pessimistic assessment of the situation made by the Director General of FAO:

'Il ne fait aucun doute que le développement et l'introduction des variétés à haut rendement constituent un événement technologique de la plus haute importance, qui nous permet d'espérer que nous serons, en définitive, à même de conjurer de ce monde le spectre de la famine. Mais, sans même parler du formidable appui matériel et politique que réclament ces variétés, on peut dire sans crainte de jouer sur les mots qu'elles contiennent les germes de nouveaux dangers. Nous avons déjà constaté que, comme elles sont, immédiatement plus efficaces dans les régions irriguées que dans les régions sèches ou non irriguées et comme elles profitent aux agriculteurs riches tout en laissant les plus pauvres dans la même condition qu'avant, elles risquent non seulement de perpétuer, mais même d'aggraver les inégalités sociales existantes. En ootre, il est pratiquement certain que l'accroissement de production qu'elles permettrent d'obtenir aggravera encore les difficultés du commerce international des céréales si des politiques d'ajustement ne sont pas adoptées.''[38]

Effective demand for technologies

I have hitherto mostly been concerned with analysing the short-comings of the supply of technologies, insisting on the problem of transfers from abroad, as the output of local institutes of research and engineering offices has been up to now, on the whole, negligible, it is time now

---

[38] A. H. Boerma, Discours Prononcé à l'Occasion de la 18e Conférence Générale de la Fédération Internationale des Producteurs Agricoles, Paris, 14 May 1971, p. 10.

to turn to the demand. No successful TPs can be devised without inquiring into the reasons of the present lack of concern of Latin American entrepreneurs for domestic research. This implies looking into the business environment and the forces which shape the entrepreneurial decisions.[39]

The situation may be summarized in the following way:[40]

(a) those who have easy access to public sources of capital are flooded with it. For them capital for investment is neither scarce nor expensive, as rates of interest are heavily subsidized and endemic inflation in some cases allows them to get loans at negative rates of interest.

(b) On the contrary, working capital is hard to obtain and expensive.

(c) As social charges are made proportional to the wage bill (instead of being financed out of a higher general tax on value added), entrepreneurs are inclined to consider that labour costs run high, even though wages may be quite low; the preoccupation with possible social conflicts in the factory reinforces the propensity to substitute capital for labour.

(d) Fiscal incentives are all directed towards capital expenditures.[41] Endemic inflation seems to be working in the same direction, although its ultimate impact on the value of industrial assets is hard to estimate.

(e) In most countries, foreign exchange and trade policies favour imports of equipment without sufficient selectivity, both with respect to the uses of such equipment and the availability of alternative technologies with lesser import content.

(f) Protection accorded to domestic industries for balance-of-payments reasons amounts in reality to a positive discriminatory control, as windfall profits accruing to those who produce import substitutes are not wiped off by adequate taxation.[42] To this I should add that, to the

[39] The importance of such an analysis has been stressed by M. Halty Carrère, *The Process of International Transfer of Technology: Some Comments Regarding Latin America*, Pan-American Union, Washington, 1968, p. 2.

[40] See for a country study *Hacia el Pleno Empleo*, *op. cit.*, and also G. Myrdal, *Asian Drama*, New York, 1969, which in spite of its geographical concentration contains many valid general points. See also Chapter 9.

[41] A recent United Nations Report (Document E/4988) submitted to the Economic and Social Council concluded that the structure of most tax incentives in developing countries is biased towards capital-intensive investment (UNCESI features, ESA/43, 18 June 1971).

[42] See G. Myrdal, "A note on positive operational controls", Appendix 8 to *Asian Drama*, vol. III, New York, 1969, pp. 2077–2108.

extent to which this protection is granted to foreign-owned industries expatriating their profits and using expensive imported inputs, the measure proves also self-defeating with respect to the balance-of-payments criterion.

(g) Protection from outside competition, reinforced by the imperfect market structure (a consequence, *inter alia*, of the skewed income distribution which restricts the outlets for all industrial commodities, as well as of the technologies employed), leads to a price formation system guaranteeing high profits to highly inefficient industries. Entrepreneurs are not really concerned by costs, as the volume of their profits is by and large proportional to the costs involved. In those Latin American countries where control of industrial prices is being attempted, it consists in most cases in checking whether the costs were really incurred and in forcing the entrepreneurs to squeeze them by delaying authorization for increases in prices, motivated by inflationary increases in the cost of inputs. But no attempt is made to look at the roots of the problem. The result of this policy is that the main effort of the entrepreneur goes once more towards reduction of the labour intake, rather than to the limitation of payments abroad. Paradoxically enough, registration of contracts for imports of foreign technology becomes for the entrepreneur a guarantee that he will get foreign exchange for his payments abroad; the most controversial part of his costs is the best protected against rationalizing measures on the part of the State.

Under these circumstances, it is no wonder that the effective demand for industrial technologies discriminates against domestic sources of supply, to the extent to which they might operate. It is addressed almost in its entirety to foreign sources of supply and gives preference to capital-intensive technologies. This is the more so, because the supply of equipment and of technologies readily available on the market is precisely of such a nature, that foreign aid and credit facilities are extended to Latin American countries for such purchases, while practically no assistance whatsoever comes to strengthen the domestic supply of technologies.

Two additional, reinforcing circumstances are discussed below:

(h) The first is the preeminence of product technologies over process technologies. Shopping abroad consists of looking for new products and accepting the process technologies which happen to be available for the chosen product. If such technologies impose a minimum scale of production far superior to the market possibilities, Latin American industrialists can afford, within the price formation system and market structure described above, to underutilize their installed capacity. The cost will be shifted to the public, and to the extent to which profits are calculated as a mark-up over costs the idle capacities will even yield profits, not to speak of other advantages accruing from the size of installed capacities and of the volume of investment involved, such as side profits during the construction of the plant, value of the land and buildings, access to larger credits, etc. As a matter of fact, one of the salient features of Latin American industrialization over the last quarter of a century has been the conjunction of high investment with a persistent underutilization of installed capacities.

(i) The second is no more of an economic but of a psychological nature: Latin American entrepreneurs and a substantial part of public opinion, submitted to a continuous flow of cultural and commercial propaganda, seem to be, at present, very sensitive to the "demonstration effect" of modern technology employed in highly industrialized countries. The concept of one absolute and universally valid scale of technological values has been internalized to such an extent that considerable prestige is attached to using the most up-to-date labour-substituting technologies, even though it may prove clearly detrimental to the social interests. This state of mind ties up with the mystique of high rates of growth, already referred to, without any concern for employment criteria and social distribution of income. This applies to the public and private sectors alike and even in such areas as public works, which had been used in developed countries to ease the pressure of unemployment, the fashion is for highly capital-intensive and labour-saving technologies.

(j) We may now turn for a moment to the demand for modern technologies in agriculture. Once more, the analysis must proceed by looking at the institutional set-up. Broadly speaking, we may distinguish four categories:

(i)   The great mass of poor farmers, who do not have access nor the possibility of using modern inputs and whose condition is likely to worsen very much under the impact of the "green revolution" (see the previous section). Job opportunities will not increase and the competition of big farmers will become tougher.

(ii) Latifundistas, who exploit their land in a traditional manner and are rather resilient to technological change because of the peculiar combination of low outputs per acre, still lower labour costs, and large land tracts, which gives them a high volume of profits with very little working capital (whatever is needed is supplied by banks) and practically no new fixed investment.

(iii) A stratum of larger farmers, conveniently located with respect to urban markets and infrastructural facilities, and therefore well positioned to seize advantage of that peculiar mix of opportunities created by new technologies and State assistance in the form of cheap (or free) irrigation, improvement in transports, more credits, and low agricultural taxes. Their demand for modern technologies is high, in spite of the fact that the prices of modern inputs produced by inefficient industries are high compared to the level of agricultural prices.

(iv) Large enterprises, usually linked to food-processing industries and marketing circuits, decided to make the best use of modern techniques to wipe off smaller competitors.

Of course, the ten points made above need to be checked by means of surveys conducted in each Latin American country, so as to take into consideration all local specifications and the intensity of each distortion pointed to here. It is only against the background of detailed empirical knowledge that it will be possible to lay down TPs really conducive to economic development. The following conclusions seem, however, to reflect fairly well the situation prevailing in most countries:

(a) The present configuration of market forces creates a strong effective demand for imported capital-intensive technologies. Even in those areas where the range of technological choices is fairly extensive (e.g. in public works, construction,[43] agriculture) the opportunities to choose

---

[43] A recent study based on the experience of Peru as compared with information from Colombia, Mexico, and Venezuela pointed to a disquieting trend towards labour-saving innovations in construction. See W. Paul Strassman, "Innovation and employment in building: the experience of Peru", *Oxf. Econ. Pap.*, **22**, no. 2, July 1970.

technologies more conducive to the implementation of employment targets and social goals are foregone.

(b) Under certain circumstances TPs devised merely to satisfy the existing demand for technologies would contribute to an increasing distortion of the development pattern. The gap between the proclaimed social goals and the reality would grow ever larger, and the present pattern of growth without employment, increasing disparities in incomes, and polarization of agriculture would be strengthened. The situation is somewhat similar to that prevailing with respect to manpower, described in the following way by P. H. Coombs: "There is a wide disparity between the manpower *needed* for economic growth and the manpower *actually demanded* by the market."[44]

(c) Thus TPs congenial with meaningful development cannot be merely grafted upon the existing structures;[45] they must form an integral part of a comprehensive "package" of measures acting at the same time on the demand for and on the supply of technologies. In a mixed economy this calls for a change in the business environment; so long as this is not done entrepreneurs will persist in their present attitudes, and for good reasons. In other words, TPs must be harmonized with fiscal, trade, financial, and social policies. Operational controls, as rightly stressed by Myrdal, must be approached in a systematic way.[46] Different solutions are certainly envisagable, depending on political preferences, the degree of boldness of the proposed structural change, and also administrative convenience; but whatever the choice, it will always be necessary to conceive and apply a consistent mix of policies and controls and not a set of separate measures.

However, the action on the supply side requires as a prerequisite in most Latin American countries the building of an appropriate institutional framework. It will not be enough to strengthen the capacity of the local research infrastructure, nor to lay down general science policy principles. The example of India is in this respect very instructive. That country has at present little less than a million scientists, technolo-

[44] P. H. Coombs, *The World Educational Crisis—A System Analysis*, London, 1968, p. 89.

[45] Hence some apprehension about the working of the Estatuto Andino Sobre Capitales y Tecnologia.

[46] G. Myrdal, *op. cit.*

gists, and technicians, and an annual turnout in 1968 of 123,000 at the level of graduates and above.[47] In absolute terms it is the largest in the world after the United States and U.S.S.R. (and perhaps China). And yet, the contribution of local science and technology to the Indian industrial development has been disappointing, because of the following reasons: lack of appreciation of the role of indigenous R and D effort on the part of the government and industries, both public and private; lack of correlation between the structure of R and D and that of industries; the preference of private industries for foreign collaboration agreements, in many cases repetitive, costly, and demoralizing for local research; lack of clarity in research aims.[48] Hence the demand of Indian scientists and technologists to supplement the Science Policy Resolution with a Technology Policy Resolution, which affirms the country's determination to achieve self-reliance and formulates a very selective approach towards the import of foreign technology, which must be followed by local research along the Japanese example.[49]

Once more, the approach must be systematic and the institutions created for the supply of technologies should also be entrusted with some responsibility with respect to policies devised to change the pattern of demand. The next section will be devoted to an examination of this matter.

Shaping the institutional framework for TPs and choosing the operational controls

Throughout this section we shall assume that the following objectives are pursued by means of TPs:

(a) Modernization, expansion, and diversification of the economy, keeping in view higher outputs and a more equitable distribution of the same and realizing, therefore, the need to harmonize growth with employment targets.

[47] Data quoted by A. Rahman, "Technology and industrial growth", *Commerce*, annual number 1969.
[48] *Ibid.*
[49] B. M. Udgaonkar, "Implementation of the scientific policy resolution", *Economic and Political Weekly, Bombay*, 26 December 1970, p. 2091.

(b) Progressive overcoming of technological dependence by performing a breakthrough in domestic research and according protection within reasonable limits to infant domestic technology.

(c) Efficient handling of imports of technology by identifying the range of available alternatives, choosing the most suitable kinds and sources of supply and minimizing the foreign exchange cost.

What set of institutions is necessary to carry out such policies? The lower part of Figure 10.2 provides an answer quite similar to proposals put forward by OAS[50] and several Latin American scholars.[51]

To co-ordinate the whole operation, a high-level organ, called here the Agency for Technological Development, is necessary. It should have a ministerial or similar status. The agency should be entrusted with the supply of technologies both from local and foreign sources and, at the same time, have an important voice in the implementation of policies meant to shape the pattern of the demand (to be discussed later on).

In all its activities the need for reliable independent information about sources of know-how, the range of available technologies, and the costs involved will be obvious. Hence the importance attached in our organigram to Technological Documentation Centres. The less research is developed, the more important it becomes to build up well-staffed documentation centres and to grant to its personnel the possibility of frequent travel abroad.

From all that has been said in this chapter, it follows that foreign operations in the realm of technology must be carefully screened. Hence the need for a specialized body for foreign operations, which for administrative convenience may be located inside the institution entrusted with control of external trade and financial operations, but should enjoy a certain autonomy and, what is more important, should be composed of a small staff of highly qualified economists prepared to go into all the complexities of trade in technology. The body should be, as a minimum, empowered to apply negative direct discriminatory controls on

[50] See OAS, Department of Scientific Affairs, *Resumen del informe de la Mision de Evaluacion de los Sistemas de Difusion de la Informacion Tecnologica en America Latina*, November, 1 and 7P.

[51] See, in particular, Helio Jaguaribe, "Ciencia y tecnologia en el cadro sociopolitico de la America Latina", *El Trimest. Econ.* **150**, 1971, p. 426.

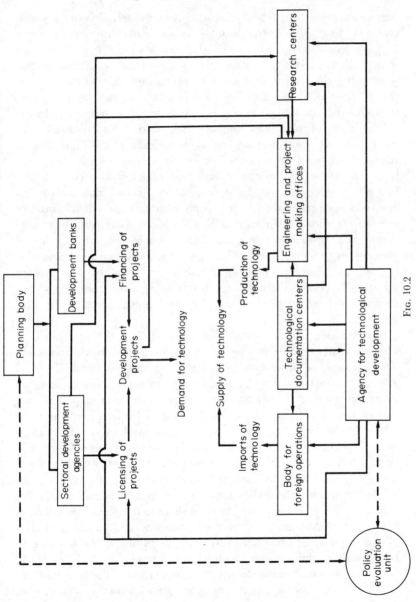

FIG. 10.2

new contracts for imports of technology and indiscriminatory controls on the existing contracts (by laying down accepted conditions and limits for payments abroad). But it could also be entrusted with positive functions, such as assistance in obtaining the most suitable technology and negotiating the contracts or even shopping abroad on behalf of the public sector and eventually private firms. In the latter case, however, it should create for that purpose a specialized agency or public enterprise.

The supply of technology from domestic sources in its ultimate form must come from engineering and project design offices. The lack of such institutions is perhaps the weakest spot on the Latin American scene and the utmost urgency should be attached to their creation, in order to decrease the influence on the decision-making process enjoyed at present by foreign consulting engineers and allied firms. We are not pleading for autarky in this field and quite obviously local engineering and project designing offices should subcontract parts of the projects to foreign firms, whenever a highly specialized knowledge is involved. They should be equally entitled to purchase technology abroad if local expertise is lacking. But the very fact of assuming global responsibility for the projects would be an important step in the right direction.

Quite obviously, the setting up of such offices is the only practical way to create a stable market for local applied industrial research. The principle of protection to domestic technology should be thus applied at two levels: first, by giving contracts to domestic engineering and project designing offices, even though at the beginning a certain cost of apprenticeship will be involved; then by insisting that these offices should closely collaborate with local research units. The strategy of the implementation of engineering and project designing offices should be carefully worked out and time-scheduled. It is not possible to enter into all fields at the same time. Specialization is called for.

This programme should be harmonized with the plans of development of the research infrastructure, and both should reflect the priorities of long-term development plans. For various reasons, it might be preferable to start by creating such offices in the public sector and to give them contracts for projects financed out of public funds. They could be thus more easily geared to the implementation of the first objective specified above: the harmonization of growth with employment targets.

The Agency for Technological Development should take a close interest in the fostering of industrial research, sharing in this respect the responsibilities with the sectoral development agencies (industrial ministries). It should, in particular, have a voice in the setting of research priorities.

Finally, a strongly staffed policy evaluation unit, enjoying a large autonomy, should be created with a twofold purpose: constant evaluation of the results brought about by the implemented TPs, so as to suggest modifications both to the Agency for Technological Development and the overall planning body; and also expert evaluation of single projects, either because of their importance or because of the suspicion that they go against the accepted policy guidelines. This screening of projects should apply alike to projects elaborated by local and foreign engineering and project designing offices, including those financed by external resources.

We turn now briefly to operational controls over the pattern of demand. As mentioned in the previous section, a whole array of financial, fiscal, trade, and social policies is called for, so as to increase the relative price of capital, suppress the disincentives towards the utilization of more labour and induce investors and industrialists to avail themselves of the domestic technology. A detailed discussion of such policies goes beyond the scope of this chapter and, to be profitable, should take one by one the situations prevailing in each country. I shall content myself with drawing the attention of the reader to two critical points where considerable improvement could be obtained without much effort.   The first refers to the financing of new projects by development banks and industrial development corporations (*corporaciones de fomiento*). At this borderline between the public and the private sectors it should be possible to offer the investor the right technological choices. After all, the bank enjoys a vantage position and it should be equipped to know what is the best solution from the social point of view. If necessary, the bank could consult the Policy Evaluation Unit and recommend specifically the use of domestic technology. Apart from this direct discretionary control, the bank could use indirect discretionary positive controls by a more selective use of preferential loans, made dependent on the technological content and the employment effects of the project. In theory, these criteria have been incorporated in the evaluation forms used in such occasions. But this has been done either mechanically or the weights attached to the technological content and employment effect are too small to have a meaningful impact on the decisions. This seems to be at least the situation with respect to SUDENE[52] and CORFO, to quote two examples. I am quite aware of the difficulties involved in multivalued choice and quite sceptical also with respect to all kinds of mechanical evaluation procedures. But it should be possible to do in this respect considerably better, once the TPs are specified and the development banks integrated into the comprehensive institutional set-up called for their implementation.

Another opportunity of screening the technological content of the project and imposing changes, if necessary, arises at the level of project licensing. The use of this direct negative discretionary control would become, however, less and less frequent if adequate indirect controls were put into use at the level of fiscal, financial, trade, and social policies, if the development banks were better geared to the implementation of TPs, and if the supply of adequate technologies was made available thanks to local research and project designing offices. Once more, I should like to insist on the need to approach the matter in a systematic way.

The above description of the institutional framework for TPs calls for two additional comments:

(a) Special treatment should be reserved for the public sector, which should be directly geared to the implementation of development goals. This is easier said than done, however, where public enterprises are for all practical purposes private businesses owned by the State and the bulk of public works is subcontracted to the private sector. Once more, to discuss the alternative organizational patterns for the public sector is beyond the scope of this chapter. An ECLA report stressed the potential role of the public sector for development, provided it could be managed as an integrated sector geared to the plan implementation. As the public or semi-public enterprise is the only viable alternative to foreign multinational conglomerates, the strengthening of the public sector could well be the best way of assisting the locally

---

[52] See J. Camara Zapata, *Croissance Économique, Changement Technologique et Emploi au Nordeste Brésilien*, EPHE, Paris 1971 (unpublished doctoral dissertation).

owned private sector to expand.[53] But, even without introducing major organizational changes, it should be possible to enforce TPs with respect to all new public investment by applying the screening procedures suggested above. If the relative price structure is amended, there should be in principle no need to use shadow prices, but in cases where some kind of shadow-pricing is resorted to, it should be possible to offer the resulting choices to the public enterprise more easily than to the private investor. With respect to public works, there should be more direct involvement in their implementation on the part of public enterprises. Moreover, contracts with private contractors might be made dependent on the choice of the most adequate technology.

(b) This ties up with the need to lay down specific sectoral TPs in a few areas, where the range of alternative technologies is large and the volume of employment quite substantial. I believe this should be done for agriculture, public works, construction, and possibly for certain industries which directly compete with cottage and small-scale traditional production. A way of making virtue of necessity and tolerating for some time technological dualism in such industries as textile, shoe-making, wood products, etc., might consist in giving subsidies to the artisan-type production financed out of additional excise duties imposed on similar products from modern industries. This policy has been applied with some success in India. The sectoral policies suggested here should have a counterpart in research programmes enjoying a high priority.

---

[53] See CEPAL, *Notas Sobre la Economia y el Desarrollo de America Latina*, no. 79, 1 July 1971, with a summary of ECLA's Report on the present and potential role of the public sector (Document CEPAL E/CN 12 872).

CHAPTER 11

Transfer of Technology and Research Priorities for Latin America—a Social Scientist's Point of View (1971)

Preliminary remarks

The less developed that research is in a country, the more it becomes important to give it adequate orientation, i.e. to lay down priorities and careful time-scheduling. Unless this is done, even a substantial increase in expenditure for R and D may not yield results. Quantitative targets do not offer *per se* any protection against wasteful uses of resources, financial and human.[1] To be meaningful, research must ultimately serve as an input both to the economic and social system and to further research. Neither of these two functions is performed automatically and quite often brilliant scientific achievements fail in this respect, so long as they are the product of isolated efforts by outstanding individuals. At best, such individuals become well known all over the world, enjoy the esteem of their colleagues in highly developed countries, publish their papers abroad, and bring in this way some prestige to their mother country. They may be compared to artists and writers, with the difference, however, that they do not find audience among their countrymen.

I do not mean that quantitative targets should be given up. In all Latin American countries a big effort is called for to channel more resources to science and technology. But planning of science should

[1] For a note of caution with respect to the application of analytical methods in planning of science and technology, see C. Maestre and K. Pavitt, *Analytical Methods in Government Science Policy: An Evaluation*, OECD, Directorate for Scientific Affairs, Paris, October 1970.

not indulge in the same mistakes as planning of education. The contents of education and the most efficient ways of conveying it have been much less discussed over the last twenty years than indices of scolarity, ratios of teachers to students, etc. We know today that this approach has proved wrong. In the same way, it is not enough to determine what share of GNP should be allocated to research. The discussion about "how much" makes little sense without inquiring at the same time "on what" and "how". The last question refers to the institutional set-up and to the critical minima of required concentration of resources.

One more reason to insist on the choice of priorities is that the first attempts in planning of science have been characterized by an almost exclusive emphasis on allocation of resources, motivated *inter alia* by the disparity in time horizons involved in economic and scientific planning; while economic planners deal with the next five or ten years the development of science requires a much longer—and bolder—view.[2]

Nor are we making a plea for a narrow, instrumentalized concept of science reduced to applied research on contract. Fundamental research ought to go on in all countries, even the smallest and the poorest, for the simple reason that its absence would upset the training of people for research, both fundamental and applied. Scientists aware of the problems of their country should also have a reasonable freedom of choice of their subjects. But three misconceptions must be dispelled.

First, it is not true that science develops along a logic of its own with no relation whatsoever to the social context in which scientists live. As René Dubos puts it: "The development of any particular field of science is profoundly influenced, of course, by forces inherent in the scientific enterprise itself....On the other hand, social forces unrelated to the logic of science play a large role, probably the dominant one, in determining which fields of science are emphasized at a given time and which are neglected."[3] Thus, "serendipity", i.e. discovery of things that were not looked for, does not seem to have played a major role in the history of science. It follows that the usefulness of useless research is debatable, mostly when resources are scarce and the minimum size of the meaningful effort large enough to undermine

[2] See J. Spaey *et al.*, *Le Developpement par la Science*, UNESCO, Paris, 1969, pp. 105–106.
[3] René Dubos, "Future-oriented science", in *Perspective of Planning*, ed. by E. Jantsch, OECD, Paris, 1969, p. 160.

mission-oriented research by financing non-oriented research too liberally. To this I should add that serendipity may occur also as a by-product of mission-oriented research.

Second, we should not forget that the point of departure in Latin America is an almost absolute dearth of oriented research with some non-oriented research. We should plan, therefore, for quite a period of time, for much more development-oriented research, so as to transform science and technology into an asset in the war against poverty. For the moment, Latin America is mostly feeling the backwash effects of modern science and technology. In other words, instead of treating science as part of a general cultural effort, attention should be given to its double function, already mentioned, of input to the economic and social system and to more purposive research. This change will require new and imaginative methods of planning, as science and technology planning in industrialized countries was born to attend altogether different objectives, the military effort being its prime force.[4]

Third, mission-oriented and applied research should not be considered as a poor relative of fundamental research, assuming that there is a clear-cut borderline between the two. Mission-oriented research may involve a number of intricate theoretical problems too and, in many cases, it is likely to prove much more difficult than the fundamental one, because of the need to take into consideration the whole complex web of existing interrelations.

In reality, development-oriented research implies a continuous requestioning of societal goals and means available to reach them. It thus links up with the core of long-term planning understood as a future-directed decision process.[5] To the extent to which such planning should be participatory, a continuous dialogue between planners and scientists is called for. The effort to spell out the societal goals and to derive from them the priorities for research should not be understood as a one-way process by which the social scientists and the politicians

---

[4] The United Nations Advisory Committee on the Application of Science and Technology to Development rightly recommended that the developing countries' policies of scientific and technological development "should not and must not be carbon copies of those of developed countries" (United Nations, *Science and Technology for Development*, New York, 1970, p. 8).

[5] H. Ozbekhan, "Toward a general theory of planning", in *Perspectives of Planning*, ed. by E. Jantsch, OECD, Paris, 1969, p. 151.

draw up a list of demands to be presented to scientists. The latter should be closely associated with the elaboration of a demand for science, as well as with the assessment of the uses of science. The sooner they internalize the societal goals pursued and realize that the only meaningful assessment of scientific and technological progress consists in relating it to the socioeconomic context, the more fruitful the dialogue will become for all the participants.

The purpose of this chapter is to inquire into the societal criteria, by means of which in development-oriented research priorities could be evaluated, and the various strategies open to Latin American countries, combining different forms of transfers of technology with domestic research.

Evaluation criteria of development-oriented research

The basic aim of development-oriented research should be a more efficient harnessing of available resources for the implementation of societal goals defined in terms of more output of goods and services and an equitable distribution of the same. The latter condition also implies an effective granting of job opportunities to the whole active population.

Better utilization of the pool of human resources thus implies that, whenever possible, reasonably efficient labour-intensive methods will have to be resorted to so as to maximize employment subject to the constraint of a minimum acceptable productivity of labour;[6] at the same time high priority will have to be given to the expansion of educational, health, housing, and social facilities designed in such a way as to reach those who need them most, i.e. the broad masses of poor people, both rural and urban. All estimates point to the gravity of the present unemployment crisis in Latin America. In 1960, unemployment and underemployment affected the equivalent of 27 per cent of the active population, or 18 million people. In 1970, the comparable figure was 25 million[7] and the trend is likely to continue unless drastic

---

[6] See Chapter 9.
[7] For an up-to-date discussion of the employment situation, see W. C. Thiesenhusen, "Latin America's employment problem", *Science*, **171**, no. 3974, 5 March 1971.

measures are taken to revert it: quite obviously such measures will call for a much more generalized utilization of labour-intensive methods.

Better utilization of natural resources requires, first of all, a more accurate knowledge of the same, and then imaginative ways of using them. Predatory use of natural resources should be carefully avoided, so as to minimize environmental disruption and the social costs arising out of it. Development must and can be harmonized with environmental concern.[8]

Better utilization of the existing productive capacities calls for an urgent improvement in the management of the economy and the organization of society.

Better utilization of the foreign exchange—the joker of the planning game—calls for a reduction of the foreign exchange component of the development process, i.e. for more self-reliance.

The foreign exchange gap constitutes the most severe bottleneck for several Latin American countries and the real cost of transfers of technology, when properly computed, is likely to prove exceedingly high. More self-reliance (which is not tantamount to autarky, as we shall see in the section dealing with strategies of research) is also badly needed for political reasons, as the development potential of a country may be seriously impaired by technological dependence.[9]

Finally, the usefulness of the domestic research effort should be evaluated from the point of view of its contribution to the protection of the country from the backwash effects of imported modern technology; some measure of counter-research is called for.

To sum up, self-reliance appears as the major criterion as it subsumes all the others, while among the partial criteria contributions to employment and to the balance of payments should be rated as the more important.

[8] See *Development and Environment*, Report submitted by a Panel of Experts to the Secretary-General of the United Nations Conference on the Human Environment, Founex, Switzerland, June 1971.
[9] See Chapter 10.

Some priority areas for development-oriented research

It follows that the following areas should enjoy high priority for research in Latin America, subject, of course, to corrections from country to country in order to take into consideration the specificity of each case.

LABOUR-INTENSIVE METHODS OF PRODUCTION IN INDUSTRY

The main reason for the dearth of reasonably productive methods of production, requiring a moderate capital–labour ratio, lies in the lack of research effort directed to creating them.[10] The bulk of the world's research effort goes into the creation of technologies for the highly industrialized countries. The results are diagrammatically shown in Figure 11.1. The three curves T_1, T_2, T_3 show for three successive

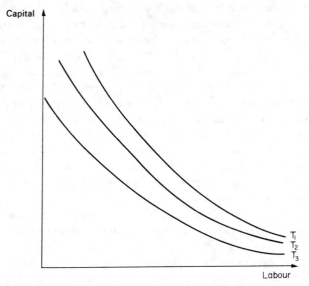

Fig. 11.1   Technological progress

[10] See C. H. G. Oldham, *Characteristics of the Process of Transfer of Technology*, OAS, CIECC/Doc. 77, 11 February 1971, p. 4.

periods of time all the available efficient technologies to produce a unit of GNP. Progress occurs mostly in the range of capital-intensive technologies.

Technological progress mostly affects the left upper part of the supply curve of technologies, i.e. highly capital-intensive technologies. It is unlikely that scientists from developed countries will take up the problems affecting the lower right part of the supply curve; the bulk of research effort must be provided by the developing countries. It should be realized, at the same time, that such industries as automobiles and durables, reputed for their technological advancement, turn out in Latin American goods consumed only by a tiny minority. Table 11.1 provides ILPES data on the consumption patterns of Latin Americans by income brackets for 1960. The lowest 20 per cent of the population spent less than 2 dollars on durables and vehicles, the next 30 per cent 4.72 dollars, the 40 per cent belonging to the third category 16.29 dollars and the uppermost 10 per cent over 100 dollars. The vast majority of Latin Americans will not be able to afford such goods for quite a long time, even on the assumption of a development path directed towards a substantial redistribution of income and a rapid increase in employment of the poorest strata. Processed food, garments, shoes, and furniture are likely to take the bulk of their expenditure. These are industries where a relatively wide range of alternative efficient technologies exists at present and, possibly, could be expanded still more. The utmost attention should be paid, at the same time, to the utilization of local materials, so as to open new markets for the primary activities and to reduce the foreign exchange component. In other words, industrial research should endeavour to combine three criteria discussed in the previous section: labour-intensive bias, better utilization of local resources, and import substitution.

The same goes for certain capital goods industries, such as implements for agriculture, certain kinds of machinery, and some inexpensive durables (bicycles, radio sets, and also a really popular refrigerator, etc.).

Industrial research should, furthermore, pursue an additional goal: reduction of the minimum viable scale of production so as to foster, whenever possible, small-scale decentralized industries. Rural industries providing employment for the agricultural population in the slack season should be given a much more serious consideration than hitherto. Their

Latin America: Consumption structure and other information relating to income brackets, [a] 1960

CIIU	Details	Categories				
		I	II	III	IV	
	Proportion of the population in each category in 1960	20	30	40	10	100
	Proportion of total personal income received	5	13	41	41	100
	Total personal income received (in millions of dollars)	3.990	10.360	32.690	32.680	79.720
	Average annual income per capita (in dollars)	100	173	410	1.640	400
	Percentage of personal income allocated to consumption	95	90	75	60	71.8
	Total private consumption (in millions of dollars)	3.790	9.330	24.510	19.610	57.240
	Proportion of total consumption (in percentage)	6.6	16.3	42.8	34.3	100.0
		Consumption structure percentages				
	Unmanufactured agricultural foods	76.5	11	5	2	
20–21–22	Foods, beverages and tobacco	8.5	42.0	39	28	
24	Clothing and footwear	10	10	13	13	
26	Furniture	—	2	2	1	
31	Pharmaceutical and toiletry products, medicines	1	5	5	5	
35–36–37	Durable items	2	3	3	5	
38	Vehicles	—	0.3	2.3	5.2	
32–39	Household cleaning articles	1	5	4	4	
	Others	—	1.7	2.7	8.8	
	Services	1	20	24.0	33	

Source: ILPES based on family budget information.
[a] All figures and percentages in this table have been rounded off.

apparent inefficiency vanishes to a great extent when the costs of urbanization are brought into the picture. But, for obvious reasons, the private entrepreneur will never take them into account, unless he is compelled to bear a share of the same. Instead, he is usually given fiscal and other incentives to establish himself in the town. In this way, a substantial part of the costs is externalized by the enterprise and dumped on the society at large.

LABOUR-INTENSIVE TROPICAL AGRICULTURE

In all honesty, I do not expect spectacular employment effects on the processing industry side, even granted that research will be engaged along the lines suggested above. My insistence on industrial research is motivated not so much by the expectation of quick results but by the need for a drastic change in approach and in the scale of values prevailing among industrialists and specialists in technology. On the contrary, agriculture is the most promising field in terms of employment potential, and also has in view three other criteria: social upgrading of poor people by improving their nutritional standards, balance-of-payments effects, and counter-research to prevent further displacement of natural products by synthetics.[11] Moreover, research effort in agriculture should yield results, as the point of departure is very low indeed; we continue to ignore almost everything about wet tropical agriculture. Needless to say, transfers of technology from the developed countries are ruled out, because of the difference in climatic and natural conditions.[12] One could expect, at best, that the same scientific approach could be applied. Even so, there is the danger of taking a too-technocratic view of agriculture, subestimating the impact of the institutional set-up

[11] The present environmental concern should logically lead to a restriction in the uses of certain synthetic fibres and plastics, and the natural fibres (as well as paper) might prove once more competitive, provided the social cost of disposing of the synthetic waste is included into the calculation. Development and environmental protection could thus go hand in hand. This point was made forcefully at the fifty-sixth Session of the FAO Council, in June 1971, by the representative of India, T. N. Saraf (FAO Press Release 71/90).

[12] This point is emphasized even by Roberto de Oliveira Campos, who otherwise firmly believes in the virtues of the transfer of technology in processing industries (see his paper, "O desafio ambiental: sua importancia para os paises em desenvolvimento", *O Estado de Sao Paulo*, 12 May 1971).

and of the sociocultural context on the behaviour of farmers. The so-called "green revolution" is at a crossroads. Unless drastic measures are taken to control its bias towards excessive mechanization and the almost exclusive concentration of its effects in a layer of large and already prosperous farms, it may sharpen still more the concentration processes in the countryside both in terms of land and of income. While adding to the marketable surplus of agricultural produce and to the prosperity of a few, it may bring more misery and less employment for the mass of poorer peasants. Hence there is a need to study the problems of agriculture in a comprehensive and interdisciplinary way, by combining research on labour-intensive technologies with a detailed analysis of the social and economic conditions of the countryside.

RESOURCE-BASED INDUSTRIES[13]

The importance of *mining* for several Latin American countries as a source of income, and still more of foreign exchange, contrasts with the lack of systematic research related to this industry, which suffers from almost complete technological dependence. Research is urgently called for, as a pre-condition to improve, as a first step, the bargaining power of the Latin American countries with respect to foreign technology suppliers, the capacity to adapt technologies purchased abroad, and then to support the expansion of locally owned mining industries. The research effort must go in several directions:

(a) Careful inventory of the mining resources.
(b) Elaboration of technologies best suited to local conditions.
(c) Research on new uses of the minerals (forward linkage).

[13] The very concept of natural resources is essentially cultural (in the anthropological meaning of the term) and related, on the one hand, to new ideas of how to use them and, on the other, to the creation of new needs. See the following statement by Marcos Kaplan: "The role of an autonomous, scientific and technological strategy would exist even if we were able to create new natural resources in order to adapt them to new conditions of international trade, or if we were able to develop a rate of demand which does not exist at present because we have not been able to create our own supply" (*Problemas de Política del Desarrollo Científico y Techologico Referido al Caso Latinoamericano*, paper read at the Centro de Estudios de Post-Grado, Facultad de Ciencias Económicas y Sociales, Universidad Central de Venezuela, Caracas, 8 December 1970).

(d) Research on equipment needed by the mining industries (backward linkage).

(e) Counter-research on potential substitutes.

Once more, an interdisciplinary approach is called for. The analysis of the world markets, keeping in mind the opportunities for joint action on the part of the developing countries, should be viewed as an integral and important part of the research programme.

Forestries should be given a high priority in research for reasons opposed to mining: their contribution to the income of Latin America is much too low. They may well constitute the most persistently under-utilized resource of the continent. New methods of treatment of wood should give it a second youth as a building material.[14] The growing environmental concern in developed countries and the difficulties caused by plastic waste disposal speak in favour of paper and similar products. The leaf protein may become, in the not-too-distant future, a marketable commodity. Several extractive industries could be expanded, as they provide natural products for which there will be a growing market in rich countries, more and more preoccupied with the harmful effects of many synthetic products.

Fisheries recommend themselves as a privileged area of research both for balance-of-payments and social reasons. Once more, we are in the presence of a potential source of income and of improvement in nutritional standards not very well assessed as yet. For instance, the inland waters have barely been investigated, not to speak of the possibilities of fish and crab breeding. Fishing and fish-processing industries belong to the group where a considerable range of alternative reasonable technologies could be developed, including labour-intensive ones. The same applies to industries turning out equipment for the fishermen, such as boats, nets, etc. This opportunity should not be missed.

CONSTRUCTION, HOUSING, PUBLIC WORKS

Many employment opportunities are being foregone, at present, in Latin America by favouring capital-intensive methods of construction

---

[14] A United Nations meeting in July 1971 in Vancouver (Canada) discussed new and improved ways of using wood in housing, particularly in developing countries (UN-CESI Features ESA/44, 24 June 1971).

and public works execution. And yet this is an area of economic activity, where the quality of the output depends little on the methods of production and materials employed. Latin American entrepreneurs are proud to imitate techniques used in the most industrialized countries[15] and governments give them support in this, oblivious of the fact that in the thirties public works had been resorted to on a massive scale as a measure to decrease unemployment created by the "great crisis". To this I should add that a good deal of development in the USSR and East-European peoples' democracies was equally obtained, in a first stage, by extensive methods, i.e. by the expansion of employment, rather than by marked increases in labour productivity; infrastructural works and reconstruction, as well as expansion of towns and industries, played a substantial part in this first stage.

Two arguments speak forcefully in favour of research on the most appropriate methods of construction and public works organization:

(a) The growing environmental concern, in the context of the Latin American countries, should express itself in more public works to control the backwash effects of big development projects, such as dams, multipurpose valley schemes, etc., to remove the consequences of predatory exploitation of natural resources and to reduce the disruption of the social environment arising out of disorderly urbanization processes. Such works are by nature more amenable to experimentation with labour-intensive methods than any other area of the economy, with the exception perhaps of agriculture.[16]

(b) The housing deficit is rapidly increasing, as it has been estimated that urban "marginal population" is growing at 15 per cent per year. The number of favelados in Rio de Janeiro increased from 400,000 in 1947 to 900,000 in 1961, in Mexico from 330,000 in 1932 to 1,500,000 in 1966, and in Lima from 114,000 in 1957 to 1,000,000 in1969. Buenaventura in Colombia probably holds the record for the highest percentage of a city population living in slums: in 1964 it was 80 per cent

[15] In an interview granted to *Revista Banas* (25 January 1971) Sebastião Camargo Corrêa, the biggest contractor in public works in Brazil, proudly stressed that unqualified workers were less than 2.5 per cent of his employment roll.

[16] See I. Sachs, *Environmental Quality Management and Development Planning, Some Suggestions for Action*, paper presented by the UNESCO Secretariat to the Panel of Experts on Development and Environment, Founex, Switzerland, June 1971.

out of a population of 110,000.[17] There are practically no chances of solving the housing problem by conventional means on a world scale. According to the ECA's estimates with respect to Africa, where the situation seems to be less drastic than in most Latin American countries, it would be necessary every year to invest 10 per cent of the national income of the African states to keep the housing problem in towns and countryside under control on the conservative assumption of a cost of 1,500 dollars per urban dwelling and 500 dollars per rural dwelling, plus an equivalent amount to finance the necessary infrastructure and minimum amenities.[18] The United Nations Centre for Housing, Building and Planning has estimated that 1.4 billion new homes will be needed world-wide by the year 2000. To achieve this goal would require an increase of from three to five times the present rate of construction.[19]

Under these circumstances, it is necessary to look for unconventional methods as part of an effort to directly improve the living conditions of the population, while simultaneously increasing employment. Research must explore four topics: reasonably efficient methods of labour-intensive construction; the uses of local building materials, in particular timber and wooden products, obtained whenever possible by labour-intensive methods; designs best adapted to local climate and cultural traditions; and participation of the population concerned in designing and implementation of urban and rural housing schemes.[20]

SOCIAL-ORIENTED RESEARCH

With the exception of medical research centred on tropical diseases and some isolated experiences in non-formal adult education, in social services Latin America has been following the patterns set out by the

[17] Data from United Nations sources are quoted in *Environmental Costs and Priorities*, background paper prepared by the Secretariat of the United Nations Conference on the Human Environment for the Panel of Experts on Development and Environment, Founex, Switzerland, June 1971.

[18] Estimates quoted in "Urbanisation in Afrika", supplement to *Afrika Heute*, September 1970 (reproduced in *Problèmes Economiques*, no. 1225, 24 June 1971).

[19] UNCESI Features ESA/44, 24 June 1971.

[20] The four approaches are harmoniously blended in Hassan Fathy, *Construire avec le Peuple*, Paris, 1971. This book describes a pioneering but unsuccesful effort by a leading Egyptian architect.

industrial countries. In other words, the opportunity of loading the social welfare function with a lot more public health, nutritional, educational, and environmental services performed by labour-intensive methods has been foregone. The wrong pretence of emulating the developed countries in standards of excellence provides in reality an excuse to offer social services to a minority of privileged people. In no other field is the need for original research more pressing. The economics of labour-intensive social services is simple enough and, at any rate, easier to cope with than the heavy burden of redundant administrations. But technologies and organizational patterns are badly lacking for rural para-medical and nutritional services,[21] based whenever possible on active participation of the populations concerned and using local resources, including locally grown unmarketable food supplies. In addition, education requires a profound re-thinking, first with respect to its contents and then to the pedagogic methods, which should be active to the fullest extent and, at the same time, should avail themselves of the new possibilities offered by modern communication media. How to combine all these elements into a homogenous programme is a challenge to Latin American educators and social welfare specialists.

PLANNING AND MANAGEMENT OF THE ECONOMY

Elimination of waste and a fuller utilization of the existing capacities of production improves the economic performance without additional investment.[22] The resources thus saved can be invested into new plants and the economy can then grow at a higher rate without sacrificing its consumption standards. Hence we see the importance of research on planning methods in mixed economies and on management of the

---

[21] For a very convincing plea in favour of para-medical services, see O. Gish, "Health planning in developing countries", *J. of Dev. Stud.*, **VI**, no. 4, July 1970. Nutrition should no longer be considered an economic factor but rather, like education and health, one of the essentials of life to be provided free to vulnerable population groups in cases of extreme necessity. At any rate, people should be educated for and assisted in making the best use of the locally available resources. See R. Korte, *Report and Summary of Discussions*, from the Eighth Pugwash Symposium on Overcoming Protein Malnutrition in Developing Countries, Oberursel, May 1970.

[22] The last report of the Inter-American Bank insists on making, whenever possible, a more intensive use of the existing equipment by working on two or even three shifts (*Progreso Socio-Economico en America Latina*, Washington, 1971, p. 16).

TABLE 11.2
Some research priorities

Problem area	Societal goals						Interrelations
	a	b	c	d	e	f	
A Industrial research	×		×	×		×	B, D, E, G, I
B Agriculture	×	×				×	A, F, H, I
C Mining			×	×		×	F, I
D Forestries	×		×	×		×	A, G, H, I
E Fisheries	×	×	×			×	A, H, I
F Public works	×			×			B, C, D, E, I
G Housing	×	×					A, D, H
H Social services	×	×					B, E, G
I Planning and management					×		A, B, C, D, E, F, G, H

a = promotion of employment   b = social uplifting
c = utilization of natural resources   d = environmental concern
e = efficient management of the economy   f = balance-of-payments improvement

public sector, which should be geared to the plan implementation, as well as on ways of inducing the private sector by an adequate mix of positive and negative, direct and indirect, controls to act in reasonable conformity with the social interest and the priorities set out in the plan. Once more, original research is called for, as the existing administrations, patterned along foreign models, were not created to serve development. A new concept of development-minded public administration is needed, as well as new models for the public enterprises. At present, they are either run on a non-economic basis—which is costly and wasteful—or given the status of public-owned but fairly autonomous businesses, administered as if they were private concerns—which means that the rationality of the enterprise often enters into conflict with the social interest. Neither of the two formulae is acceptable. Special attention should be given to ways of organizing and implementing public works and investment financed out of public resources.

Table 11.2 summarizes the argument of this section.

Strategies of research

I will now briefly discuss the various strategies of research. Quite obviously no country in the world can afford to rely exclusively on results obtained in their own laboratories. Even the USSR explicitly recognizes today the need for international co-operation in research and technology[23] and the argument applies *a fortiori* to smaller, less-developed and less-autarkically minded countries. The priorities referred to above should be taken up according to a careful time-scheduling, expressing the needs and the possibilities of each country and integrating them into a comprehensive science and technological policy.

At a given moment, the following alternatives are always open:

(a) No research at all (the needs are entirely satisfied by imitative transfer).

(b) Research on a modest scale only for teaching and information purposes.

(c) Adaptive research of different degrees of intensity and exploration of the forward and backward linkages.

(d) Counter-research, which is situated half-way between adaptive and creative research.

(e) Creative development-oriented research, as well as the exploration of the technological gaps left by foreign research (the Japanese theory of "sukima"[24].

The various alternative strategies of research consist in different combinations of these five elements. I have already discussed, at some length but in a very general way, the criteria and the priorities for (e) and (d), but the choices of specific subjects within these broad priorities and the time-scheduling call for additional analysis, based on the following feasibility criteria:

(a) The initial situation in terms of conformity of the technologies in use (if any) with the development goals.

(b) Access to alternative foreign technologies and their real cost.

---

[23] "The scientific and technological forecast should help in selecting the most promising and effective lines for development in this field, the main focal points on which to concentrate efforts, and the opportunities for international co-operation and for taking advantage of the division of labour" ("Principles and methods of long-term planning and economic forecasting in the Soviet Union", in *Long Term Planning*, United Nations, New York, 1971, p. 104).

[24] See "Japan: how the imitator shows the way", *Business Week*, 16 May 1970, (also reproduced in *Problèmes Economiques*, no. 1216, 22 April 1971).

(c) Magnitude and recurrence of the technological problem under consideration.

(d) Scale of the research effort needed, both in terms of financial and human resources.

(e) The likely economic and social impact of the research.

(f) The likely scientific impact of the research (time-scheduling in conformity with the so-called inner logic of scientific development).

In practice, this means painful arbitrations, which cannot be escaped and would be only obscured by resorting to any form of weighting the different criteria in order to get at composite quantitative indices and in this way also rate the different research projects. The only way out is an institutionalized dialogue among planners, project designers, managers, policy-makers, and scientists. In addition the exact proportions between imitative transfers, adaptive transfers, and creative research cannot be set out *a priori*. But the mix is, at present, so heavily biased in favour of imitative transfers that most certainly adaptive and creative research should be strongly favoured by development plans.

The case for international co-operation

The feasibility prospects for research, analysed for a single country, may be unfavourable, yet for a group of countries with similar problems the picture might be quite different. Hence there is a case for developing by all means scientific and technological co-operation among Latin American countries and, more generally, among developing countries at large. The United Nations should be persuaded to assist the developing countries in creating a meaningful communications network, so as to exchange experience, technologies, and technical services. All the internationally financed development projects should rely to a much greater (and growing) extent on technologies and technical services provided by developing countries. In many cases, these technologies would probably be better adapted to the needs of the recipient countries than the ones purchased in highly industrialized countries. Thus, technical services, such as project designing, should become an export item of several developing countries. These are, as a matter of fact, typically qualified as labour-intensive activities. Once the developing country has got the necessary skills—and many developing countries already suffer from unemployment of university graduates—it should be able to offer such services at very competitive prices because of the relatively low wage level.[25]

Among smaller groups of countries, such as the members of Pacto Andino, scientific co-operation should be expanded on parallel lines with industrial integration. In both cases, functional planning should be resorted to instead of taking the traditional sectoral view. In other words, all forward and backward linkages, including equipment of major activities like mining, fisheries, or forestries, should be explored in order to select the investment projects and also the research priorities to be then allocated among the member countries. Transfers of technology resulting from a rational division of labour and operated by means of mutually agreed procedures should be made free from most negative aspects, presently attached to transactions on the international market of technology. More self-reliance in science and technology, obtained on a subregional or regional level, should also yield an additional dividend: Latin America's bargaining position towards foreign technology suppliers would be considerably strengthened. We come thus to a paradox: underdeveloped countries must first insist on more self-reliance, so as to be able later on to afford to rely more on selective transfers of technology, once the basic receiving structures and the capacity for autonomous decisions have been built into their systems.[26]

[25] An article in *Economic and Political Weekly, Bombay* (10 October 1970) argued that India is well placed to export computer software. The two reasons advanced were: the availability of highly skilled programmers (it is not uncommon to find first class Master's degree-holders from the Indian Institutes of Technology willing to specialize as programmers) and the salaries level, which is approximately eight times lower than in the United States.

[26] If there is a positive lesson to draw from the Japanese experience, it is their hitherto insistence on autonomous development, which can go hand in hand with an open economy. The following comment of *Commercio Exterior de Mexico* (February 1971) prefacing the publication of a summary of the Japanese White Book on Science and Technology, deserves to be quoted in this connexion:

"There is general agreement that the experiences of the Japanese have very limited application in Latin America. Among the principal factors which prevent a direct application, four characteristics of the Japanese economy and society stand out which are not found in any Latin American country: a) the very effective role of the State in the encouragement of national development since the implementation of the first Japanese industrial development plan which dates from 1884; b) the near-autonomous development based on restrictions to the admission of foreign private capital and on large scale importing, although selective and controlled, of foreign technology; c) the creation, since the beginning of the century, of a particularly advanced educational system; d) the very effective mobilization of the internal economy by restricting consumption. Considering that historically in Latin America contrary situations have prevailed (the inefficiency of the State, development dependent on foreign capital, weak and out-of-date educational systems and the lavish consumption of the élite), it seems practical to bear in mind that our part of the world is in no condition for the important experience of Japan to be relevant."

CHAPTER 12

A Welfare State for Poor Countries? (1971)

The free-market model dies hard. Dismissed on the grounds of substantive economics as illusory, it nevertheless continues to permeate normative thinking. Hence the place of pride attributed in development planning to the increase in aggregate individual consumption realized through the market. True, targets directed at improving standards of basic consumption are important, though meaningless when stated in terms of an aggregate which fails to take into account the social distribution of income. Yet, at the same time, questions need to be asked about the desirable proportion of individual and collective consumption,[1] as well as the role to be attributed to the latter, so as to transform it into an instrument of income equalization instead of letting it become one more privilege accruing—as often happens—to the already privileged élite.

This is, of course, a relatively old issue, extensively debated by socialists of all confessions, partisans of welfare economics, and critics of the affluent society. Yet, in developed countries, the myth of consumer's sovereignty and of the preeminence of individual consumption continues to be largely accredited, or at least constitutes an article of official faith. Paradoxically enough, the socialist countries do not show interest in fostering discussion on the alternative models of consumption pattern. Rather than make explicit these fundamental ideological choices, they prefer to make the choices indirectly through current economic policy-making. Even while the Soviet Union and China pursue completely

[1] Under "collective consumption" we include both consumption proper and investment carried out to build schools, hospitals, and other social facilities, as well as public outlays on popular housing, i.e. a substantial part of the so-called "unproductive investment" in Marxist terminology.

different goals in this respect, both these countries have in common the fact that the social welfare function is not subject to discussion, except for details of implementation. To me this is like wasting the best opportunity there is to assert the capability of socialism to choose, consciously and democratically, a design for living which is different from and superior to that of the affluent societies of the West. As for the less-developed countries, I shall argue in this chapter that, for a variety of reasons examined below and in spite of the lip-service paid to it in all development plans, the problem of collective consumption and more specifically of social services has not been properly equated there—except in a few countries like Cuba and Algeria.

We are more often than we suspect prisoners of our conceptual framework and we tend to value highly what fits into that framework, while dismissing those portions of reality which do not yield themselves to conventional analysis. When it comes to quantitative thinking, our natural tendency is to overemphasize the impact of measurable factors and to exclude from the model the non-measurable variables. Material consumption and marketable services can be easily evaluated and added up. Social services are more troublesome, and their treatment in national income accounting is very unsatisfactory.

According to Marxist economists, social services should not be accounted at all, as they are financed out of a redistribution of income. As for investment in social services and housing, it is included in capital formation under the heading of "unproductive investment"—a denomination which, in spite of all doctrinal affirmations to the contrary, confers upon it the status of a poor relative of productive investment directly responsible for the growth of the GNP. Western economists include social services in the GNP, but their way of proceeding is open at least to two criticisms. No distinction is made between different kinds of social and administrative services—those of a teacher or health officer and those of a policeman—although from the point of view of the social welfare function that difference certainly matters. Besides, since no satisfactory ways of valuing non-marketable social services have been found, they are accounted for in terms of cost. Thus, whenever capital outlays are not needed, the value-added in social services is equal to wages disbursed, while in all other activities the value-added exceeds wages by the amount of profit. In other words, the relative value of social services is underestimated. This is particularly so in countries where the level of wages is low.

Quite obviously we do not have a direct way of measuring the impact of social services on peoples' welfare, but at least two indirect quantitative arguments can be advanced in favour of their re-evaluation in development planning.

(a) The physical productivity of social workers does not depend at all on their wages. That of a teacher is roughly the same all over the world, though in the less-developed countries he is paid a small portion of his counterpart's wage in the rich countries. Now, the cost of installing a plant, per unit of output, is usually considerably higher in the less-developed countries and so are the prices of industrial consumer goods. Hence, a decision at the margin to devote a higher share of the income to collective consumption, at the expense of productive investment and/or of individual consumption, yields a far more spectacular result in a poor country than in a rich one, even though the conventional rate of growth of the economy may suffer from it.

The above proposition is, of course, subject to several qualifications. First, the elbow-room for this kind of substitution is quite narrow and at no moment should it be forgotten that the planner must look at complementarities. Educating a starving population does not make too much sense, while improving the diets of rural illiterates without preparing them through education to use more sophisticated techniques and to have access to new kinds of jobs does not lead far either. Second, quantitative goals, such as in education, sound suspect so long as the content is not spelled out and efficiency examined. And in this task, quantitative education economics is a mis-leader. The ways suggested to evaluate the impact of education and technical progress on output are open to severe criticism, insofar as they imply the acceptance of the neo-classical theory of factors' income. Third, collective consumption is not a goal in itself, but a means of achieving a more equitable distribution of welfare. Forms of collective consumption, which add to the already existing distortions in income distribution, should for this reason be discouraged. But in practice, they eat into a considerable part of the resources allocated to social services and public housing. Governments find it very convenient to bestow privileges upon the élites while present-

ing them as a democratic achievement. Free higher education in countries where the majority of students come from well-to-do families is
a case in point.

(b) To the extent that technical progress does not significantly affect
social services, it may be rewarding to concentrate on social services
in the initial stages of development—even at the price of postponing
some productive investments which are likely to gain in productivity
by being delayed, given the rapid rate of technological change.

At this stage, I should like to emphasize once more that the proposed
trade-off is a very delicate choice and its scope limited, though by
no means negligible, considering the volume of social services included
in the plan and the job opportunities offered in this sector.

I therefore believe that a critical examination of the system of national
accounts and of the commonly accepted methods of measuring development (the rate of growth of GNP) should lead to the conclusion that
poor countries do not pay enough attention to social services because
of their little impact on statistical growth. At the same time, I would
dismiss for two reasons the argument, used in favour of social services,
which involves quantifying their influence on the productivity of labour.
First, I do not consider that social services are just an instrument—a
cost—of economic development; they constitute a major development
goal by themselves. Secondly, I am not persuaded at all by the possibility
of measuring the influence of, say, education on productivity, although
a correlation between the two does exist; at least the attempts to quantify
the so-called "residual factor" are theoretically very unsatisfactory.

Thinking in terms of a welfare state in a poor country may seem
preposterous for all those who explicitly or implicitly accept the simplified theory of development which makes the GNP per head the
main determinant of economic and social structure. For them, history
is bound to repeat itself: there exists but one broad pattern of industrialization and development, and, since the highly industrialized countries
started to think in terms of the welfare state only in the recent past
when their GNP per head was a multiple of what it is today in the
developing countries, the latter should wait till they are richer before
they provide more social services.

Yet, experience both in socialist and less-developed countries shows
that different paths of development are possible at similar levels of

GNP and that the historical pattern of the developed countries should not be accepted as the only possible one. Moreover, a conscious effort should be made in less-developed countries to evolve a different design of living and to project development goals inspired by an original set of values and by an analysis of the potentialities inherent to each country rather than by mere imitation. I am not pleading for originality at any price, or for pure negation of whatever comes from developed countries; but I cannot accept, on the other hand, the pattern of subservience which is implied in the theory of unilinear development.

I would submit that, in this search for a new design of living, social services, conventional and novel, could play a much bigger role than they have up to now. There is room not only for increasing education and health services but also for creating new services dealing, for instance, with nutritional problems and environmental control. At the same time, the utmost effort should be made to renew the contents and organizational structure of the conventional services. Education should not be necessarily equated with formal schooling; public health services should concentrate on the organization of an efficient network of rural health centres staffed with para-medical personnel. Dissemination of technical knowledge among peasants should not be conceived as a one-way process in which farmers have an entirely passive role to play, and in which knowledge comes only from distant laboratories; more credit needs to be given to the capacity for local innovation, the "research guerilla", as aptly called by the French anthropologist Michel Leiris.

Throughout this chapter "welfare state" is understood in a technical way and not as a political model conceived as an alternative to socialism in specific historical conditions of twentieth-century Europe. It just means that the State is entrusted with providing social services and organizing collective consumption.

It is now necessary to qualify a simplifying and comfortable assumption used in the previous paragraph, viz. the low capital–output ratio of social services. This is obviously untrue for housing and public health services as they stand today. The real question to be asked here is: To what extent is the considerable capital cost of social services motivated by passive acceptance of Western models and by a lack of adequate research to find alternative solutions characterized by less capital outlays, a higher wage component, and a growing participation of the interested communities? Many scholars are inclined to think that, even in the most developed countries, this type of research is urgently needed. The argument applies *a fortiori* to less-developed countries.

It follows that utmost priority should be given to technological research on low-cost buildings, on methods of education, on organizational schemes for para-medical services, etc. Educational priorities should be modified so as to prepare, as soon as possible, personnel for the social services and to avoid the wasteful training of highly skilled specialists who hold excellent degrees recognized throughout the world but are unable to find a job in their own country. The situation of Indian doctors is a good case in point, but similar situations arise perhaps in a less dramatic way with other specialists in most developing countries. A survey conducted recently in Mexico—a developing country known for its reasonable rates of growth—showed that the supply of chemical engineers is already reaching a saturation point and will soon lead to an imbalance on the labour market.

The tasks outlined in this paragraph are exceedingly difficult because they hit well-entrenched prejudices and vested interests. It is often argued that standards of excellence evolved in the most-developed countries should be adopted by the less-developed countries as the only way of bridging the gap and overcoming the consequences of the colonial past. But this attitude is founded on cultural dependence, the single most-powerful and devastating inheritance from colonialism. There are no reasons to believe *a priori* in the excellence of standards presently used in the so-called advanced countries. In nine cases out of ten, their suitability in a different socioeconomic context, of less-developed countries, is more than doubtful. The pursuance of policies based on these standards can only lead to one result: the creation of Western-like amenities for a tiny minority of privileged Westernized élite. If new and original solutions for social services are not found, the postulate of a welfare state in a poor country is self-defeating. It can only provide an ideological cover for a privileged stratum. But I do not see any reason why spectacular effects could not be achieved in research as outlined above in a matter of a few years through proper concentration of effort both on the national and the international scale.

One more fact militates in favour of a serious reconsideration of the place of social services in the development strategy. Experience shows that industrialization in less-developed countries is unable to solve the employment problem and that the same can be said of the so-called "green revolution" in agriculture. Quite obviously, social services could not become a major source of employment; but as already mentioned in this chapter, they could provide an outlet for some of the unemployed, mostly the educated ones. They could even have an impact on the labour market of unskilled people if popular housing schemes were given a high priority in the plans. The usual objection is lack of finances, but to the extent to which recent progress in agricultural output can be taken as an indicator of a more elastic supply of food—the basic wage good—there should be no reason for not increasing expenditure on social services over an above the limits set by orthodox budgetary policies. Resorting to deficit financing within certain limits should not be considered harmful and voluntary participation of the populations concerned should be, of course, encouraged. Social services would thus be partly financed out of newly created income and not from its redistribution. The trade-offs discussed above would lose in intensity and it should be possible even to have for a while the best of both worlds: the originally planned volume of investment and individual consumption, as well as more social services.

CHAPTER 13

Approaches to a Political Economy of Environment (1971)

The environmental revolution constitutes a challenge to the social sciences in general[1] and to economic theory in particular. Up to now, economists failed to respond to it, and pioneering books such as Kapp's *The Social Costs of Private Enterprise* did not generate the discussion they deserved.[2] Coddington goes so far as to plead guilty for the failure of the economists as a profession to integrate a major characteristic of recent technological progress into their theoretical thinking: the provision of opportunities for shifting costs from the producer onto society. According to him, the main body of economic thought is ill-adapted to coming to terms with the ecological viewpoint and, therefore, "it may even be the case that the greatest service economists can render posterity is to remain silent".[3]

This chapter will take a slightly less pessimistic view. It will be argued that a *political economy* of environment, as distinct from an *economics* of environment might be constructed, provided we recognize the need for far-reaching revisions of large chunks of theory. For obvious reasons, it cannot be done in one chapter—not at this juncture. My aim is much less ambitious: to identify some of the problem areas and to suggest a few priorities for further study. Before I turn, however, to this task, it may prove useful to clear the ground by attempting a

---

[1] See S. Tsuru (ed.), *Environmental Disruption: A Challenge to Social Scientists*, Tokyo, 1970 (Proceedings of the International Symposium organized under the auspices of the International Social Science Council, Tokyo, 8–14 March 1970).

[2] K. W. Kapp, *The Social Costs of Private Enterprise*, Oxford, 1950. The far-reaching implications of this book were underlined by J. Weiller in a review note published in *Rev. d'Histoire Economique et Sociale*, **29**, 1951, pp. 414–417.

[3] A. Coddington, "The economics of ecology", *New Soc.*, **393**, 9 April 1970, pp. 595–597.

brief classification of the main ideological trends discernible in environmental discussions. Social science production is never quite free from ideological bias and this is particularly true with respect to writings on environment, as any response in this field will perforce involve the collective action of large groups of people.[4]

The motives behind the concern

Disregarding shades, and minor differences of emphasis, the bulk of literature on environment (mostly in the United States) can be classified, for my purposes, into six groups.

(a) The *diversionists* come first, as far as publicity is concerned. This is understandable since they enjoy the support of several establishments. In their view, environmental disruption—the reverse side of the scientific and technological revolution—is taking such alarming proportions that it should become a major and constant concern for citizens, at the expense of other political preoccupations nowadays considered less important. People are called upon to organize themselves in order to protect the ecosystem. But the action they are expected to take is to be of a purely conservationist nature; no links whatsoever are established between environmental disruption and the working of the sociopolitical system. Young people in particular are exhorted to devote their exclusive attention to environment in the hope that they may thus be diverted from other burning international or social issues and that, at the same time, they will stop short of digging too deeply into the sociopolitical context of environmental disruption.

The writers who, in good faith, produce piles of gloomy books, pamphlets, and articles on the alarming state of the biosphere and the imminent disaster facing humanity in this way become involved, whether they realize it or not, in a campaign of political mystifications. For those, however, responsible for having launched it, environment, as such, matters very little indeed.[5] It is just an issue which can be easily played

---

[4] See G. Vickers, *Value Systems and Social Process*, Harmondsworth, 1970, pp. 181–183.
[5] Were this a legitimate concern, it should reflect itself in the appropriation of public funds for environmental action.

up and lends itself to exploitation as a safety-valve, because many people are disturbed by the worsening quality of their lives.

b) The attitude of *big business* towards environmental concern is ambivalent. While some industrialists fear an increase in costs, threatening their competivity,[6] others, on the contrary, approach the matter from a more positive angle. Anti-pollution for them is likely to become an important market and, possibly, an additional pretext for the spending of public funds in such a way as to increase private profits.

As one of them has put it in an article entitled "Social-sector industries: the challenge of our conscience" (*sic*): "It is interesting to reflect that perhaps in the years ahead great careers and even fortunes will accrue to those who devote their efforts to societal—*not* production—problems. Air and water and noise and landscape pollution control; housing; recreation; education; transportation; public facilities requirements—these and other social needs present a market measured in the trillions of dollars and human survival."[7]

Seen in this perspective, the index of advertisers in the *Scientific American* special issue on the Biosphere[8] makes very interesting reading indeed.

(c) For the *neo-malthusians* busy keeping the underdeveloped countries from industrializing, environmental concern is an excellent pretext, as they may now claim that not only food but also all other resources of the spaceship Earth are supposedly in short supply, to such an extent that the Earth may even prove incapable of supporting on a sustained basis a population as large as the present one.[9] Such an approach is being consistently developed by Paul R. Ehrlich among others. In a best-selling pamphlet[10] he enjoins Americans to write letters to politicians, insisting, *inter alia.*, on the following points: population is far outstripping food production, more than half of the world is hungry and many are dying of starvation; not all countries can be industrialized;

[6] See R. S. Diamond, "What business thinks about its environment", in *The Environment: A National Mission for the Seventies*, New York, 1970, pp. 55–64 (reprinted from *Fortune*).

[7] D. Carley, in *Agenda for Survival: The Environmental Crisis*, 2nd ed., ed. by H. W. Helfrich, Jr., New Haven, Conn., 1970, p. 98.

[8] *Scient. Am.*, **223** (3), September 1970.

[9] L. G. Cole, "Playing Russian roulette with biogeochemical cycles", in Helfrich (ed.), *op cit.*, p. 14. See also the findings of the System Dynamic Laboratory of MIT summarized by G. Leach in *The Observer*, 27 June 1971, and J. Forrester, *The World Dynamics*, Boston, Mass., 1971.

[10] P. R. Ehrlich, *The Population Bomb*, 13th ed., New York, 1970, pp. 117–178.

DCs (developed countries) cannot feed UDCs (undeveloped countries). In more scholarly papers he does not hesitate to ask for the stopping of aid to underdeveloped countries, unless a substantial share of the same is spent on population control: "We will have to recognize the fact that most countries can never industrialize and that giving them industrialization aid is wasteful."[11] In the same vein the Paddock brothers suggested[12] that the concept of "triage" borrowed from military medicine should be applied to aid policies. Underdeveloped countries which lag hopelessly behind in the population–food game should not be assisted, as the resources allocated to them will be wasted. They should be instead permitted to starve to death, in order to concentrate resources on better cases. The Paddocks had India in mind, but it seems that their recommendation will be first applied on a mass scale in East Pakistan, where millions of people are almost certain to die next year in the midst of world indifference.[13] The fullest presentation of Ehrlich's views is contained, however, in his well-known book *Population, Resources, Environment*.[14] The DCs are asked to "de-develop" and at the same time to share their income with the UDCs. As for the UDCs, while they wait for the de-development of the DCs, they should content themselves with a "semi-development". In a passage of his book, which brings back memories of colonial theories, he explains what "semi-development" means to him: "As examples of semi-development, Kenya and Tanzania might be semi-developed as combination agrarian-recreation areas. They, and some other African nations, can supply the world with a priceless asset: a window on the past when vast herds of nonhuman animals roamed the face of the Earth. They could also provide one of the many living stockpiles of organic diversity, stockpiles which may prove of immense value as mankind attempts to replenish the deteriorated ecosystems of the planet. These and similar areas could serve as rest-and-rehabilitation centres for people from the more frantic industrialized parts of the planet. They would also serve as guarantors of

[11] P. R. Ehrlich, "Famine 1975: fact or fallacy?", in Helfrich (ed.), *op. cit.*, p. 64.

[12] W. and P. Paddock, *Famine—1975! America's Decision: Who Will Survive?*, Boston, Mass., 1967.

[13] Provisional estimations are given in the unpublished paper by D. Thorner and K. H. Iman, *The Menace of Famine in Bangla Desh*.

[14] P. R. and A. H. Ehrlich, *Population, Resources, Environment: Issues in Human Ecology*, San Francisco, Calif., 1970.

298 Studies in Political Economy of Development

cultural diversity, as areas specifically reserved to permit peoples to maintain their traditional ways of life. . . .We need to create a demand for what Aborigines, Eskimos, Kenyans and Honduras can supply, what might be called cultural resources. These priceless resources are in short supply, they are dwindling rapidly, and they are nonrenewable. A way must be found to permit these people access to more of the fruits of industrial societies without attempting to industrialize the entire world".[15]

In short, alleging the need to protect the UDCs from the mistakes of overdevelopment and the limited resources of the spaceship Earth, Ehrlich manipulates the concepts of cultural pluralism in such a way as to propose an international division of labour closely resembling the relationship between the public and animals in a zoo. Once more, his conclusions have little to do with the environment as such, merely used by him to sell, in brand new packaging, an unsophisticated version of colonialist paternalism.

(d) I shall now turn to those who really mean environment when they speak about it. In most developed countries, environmental concern materializes in some kind of *institutionalism*. Even people who are not prepared to go deeply into the social and political roots of environmental disruption, but content themselves with a more phenomenological approach to this matter, insist on the need to create special environmental agencies and on the enacting of legislation to make their action at all possible.

Although the scope and the type of collective action proposed varies from case to case, all the institutionalists have at least one thing in common: they all emphasize the inadequacy of the individualistic approach and the urgency of building into the capitalist societies more social controls on private enterprise as well as on public services very much in line with Galbraith's criticism of the affluent society.[16]

(e) The last two trends are both *radical*, and they define themselves in opposition to one or more of the trends described above. Strangely enough the radicals split into two diametrically opposed positions.

Several authors consider environmental concern as a non-issue or a false issue for the workers and the masses of poor people. The arguments

[15] *Ibid.*, p. 313.
[16] See J. K. Galbraith, *The Affluent Society*, London, 1958, and in particular chap. 18 on the theory of social balance.

invoked vary in kind. It is thus claimed that preoccupation with enviroment is a typically middle or upper class problem. Poor people do not care about the pollution of Florida or Monte Carlo beaches because they never go there. "Conservation is an essentially conservative issue."[17] The motives of the "divertionists" are forcefully exposed and the new version of solidarism wrapped in environmental concern rejected. At the same time, it is feared that environmental quality management will be financed out of resources which could be better used in a genuine war against poverty. Poor people will bear a substantial part of the cost of such operations. Moreover, they would be the first victims of the policies devised to slow down the rate of growth in order to improve the quality of life (whose life?).[18]

The radicals' refusal to play the environmental game of the rich

[17] G. Marwell, "Who is worried about the environment?", *Bull. of Peace Proposals*, **2**, 1970, p. 187.

[18] Three excerpts from a speech delivered on the Earth Day in Harvard University by George Wiley, director of the National Welfare Rights Organization are instructive (*Earth Day: The Beginning: A Guide for Survival*, ed. by National Staff of Environmental Action, New York, 1970):

"Are you going to ask the poor people in this country to bear the cost of cleaning up air pollution and doing something about other environmental problems? In all likelihood a good many of the approaches that you are likely to take are going to be paid for directly at the expense of the poorest people in this country. This will happen in a number of ways. It will happen, for example, because most of the systems of controlling air and water pollution, if they are imposed, will simply be passed along to the consumer in higher costs. The poor people, the people at the bottom of the economic ladder, will essentially be given a regressive tax—they will be asked to pay the same price you pay in terms of higher costs for such basic things as electric power, heat for homes, and other commodities essential to life itself. Unless some serious planning is done, it is going to be the poor people who pay for those things you do" (p. 214).

"*Is the ecology movement planning to place any serious priority on the problems of environment of the ghetto and the barrio, of our urban areas, where pollution is worse? You must not embark on programs to curb economic growth without placing a priority in maintaining income, so that the poorest people won't simply be further depressed in their condition but will have a share, and be able to live decently*" (p. 215).

"*It is going to be necessary to have substantial government expenditures for the programs of environmental control or, indeed, of industrial control. That means that you will be directly competing with poor people for very scarce government dollars.* And if you are not in a position to mount a confrontation with the military-industrial complex, if you are not prepared to join with poor people in saying that this war in Vietnam has got to end, that we've got to stop US military imperialism around the world, we've got to cut out the vast and wasteful military expenditures; if you are not prepared to say that *we want to put a priority on dealing with urban environmental problems; if you are not prepared to put yourselves and your movement and your organization on the line for those things, quite clearly poor people will pay the cost of your ecology program*" (p. 216).

people finds its counterpart in the UDCs' fear that environmental concern will be used as a pretext to distract them from development, that it will become one more obstacle to growth invented by outsiders unable (or unwilling) to understand the UDCs' specific problems and priorities. The neo-malthusian writings discussed above are not designed to dispel such misgivings.[19]

(f) The second radical trend (quite influential in Japan, but also present in other countries) takes a quite different and positive view. It insists, on the contrary, that environmental disruption is the poor man's concern as he is the one most severely hit. The issues so widely discussed today are not at all new and the working class has been exposed to all kinds of environmental hazards since the beginning of the industrial revolution. Moreover, if pertinent questions are asked about the way in which social costs arise and are treated in different socioeconomic systems, environmental concern may act as a powerful eye-opener. As an anarchist theoretician put it, ecology is by its nature a science "critical on a scale that the most radical systems of political economy failed to attain".[20] Finally, environmental concern, far from pushing people away from other burning issues, may act as a powerful lever for mass action, which will challenge at the same time all the evil aspects of the existing social organization.

In the second part of this chapter I shall explore some of the questions and revisions suggested in the realm of political economy by the positive radical approach.

Problem areas

THE DEFINITIONAL TRAP

As usual, the definition of the scope of the subject I am dealing with in this chapter presents conceptual difficulties. It is easy to define

[19] In a recent panel on development and environment, organized by the Secretariat of the United Nations Conference on the Human Environment (Geneva, June 1971) several speakers expressed the concern of UDCs of seeing environmental concern used as a pretext to slow down the pace of their development. Whatever the merits of this attitude, politically, it is one to be taken into account.

[20] M. Bookchin, *Ecology and Revolutionary Thought*, New York, 1970, p. 6. Bookchin goes on to say that ecology is also an integrative and reconstructive science and that by insisting on the crucial role of diversity it lends itself to a libertarian interpretation, in which appear the concepts of a balanced community, face-to-face democracy, humanistic technology, and de-centralized society.

it narrowly as being merely the *economics of pollution*, but this means abandoning the most precious part of the concept of environment, namely its all-inclusiveness. The alternative is, therefore, to include in the political economy of environment all the side-effects of economic activities which are disregarded by economic agents, as well as the economic feedback of the environmental changes thus provoked. In other words, the political economy of environment should explore the consequences of insulating, for the purpose of economic decisions, a given subsystem and of referring exclusively to it as a framework for economic rationality. This is in line with the social and historical nature of political economy, since in different historical contexts and under different socioeconomic regimes the isolation of subsystems takes different forms. Wildavsky is, therefore, correct in saying that "the old economics was mostly economics. The new economics is mostly politics."[21] But two other difficulties are likely to arise. On the one hand, the political economy of environment broadens its scope to the point of including both the economics of natural resources and social conditions of life—subjects which are not new at all. On the other, it may prove a dismal science if people are persuaded to use more comprehensive models for their decision-making. Its subject matter, like the *peau de chagrin*, will be shrinking ever more, to disappear altogether the day the decision-making process is brought within the global system, considered in its entirety.

We need not bother too much, however, about either of these two points. Looking at old themes from a new and more global vantage point might prove quite useful, though the moment of really using the spaceship Earth as the framework for all decision-making has not arrived as yet. For the time being, environment appears, then, as the moving half-light between the isolated subsystem and that part of the rest which has become too important to be disregarded altogether, but has not been included, for the time being, in the expanded subsystem.

SOME THEORETICAL IMPLICATIONS

The tentative definition sketched above enhances the need to come to grips with two heroic and often unspoken assumptions of economists

[21] A. Wildavsky, "Aesthetic power or the triumph of the sensitive minority over the vulgar mass: a political analysis of the new economics", in *America's Changing Environment*, ed. by R. Revelle and H. Landsberg, Boston, Mass., 1970 p. 147.

as a profession. The first postulates the possibility of a two-stage reductionism: all things can be reduced to their economic dimension and the economic dimension yields itself to a quantitative treatment; a market or a quasi-market value can always be found or estimated. The second takes an associationist approach to build macroeconomics from microeconomic considerations. But we must now reintegrate a direct reflexion on use values[22] into economic or rather social science thinking[23] and seriously consider the possibility of finding in economics a "gestalt" approach. In other words, reflexion on environment might provide new arguments for those who inveigh against the tyranny of the "obsolete market mentality"[24] or, at least emphasize the preoccupation of the economist with the supply of non-marketed goods and services.[25] How far should we go along these lines? Shall we be compelled to re-examine the very foundations of our discipline?

The profession is split on this issue. The majority tries to avoid taking such a radical position and, consequently, employs the best of their brains on patching up the existing models and paradigms of thought. Externalities are fitted into the traditional market model and any means will do to estimate prices or quasi-prices. A minority seems ready, however, to recognize the limitations of the economic approach, although it realizes that in doing so, it is undermining the vested interests of the profession.

There is still an intermediate position, held by those who recognize the importance of the "side-effect" syndrome: "Gains are reaped and costs are incurred, but there is no market that relates the two. Most importantly, the costs that arise are borne not by those that cause them but by others who happen to be around but are outside the process—

---

[22] The remarks on the subject contained in Marx's *Grundrisse* seem to offer an excellent point of departure. See *Fondements de la Critique de l'Economie Politique*, vol. 2 Paris, 1968, pp. 220–223.

[23] Myrdal is right in emphasizing that the distinction between "economic" and "non-economic" factors should be transcended, the only scientific dichotomy being relevant and less-relevant factors. See G. Myrdal, "Cleansing the approach from biases in the study of underdeveloped countries", *Social Sci. Inf.*, **8** (3), 1969, p. 16.

[24] *Cf.* K. Polanyi, "Our obsolete market mentality", in *Primitive Archaic and Modern Economics: Essays of Karl Polanyi*, ed. by G. Dalton, New York, 1968, pp. 59–67.

[25] See N. Wollman, "The new economics of resources", in Revelle and Landsberg (eds.), *op cit.*, pp. 131–145.

bystanders so to speak."[26] But quantification in market or quasi-market values seems preferable to them—even though obtained by simplifications and abiding by discredited models—than no quantification at all.

PLANNING: PROBLEMS OF METHOD OR OF INSTITUTIONS?

The same debate continues with respect to environmental planning. On the one hand are those who consider the existing tools, such as cost-benefit analysis and input-output tables, as capable of taking care of the envrionmental dimension, subject to some adjustments.[27] On the other, we find a growing number of authors warning against the illusion of finding suitable analytical methods for optimizing choices, once the environmental dimension is brought into the picture.[28] In between are the defenders of cost-benefit as a preferable alternative to no analytical method at all.[29] Their arguments are of a twofold nature.

---

[26] H. S. Landsberg, "The US resource outlook quantity and quality", in *ibid.*, p. 123.

[27] An example of environmental cost-benefit taken to its extremes is offered in the procedures now under elaboration at the World Bank. Their complexity might have, as a first effect, a considerable slowing down of project elaboration, without necessarily taking into consideration the most sensitive aspects of the assessment, namely the interplay of natural and social environment. For the application of input-output, see W. Leontief, "Environmental repercussions and the economic structure: An input–output approach", in Tsuru (ed.), *op. cit.*, pp. 114–134 (see footnote 2). For a more imaginative extension of the input–output paradigm so as to englobe the wastes, see A. Kneese, R. U. Ayres, and R. C. d'Arge, *Economics and the Environment: A Materials Balance Approach*, Washington, D.C., 1970.

[28] A general warning against too many expectations attached to analytical methods is contained in two very important recent studies, the Report of the National Academy of Sciences on *Technology: Processes of Assessment and Choice*, Washington, D.C., 1969, and OECD, *Analytical Methods in Government Science Policy: An Evaluation* (by C. Maestre and K. Pavitt), Paris, 1970. See also OECD, *Science, Growth and Society: A New Perspective*, Paris, 1971. The first and the third documents were prepared by panels presided over by Harvey Brooks.

[29] Two recent United Nations documents contain a very frank assessment of the heroic simplifications underlying cost-benefit analysis: arbitrariness involved in the consideration of remote effects, the need to assume that prices reflect values and the market is perfect, resorting to the concept of the "willingness to pay", the impossibility to find a fully plausible, democratic social welfare function (Arrow's theorem), the arbitrariness of the rate of discount of the future with respect to the present, etc. The authors consider, however, that in spite of being "philosophically" weak cost-benefit analysis can be reasonably well applied (ECE Conference on Problems Relating to Environment, *An Introductory*

Studies in Political Economy of Development

They consider imperfect quantification, in spite of all, to be a useful obstacle to discretionary policy decisions. Moreover, they insist that qualitative assessment of alternatives anyhow involves implicit quantitative valuations and trade-offs which can be spelled out *ex post*.

Neither of the two arguments seems convincing to me.

It is an altogether different matter to spell out, formally, the results of a complex assessment and to use simplified quantitative criteria as a basis for the assessment. In the latter case, the analyst is likely to fall prisoner to his own conceptual framework; the quantifiable aspects are important because they yield themselves to analytical treatment, while all non-quantifiable variables become unimportant because they prove intractable. Besides, experience shows how often and how easily analytical methods are manipulated to justify discretionary policy decisions. One might say, of course, that bad uses of a good method do not disqualify the method, but the economist should also be concerned with the uses of his science.

For these and other reasons, which need not be adduced here, many planners have been arguing that cost-benefit analysis can only be applied to the assessment of technological alternatives to achieve a given output, but not for the choice of the output-mix.[30] The broadening of the social goals of development by emphasizing the environmental concern strengthens their argument.

We are, thus, apparently left with a vacuum. If cost-benefit is discredited, what should be proposed instead?

At the most general level, it seems reasonable to challenge the role of optimization as the central concept of planning and to reconsider the dialectics of goals and means in the context of heuristic rather than formal methods[31] of multipurpose planning. In other words, it is necessary to look at the planning process as "an iterative exchange

---

Review of Attempts to Incorporate Environmental Issues into Socio-economic Thinking as Presented in Recent Literature and *The benefit-cost Analysis of Environmental Pollution*, Prague, May 1971).

[30] This had been, *inter alia.*, Kalecki's approach who, on the other hand, used to insist on the need to apply "variant thinking" at all stages of planning procedures without necessarily resorting to formal methods.

[31] See the stimulating article by G. Kade, "La théorie économique de la pollution et l'application de la méthode interdisciplinaire à l'aménagement de l'environnement", *Rev. int. des Sci. Sociales*, **22** (4), 1970, pp. 613–626.

of information between agents and a central administrative body or as a bargaining discussion between representatives of various social groups, a discussion that follows some institutional rules".[32] The way out of Arrow's dilemma must be sought on an institutional level. Participatory technology is being proposed as a countervailing force to technological alienation in contemporary society.[33] Participatory planning may prove to be the only workable method of integrating environmental concern into planning. The quality of life being, after all, a fairly subjective concept, those who live it should be closely associated with all stages of environmental planning and its implementation.   At the level of operational concepts, environmental planning is likely to adopt a *normative* approach, laying down *social minima* as attainable goals expressed in a mixture of environmental and social indicators.[34] Normative planning has a bad reputation, on account of a not-too-commendable record in some countries. The more important it is, therefore, to begin imaginative work on this subject, linking it with the institutionalization of genuinely democratic planning procedures.

THE ACTORS IN THE ENVIRONMENTAL GAME

While the problems discussed above are of a general nature, the political economy of environment has also a more specific area of its own. It should try to identify the winners and the losers of the environmental game in different historical contexts and under different sociopolitical systems. The actors are easy to identify: enterprises, governments and people. But the game is a very complex one (it is certainly not a zero–one game) and the interests involved are not always transparent.[35] We should thus aim at having a distinct political economy of environment both under capitalism and under socialism. In both cases the reasons for the externalization of costs by economic agents might be different. Internalization of profits and externalization of costs is in-

---

[32] E. Malinvaud, "A planning approach to the public good problem", *The Swed. J. of Econ.* **73** (1), 1971, p. 97.

[33] J. D. Caroll, "Participatory technology", *Science*, **171**, (3972), 19 February 1971, p. 647.

[34] This point has been emphasized in several papers by W. Kapp.

[35] To give just one example, J. Ridgeway in his book *The Politics of Ecology*, New York, 1970, tried to link environmental disruption with the policies pursued by international corporations in control of fuel resources.

herent in the working of the capitalist enterprise under unhampered market conditions. The real problem is to know how effective the controls imposed by the State are likely to be and how far the latter is willing to go.[36] Now, in a collective socialist economy theoretically there should be no environmental disruption, except when it is deliberate or unexpected. Deliberate environmental disruption may occur when the short- and medium-range rate of growth of the economy becomes the only criterion of development, whatever the immediate social costs incurred and the degree of mortgaging of resources for the future. Single-purpose planning proves destructive in all circumstances.

The underdeveloped countries have some specific environmental problems. These are closely linked with the colonial and the post-colonial international division of labour,[37] the massive destruction of environment brought about by monocultural exploitation of natural resources, as well as with the consequences of the transplantation of the industrialized world's consumption patterns. Moreover, considerable damage to environment accompanies several big development projects. The reasons may be threefold (besides the deliberate trade-off): inadvertence (lack of expertise), convenience (on financial or administrative grounds so as to make it somebody else's headache), or lack of sociological

---

[36] The prospects for the United States are summarized in the following way by a radical author: "Recent financial reports indicate that the business of pollution control will in fact make a profit out of pollution while at the same time generating more pollution; more growth will be the remedy applied to the perils of growth. In short, that advertising will continue to cost more for business than research, that the consumers will be passed on any costs of 'pollution control', and that federal agencies, new or old, will continue to operate as captives of the industry they are to regulate" (B. Weisberg, "The politics of ecology", in *The Ecological Conscience-values for Survival*, ed. by R. Disch, Prentice-Hall, Englewood Cliffs, N. J. , 1970, p. 157.

[37] The historical perspective on a world-wide scale is aptly described by G. Borgstrom: "The harvest of the seas", in Helfrich (ed.), *op. cit.*, p. 76. "In the last 300 years, the white man has mobilized the grasslands of the world to his benefit. He has gone all over and taken the prairies and the pampas, the grasslands of Australia, many of the grazing grounds of Africa, including the South African veld; all this chiefly for his own benefit. He has taken very little account of the people who were there originally; he has killed them off, chased them away, or provided them with calories devoid of adequate amounts of protein.

"Seen in this perspective, the present large-scale exploitation of the oceans might be called our latest big swindle. As Western white men, this time we are going out to the grasslands of the oceans: the plankton pastures. We are mobilizing them, not to feed the hungry, not to feed the continents closest to these lush pastures, but to feed ourselves."

imagination (inability to understand the interplay of natural and social factors).[38]

Suggestions for further research

In the light of the above considerations, and having immediate feasibility in view, the following four areas are proposed for the organization of research projects:

(a) Adding to social indicators a set of environmental indicators. This implies, in the first stage, a joint effort on the part of scientists, physicians, and social scientists and, then, an exercise in the methodology of planning, if the indicators are to play an operational role. Attention should be paid not only to social minima and to critical points, but also to the behaviour of the variables (morbidity is a poor criterion by which to describe a state of health; psychological stress is certainly no less important than nervous breakdowns, etc.).

(b) Evaluation of recent trends in long-term planning, both with respect to methodologies and institutional arrangements aimed at integrating environmental concern into planning procedures. Once more, this subject should be approached in an interdisciplinary way. A very interesting by-product of research in this area could well be the assimilation, by economic planners, of new ideas in planning advanced by architects, urbanists, specialists in OR, and social workers. The need clearly to differentiate the paradigms of medium-range and long-range planning could be taken as a working hypothesis.

(c) To the extent that the institutional set-up for environmental planning should be participatory, its long-run success will be conditioned by the educational system's capacity to train and motivate people for genuine participation in public affairs. The implications of the environmental concern and of participatory planning for education should be spelled out. The project should try to convey to educational specialists the postulates of environmental planners.

---

[38] For more details see the paper prepared by this author for UNESCO, *Environmental Quality Management and Development Planning: Some Suggestions for Action*, submitted to the United Nations Panel of Experts on Development and Environment which met in Geneva in June 1971, published in *Econ. and Political Weekly*, **6** (30–31), 1971 (special issue).

(d) Several big development projects in the UDCs, implemented with foreign assistance, proved quite destructive of natural environment and ill-adapted to social environment. Environmental audits of such projects are, therefore, urgently needed in order to identify the sources of bad planning and to propose remedial measures. Such measures should, whenever possible, be based on labour-intensive methods and could, at the same time, become pilot projects in participatory planning. The bulk of this research should be carried out by the countries directly concerned. But broad international co-operation is called for.

Bibliographical Notes

1. *Some Considerations on Long-term Planning in Mixed Economies*, Report on the Third Inter-Regional Seminar on Development Planning organized by the United Nations Department of Economic and Social Affairs, Santiago, Chile, March 1968 (ISD-P. 3/A/R.10). Also published in *Econ. and Political Weekly, Bombay*, special number, July 1968.
2. *Industrial Development Strategy*, by Ignacy Sachs and Kazimierz Laski, United Nations Industrial Development Organization, Vienna, published in *Industrialization and Productivity*, bull. 16 (Sales no. E. 70.II.B.31), New York, 1971 (Paper not included in the French volume).
3. *Development Planning and Policies for Increasing Domestic Resources for Investment (with special reference to Latin America)*, Report on the Third Inter-Regional Seminar on Development Planning organized by the United Nations Department of Economic and Social Affairs, Santiago, Chile, March 1968 (ST/TAO/SER.C/110, Sales no. E.69.II.B.33), New York, 1970 (in English and in Spanish).
4. *Levels of Satiety and Rates of Growth*, in *Problems of Economic Dynamics and Planning. Essays in Honour of Michal Kalecki*, PWN–Polish Scientific Publishers, Warsaw 1964.
5. *The Significance of the Foreign Trade Sector and the Strategy of Foreign Trade Planning*, Report on the First Inter-Regional Seminar on Development Planning organized by the United Nations Department of Economic and Social Affairs, Ankara, Turkey, September 1967 (ST/TAO/SER.C/91, Sales no. 67.II.B.5), New York, 1967.
6. *Forms of Foreign Aid*, by Michal Kalecki and Ignacy Sachs, Paper prepared for the European Coordination Centre for Research and Documentation in the Social Sciences (Vienna) in connexion with a Research Project on Comparative Forms of Assistance to Countries Undergoing Development, 1965; also published in *Social Sciences Inf., Paris*, **V** (1), March 1966.
7. *Problems of Implementation of Industrialization Plans*, Unpublished paper prepared on the request of the United Nation Industrial Development Organization (1970).
8. *Transfer of Technology and Strategy of Industrialization*, Paper published in *Econ. and Political Weekly, Bombay*, **V** (29–31), special number, July 1970. Also published in Spanish in *Comercio de Tecnologia y Subdesarrollo Economico*, ed. by Miguel S. Wionczek, Universidad nacional autónoma de México–Coordinacion de Ciencias, Mexico, 1973.
9. *Selection of Techniques : Problems and Policies for Latin America*, Paper published in English and in Spanish in *ECLA Bull., New York*, **XV** (1), 1970.
10. *Technological Policies for Latin American Development*, Paper prepared for the Department of Scientific Affairs, Organization of American States (OAS), Washington, D.C., July 1971. Also published in Spanish in *Vision Latinoamericano sobre Ciencia y Tecnologia*, vol. II, OAS, Bogota, 1972.

11. *Transfer of Technology and Research Priorities for Latin America: A Social Scientist's Point of View*, Paper prepared for the Department of Scientific Affairs, Organization of American States (OAS), Washington, D.C., July 1971. Also published in Spanish in *Vision Latinoamericano sobre Ciencia y Tecnologia*, vol. II, OAS, Bogota, 1972.
12. *A Welfare State for Poor Countries?* Paper published in *Econ. and Political Weekly, Bombay,* **VI** (3, 4, 5), annual number, January 1971.
13. *Approaches to a Political Economy of Environment*, Article prepared for the Symposium on Political Economy of the Environment: Problems of Methods, organized at the Maison des Sciences de l'Homme in Paris, July, 1970; published in *Political Economy of the Environment: Problems of Methods*, ed. by Mouton Paris, The Hague, 1971. Also published in *Social Sciences Inf.*, Paris, **IO** (5), 1971.

Index